The Social Psychology
of School Learning

EDUCATIONAL PSYCHOLOGY

Allen J. Edwards, Series Editor
Department of Psychology
Southwest Missouri State University
Springfield, Missouri

In preparation:

Herbert J. Klausmeier and Thomas S. Sipple. Learning and Teaching Concepts: A Strategy for Testing Applications Theory

Published

James H. McMillan (ed.). The Social Psychology of School Learning

M. C. Wittrock (ed.). The Brain and Psychology

Marvin J. Fine (ed.). Handbook on Parent Education

Dale G. Range, James R. Layton, and Darrell L. Roubinek (eds.). Aspects of Early Childhood Education: Theory to Research to Practice

Jean Stockard, Patricia A. Schmuck, Ken Kempner, Peg Williams, Sakre K. Edson, and Mary Ann Smith. Sex Equity in Education

James R. Layton. The Psychology of Learning to Read

Thomas E. Jordan. Development in the Preschool Years: Birth to Age Five

Gary D. Phye and Daniel J. Reschly (eds.). School Psychology: Perspectives and Issues

Norman Steinaker and M. Robert Bell. The Experiential Taxonomy: A New Approach to Teaching and Learning

J. P. Das, John R. Kirby, and Ronald F. Jarman. Simultaneous and Successive Cognitive Processes

Herbert J. Klausmeier and Patricia S. Allen. Cognitive Development of Children and Youth: A Longitudinal Study

Victor M. Agruso, Jr. Learning in the Later Years: Principles of Educational Gerontology

Thomas R. Kratochwill (ed.). Single Subject Research: Strategies for Evaluating Change

Kay Pomerance Torshen. The Mastery Approach to Competency-Based Education

The list of titles in this series continues on the last page of this volume.

The Social Psychology of School Learning

EDITED BY

James H. McMillan
Department of Educational Studies
Virginia Commonwealth University
Richmond, Virginia

1980

ACADEMIC PRESS

A Subsidiary of Harcourt Brace Jovanovich, Publishers

New York   London   Toronto   Sydney   San Francisco

ACADEMIC PRESS, INC.
111 Fifth Avenue, New York, New York 10003

United Kingdom Edition published by
ACADEMIC PRESS, INC. (LONDON) LTD.
24/28 Oval Road, London NW1 7DX

Library of Congress Cataloging in Publication Data
Main entry under title:

The Social psychology of school learning.

(Educational psychology series)
Includes bibliographies and index.
1. Learning, Psychology of––Social aspects.
2. Social psychology. I. McMillan, James H.
LB1051.S6435   370.15'23   79–6797
ISBN 0–12–485750–7

PRINTED IN THE UNITED STATES OF AMERICA

80 81 82 83   9 8 7 6 5 4 3 2 1

Contents

chapter 3

Classroom Expectations: Teacher–Pupil Interactions 79
THOMAS L. GOOD

chapter 4

*Group Processes: Influences of Student–Student
Interaction on School Outcomes* 123
DAVID W. JOHNSON

chapter 5

The School Organization 169
RICHARD A. SCHMUCK

chapter 6
Attitude Development and Measurement   215
JAMES H. McMILLAN

List of Contributors

Numbers in parentheses indicate the pages on which the authors' contributions begin.

IRENE HANSON FRIEZE (39), Learning Research and Development Center, University of Pittsburgh, Pittsburgh, Pennsylvania 15260

THOMAS L. GOOD (79), Center for Research in Social Behavior, University of Missouri—Columbia, Columbia, Missouri 65201

DAVID W. JOHNSON (123), Department of Social, Psychological, and Philosophical Foundations of Education, University of Minnesota, Minneapolis, Minnesota 55455

JAMES H. McMILLAN (1, 215), Department of Educational Studies, Virginia Commonwealth University, Richmond, Virginia 23284

RICHARD A. SCHMUCK (169), Center for Educational Policy and Management, University of Oregon, Eugene, Oregon 97401

Preface

There is a growing awareness among educational researchers that the social environment of the classroom and school is an important variable in explaining and predicting student learning. Despite the perspective and methodology social psychology provides for researching this variable, there is a lack of theory building, frameworks, and models to study social interaction in educational settings systematically. This book helps fill this void by analyzing and integrating studies of social-psychological factors within the school that influence student behavior and learning.

The purpose of this book is to examine how student interaction with other students, teachers, and groups, and the organizational aspects of schooling affect student learning and the perceptions students have about appropriate behavior. Several other books have been written that attempt to integrate social psychology and education, but most of these texts summarize social-psychological research and then suggest possible implications for education. This approach has not been, in the main, very useful. Social psychologists have stressed fundamental research, and the results of their studies have been difficult to apply to educational settings. Also, previous texts have treated the social psychology of education as a series of discrete areas, with little or no integration of the research across topics. This book is unique in its emphasis on recent applied educational research, which is social-psychological in nature, and in its conceptual framework, which integrates each chapter to provide a holistic and meaningful perspective on the pervasive influence of personal interaction with others on learning.

The content of the book is not all-encompassing. The emphasis is on school-based research, which has direct relevance for pupil learning, rather than on providing a macro-perspective of social influences. Chapter 1 provides an overview of the book, detailing the usefulness of a social-psychological approach to school learning. A cognitive social-psychological model of learning is presented in this chapter which organizes social interaction factors that influence student behavior and learning. Chapter 2 examines the popular field of attribution, emphasizing how attribution affects interpersonal interaction and how social-psychological factors, in turn, influence the attributional process. Chapter 3 is concerned with pupil–teacher interactions, especially the dynamics of teacher expectancies, while Chapter 4 focuses on student–student relationships and group processes. Chapter 5 provides convincing evidence of the effect of organizational characteristics on student learning. Chapter 6 summarizes research on how pupil attitudes are learned and suggests new methodological procedures for measuring pupil attitudes. Each of these chapters, written especially for this book, critically analyzes applied research and integrates the area with the model of learning presented in Chapter 1. Each chapter also discusses implications for teaching and presents suggestions for future research.

The book is intended for professors, researchers, school personnel, and others concerned with current social-psychological knowledge and research applied to school learning. The book can be used as a supplement in many graduate courses in education, such as educational psychology, learning, sociology of education, and foundations of education, and could be used as the primary text in a graduate course in the social psychology of education. Psychology instructors could use the book as a supplement, especially in social psychology graduate courses, and education professors will find the information valuable for teaching undergraduate courses in learning and educational psychology.

We believe this book presents knowledge and ideas that will result in the systematic study of how interpersonal interactions affect pupil learning, and provides pragmatic suggestions for immediately improving learning from a social-psychological perspective.

As editor, I was fortunate to work with a helpful and understanding publisher, and to collaborate with exceedingly capable and cooperative authors. Many colleagues at the University of Iowa and the University of Colorado at Denver provided needed criticism and assistance, and I am grateful for their help. Finally, I am thankful for the exemplary work of Tracy Carlson, whose typing, proofreading, and patience was essential.

The Social Psychology
of School Learning

chapter 1

Social Psychology and Learning

JAMES H. McMILLAN

INTRODUCTION

As a teacher I have been challenged to explain why and some-times perplexed by the fact that the same course, taught to two different classes in the same way, can have very different outcomes. One class seems to respond better, to ask more stimulating questions, and to be more alert than the other class. At the end of a semester I think of one class very fondly as a group of people who became a cohesive, happy unit and shared my positive feelings about the course. I remember the other class more as work, with few satisfactions or rewards for me or the students. Most teachers have experienced these feelings, and yet I sense that reasons for the differences are often glossed over.

As a student I have a different set of recollections. I remember walking into a classroom and, as discreetly as possible, looking around at others to help me decide what I should do. I would begin by searching for someone who seemed to know how to behave, someone secure and confident. Imitating that person's behavior, I would wait anxiously for the teacher, not yet knowing whether it was best to sit in the front of the classroom, in the middle, or at the back. When the teacher finally arrived, I began to note mentally all the "right" and "wrong" things to do in the class.

These examples are salient in my perspective of the teaching–learning process, and each emphasizes in a different way the pervasive importance of interpersonal interactions in determining behavior. For the teacher who experiences different outcomes with various classes, the obvious explana-

1

THE SOCIAL PSYCHOLOGY
OF SCHOOL LEARNING

tion is that the students who comprised each group were of different backgrounds, orientations, personalities, and other traits, and that these group differences affected the outcomes of the classes. Moreover, the students may behave quite differently in two or more classes for the same reasons: A different group of students and a different teacher in each class promotes various "environments," and each environment demands different behavior from the student. This may be an adequate explanation for the teacher or student, but it does not go deep enough in identifying what affects behavioral patterns of students in different environments. It is the formalization of the behavioral decision-making process that is at the heart of this book. That is, what are the specific, quantifiable reasons for a student to behave in a particular way? What impact does the ubiquitous process of interpersonal interaction have on determining behavioral decisions, and what are the characteristics of individuals that determine the nature of interactions with others? More specifically, what school-learning behaviors can be analyzed through this approach? The purpose of this book is to examine variables in both the individual and the school environment that are integral to the interactive process and that influence the decisions students make about learning behavior.

It is self-evident that the school environment comprises social interaction of individuals in a particular situation: talking, responding, listening, obeying, or in other ways reacting to and being influenced by others. Viewed in this way, education is clearly a social psychological phenomenon: the study of how the social environment interacts with the individual to affect behavior. This perspective is stated emphatically in the following:

> Why do human beings behave as they do? When we approach this question, the vital point is that behavior is always simultaneously situational and personal. We cannot answer the question by use of the constructs derived from either psychology or sociology nor by adding attention to a few variables derived from the discipline that is not an essentially different unit of analysis: individual behavior in the social context [Yinger, 1969, p. 171].

The major areas of social psychology seek to identify and interpret individual and environmental factors involved in interpersonal interaction. This has been accomplished through combinating and integrating several behavioral sciences: psychology, which focuses on the individual in isolation from others; sociology, which examines social systems apart from individuals; and anthropology, which concentrates on cultural development. Indeed, interactional or social psychology is a major field of study, with a substantial body of theory and research (Magnusson & Endler, 1977). And yet, the art of teaching–learning in schools has not been given much attention by social psychologists. In this introductory chapter social psychology is examined as a field of study for educators. This overview is necessary to provide the basis for the model of cognitive social psychological learning around which the remaining chapters are organized. It is not the intent of this book to explain pupil behavior in the social setting of the school. Rather we shall examine variables in social interaction that affect pupil decisions to engage in specific learning behaviors.

THE SOCIAL PSYCHOLOGY OF EDUCATION

Charters (1973) has nicely summarized the field of social psychology and its potential relevance for education. He characterizes it as "a burgeoning field of scholarly activity . . . right at the doorstep of education [p. 70]." Charters delineates five dominant themes in social psychology, organized and defined to relate to educational problems. It is useful to examine these themes in order to understand what social psychology entails, beyond its broad definition.

1. *A focus on individual behavior at a molar level of organization.* Social psychologists are concerned most with establishing general laws of behavior and they concentrate on enduring, predictable patterns of behavior rather than isolated, individual instances. This is necessary to describe conditions that provide consistency in behavior.

2. *A strong phenomenological component.* In explaining behavior, the emphasis is on the perceptions of individuals: how they see and interpret a situation. This view stresses selection and organization of information from the point of view of the individual, and, as such, it is integrated with cognitive psychology. Recent research in attribution by psychologists and educators is a good example of applying the phenomenological perspective.

3. *Emphasis on the affective, the motivational.* Despite the cognitive approach inherent in a phenomenological emphasis and the abundance of research in cognitive dissonance, social psychologists have been most concerned with attitudes, feelings, affective states, and motivation. It is the "attitude" and feelings that mediate between cognitive perception of events in the environment and behavior. As such, the affective acts as a screen or filter—a disposition to respond positively or negatively in a situation. Unfortunately, educators have been content to accept a general definition of "attitude," ignoring its complexity. This is one reason, explored in greater depth in Chapter 6, why attitudes have always been important but misunderstood with respect to how they develop, measured poorly, and rarely altered by innovative instructional programs or curricula.

4. *The power of the group.* Social psychologists concentrate their study on those people who have immediate proximity to an individual—those people with whom the person interacts daily. This is reflected in a preponderance of research on the effect of the "group" on individual behavior. Not only are the attributes of groups important, but so are the organizational characteristics within which the group is formed. Thus, there is a stress on "roles" and "positions" as they affect group processes.

5. *The stress on uniformity, not individuality.* Social psychologists focus on interpersonal research designed to explain why people behave in similar ways. Thus, many studies have been concerned with conformity, power and influence, persuasion, reference groups, group leadership, and other areas to seek to explain why people are alike.

Throughout all these areas there remains an overriding emphasis on interpersonal interaction—what shapes it, what effects it has on subsequent behavior, how to analyze it, and how to influence it. Each area and subarea of research is designed to contribute to an overall understanding of behavior in social situations. Individual learning behavior in educational environments is obviously an example of the kind of situation that appeals to social psychologists; however, social psychology is a relatively young science which has preferred controlled experimentation to applied research. Thus, whereas the interests of social psychologists should have great relevance for educators seeking to understand student behavior, few of the principles and concepts developed through social psychological research have been of any pragmatic use to educators. Some educators have attempted to apply social psychology to education, and, in the past decade, the social psychology of education, or educational social psychology, has emerged as a recognized field of study (Bar-Tal & Saxe, 1978; McMillan, 1978).

Although Charters was not optimistic about the social psychology of education as a distinct, separate field of study in 1973, recent educational research suggests that many concepts of social psychology can be meaningfully applied to education. The first comprehensive review of the social psychology of education was done by Jacob Getzels (1969) and appeared in Volume 5 of *The Handbook of Social Psychology* (Lindzey & Aronson, 1969). In his review, Getzels suggests a definition for the social psychology of education by presenting a matrix of 21 social-psychological topics and 10 educational settings, developed by Miles and Charters (1970). He characterizes the field at that time as a "grab-bag" of social-psychological notions and data relevant to education but unrelated in any systematic way. He attempts in his article to provide a synthesizing framework for the field, and reviews an impressive amount of research. However, there remains the impression that this "field of study" fails to be distinct because the basic research and concepts of social psychologists do not integrate well with the applied research and unique problems of educators. Earlier definitions of the social psychology of education reflect this same dichotomy. In 1963, the first published book in the field gave the following definition: "The social psychology of education studies interaction and its social products in the context of educational settings and issues [Charters & Gage, 1963, p. xv]." Backman and Secord (1968) define the field broadly as a view of "the educational process through the eyes of a social psychologist [p. 1]." More recent definitions include:

> In our presentation of a social psychology of education, we have attempted to give some understanding of the interpersonal forces which lead to the maintenance of existing school practices and those that lead to disruption and/or changes of practices [Guskin and Guskin, 1970, p. 186].

> This book is designed to provide an introduction to the social psychology of education by presenting the relevant social psychological theory and research and its implications for education and providing the conceptual tools needed to diagnose and solve educational problems from a social psychological point of view [Johnson, 1970, p. iii].

> The social psychology of education focuses on the relation between the individual and the social psychological setting of the school [Bany & Johnson, 1975, p. 1].

In each of these definitions, the approach is to apply social psychology to education, which means discussing social-psychological research in the context of educational settings. This has been a difficult way to develop the field, since most social-psychological research is intended to build theories of human behavior, not to solve particular problems and concerns of teachers and administrators. For example, the well-known Lewin, Lippit, and White (1939) studies on leadership style have been used extensively to imply that democratic, autocratic, or laissez-faire teacher leadership result in particular student outcomes. While these different styles may indeed produce the predicted outcomes, there is little applied research in schools to confirm this finding. This basic approach is exemplified in the sources cited by books in the area. In a recent comprehensive text,[1] *Educational Social Psychology* (Bany & Johnson, 1975), 35 out of 270 references were in education journals or books. Johnson's 1970 book, *The Social Psychology of Education*, contained 120 education references out of 365. However, Bar-Tal and Saxe (1978), in examining four well-known journals, report an increasing number of studies concerned with social psychology in education from 1965 to 1975.

Since social psychology is such a large area of study with many subspecialties, various authors of the social psychology of education tend to emphasize different areas. Table 1.1 summarizes to what extent various

[1] An even more recent text is by D. Bar-Tal and L. Saxe, *Social psychology of education: Theory and research*, New York: Halsted, 1978.

Table 1.1

AREAS OF EMPHASIS IN SELECTED TEXTS IN THE SOCIAL PSYCHOLOGY OF
EDUCATION[a]

Social-psychological areas	Author				
	Bany & Johnson	Johnson	Backman & Secord	Guskin & Guskin	Miles & Charters
Group dynamics	3	3	3	2	3
Conformity	3	1	0	3	1
Leadership	3	3	1	3	3
Communication	3	1	2	3	2
Attitudes	3	1	2	2	2
Social motivation	3	3	1	2	1
School as an organization	1	3	3	2	2
Social-psychological learning	1	3	2	3	2
Role theory	2	3	3	3	2
Organizational change	1	3	0	3	3

[a]3 = stressed a great deal; 2 = stressed somewhat; 1 = slightly stressed; 0 = not covered at all.

books in the field emphasize the social-psychological areas. In addition, each book organizes the areas in different ways. The Johnson and Guskin and Guskin books emphasize the school as an organization, and use roles, norms, and structural characteristics and climates to organize their writing. Johnson also integrates social-psychological problem solving methods with knowledge and concepts as an approach that educators can employ. Bany and Johnson emphasize the interaction or organizational dynamics between individuals and groups, but they concentrate on topics related to group development and influence. Miles and Charters use yet another set of criteria, stressing methodology and theoretical significance to form a broad range of educational phenomena that may be studied social-psychologically. Backman and Secord analyze the interaction of personalities with the social system and culture, defining each factor and examining the student outcomes.

Thus, while there is a central theme that dominates the social psychology of education—the development and influence of interpersonal interaction within educational organizations—each source in the field emphasizes different areas. This is especially true for pragmatic suggestions and ideas derived from the research for teachers. The focus of this book is unique in the context of others written in this field. The material is integrated with a unifying concept, a social psychology of learning behavior. Rather than viewing social psychology applied to education, the contributors to this book develop a model of learning and examine how selected social-psychological phenomena are related to this model. Thus, the emphasis is on cognitive and affective learning behavior, and on the way social interactions in the school affect this behavior. We will examine how students interpret interpersonal interactions and the influence of these perceptions on learning. Furthermore, we will analyze aspects of the educational environment which have an impact on the nature of these interpersonal interactions. While basic social-psychological research cannot be ignored in this process, the emphasis is on applied educational research related to our areas. This approach is possible because of the increased interest of educational researchers in social-psychological phenomena, and will, we hope, result in realistic approaches to promote more effective pupil learning in schools.

A SOCIAL PSYCHOLOGY OF LEARNING

The notion of learning developed and critiqued in this book is based on the observation that behavior is influenced by multiple variables in both the individual and the environment. Learning cannot be conceptualized or studied as an outcome affected by a single or even a few variables. Many factors, changing in different settings, will determine whether a student will decide to study for an upcoming test or visit with a friend and how effective a behavior modification or discovery method of instruction will be with particular students. This implies that learning behavior is both a process and a product, and both these aspects need to be considered in understanding learning. Several noted educators and psychologists have stressed the need to perceive learning behaviors in this way. Although each author derives conclusions from different sources, the implication is the same: The nature of personal interaction with the social environment will determine behavior. It is a multidimensional view, stressing the unique contribution of individual differences and the variety of situations in which people interact with others. Moreover, it is a way to combine person variables (psychology) with situation variables (sociology) to understand behavior.

Magoon (1977) has pointed out how the writings of several prominent educational researchers, including Cronbach (1975), Berliner and Gage (1976), and Stephens (1967), suggest the need for a different focus in educational research. Each delineates the failures of a reductionist approach to the research on learning, while stressing the need to consider the effect of different situations, as interpreted by the learner. The research on Aptitude Treatment Interactions is a good example of traditional research methods, which have been, in the main, disappointing (Bracht & Glass, 1968; Cronbach, 1975; Cronbach & Snow, 1977). According to Magoon (1977), there is a need to concentrate on how pupils construct and interpret their learning environment. He suggests that this focus, based on an integration of cognitive psychology and sociology, will provide a more accurate understanding of complex human behavior. He uses the term "constructivist" research, "where the constructed reality/meanings of the observed participants are the primary focus [p. 670]," to identify this approach. The notion is based on the importance of what an individual constructs in his mind, as influenced by the situation. As such, "context" of behavior is not what is viewed by the researcher, but what is perceived by the subject. In the words of Magoon, constructivists assert that

> The central virtue of their view is the assurance that research investigations would include an account of the social context of the phenomenon. It would require researchers to approach the phenomena as social psychologists, sociologists, and social anthropologists, with corresponding attention to social definitions, rules, norms, values, etc. [p. 657].

Magoon suggests that a few researchers have successfully employed this approach by using a variety of ethnographic techniques. Wilson (1977) cites several educational studies that have employed ethnographic methods to collect data, and he believes this approach to research in education is growing. In his review of ethnographic techniques, Wilson summarizes how two assumptions: (a) "that human behavior is complexly influenced by the context in which it occurs [p. 253]," and (b) "the social scientist cannot understand human behavior without understanding the framework within which the subjects interpret their thoughts, feelings, and actions [p. 249]," underlie the rationale for using this approach. He stresses how these assumptions about human behavior may be quite different from the traditional view of educational researchers. This approach, which is also referred to as participant observation, or as anthropological or phenomenological research, assumes that the social situation consciously or unconsciously shapes behavior. Thus, the "researcher" is constantly aware of how he or she may affect subject responses and uses many sources of data in the situation, including the perspectives of individual subjects. Wilson notes that ethnography has been used by anthropologists and social psychologists for many years, with great success. However, only recently has education employed this approach. Two reasons for the recent interest by educators seem likely: Traditional educational research has been less than successful and new approaches are needed, in the case of ethnography forcing a different view of human behavior; and as educators realize the need to consider the complex interaction of person and situation variables, ethnography provides the tools to collect this type of data.

Urie Bronfenbrenner (1976) has also argued for a new focus for educational research. He refers to his approach as the "ecology of education" and suggests that by studying two sets of relationships in the educational setting (a) the relation between characteristics of learners and the environments in which they live; and (b) the relation between various environments, progress in educational research will be enhanced. Based on the work of Kurt Lewin, Bronfenbrenner suggests a methodology to examine what he refers to as the "dynamic relation between person and situation [p. 6]." He believes that through systematic analysis of the relation that exists between students and their environmental milieu, the researcher will better understand how the situation affects the learner, and vice versa. To provide further theoretical validity for his approach, Bronfenbrenner delineates the following propositions:

1. Research must investigate real-life situations, unencumbered by the presence of researchers or conditions that alter the social meaning for the participants. This "requirement . . . applies to all elements of the setting: place, time, roles, and activities [p. 7]."
2. An ideal to strive for is avoiding the extraneous factors in research; conditions that alter the natural setting. Such an emphasis is necessary to provide "ecological integrity" of the setting.
3. Ecological validity is maintained when the criteria used are characteristics of the social and cultural context, which are natural to the participants. He calls this "contextual validity."
4. The experimenter must assess the subjects' definition of the setting to establish constructive validity in the research. By assessing what the participants perceived in the conditions of the research, and by examining these perceptions to see if they are consistent with the conceptual definitions of the experimenter, constructive validity can be assessed. He refers to this requirement as "phenomenological validity."
5. The researcher must give as equal attention to examining the properties of the setting as he does to the behavior of the participants. This provides the data to analyze the relation between the subjects and setting. He calls this "setting analysis."

Furthermore, Bronfenbrenner goes on to list 15 additional propositions, but these 5 provide the ideas that are the most relevant for this discussion. These propositions form a distinctive research model and together they emphasize the need to consider the meanings that individuals give to various stimuli in their environment—for it is only through these propositions that the setting itself and its impact on behavior can be assessed. Bronfenbrenner is certainly not alone in his criticisms of "laboratory" research, but he offers an alternative to the emphasis on studying changes in the behavior of subjects. He suggests in further propositions the need to examine reciprocal processes of impact, the larger social system influencing the setting and participants, the affect of several settings, and other principles for those interested in conducting ecological research. Whereas it is probably impossible to meet all the requirements he believes are necessary, his overall message is clear: Educational research must attend to the systematic study of real-life settings and the impact of the setting on behavior itself. Learning behavior, more specifically, cannot be understood or predicted until these variables are accounted for.

Walter Mischel has taken a slightly different approach to research than either Magoon or Bronfenbrenner (Mischel, 1977, 1973). Mischel discusses the importance of situation and person variables in the context of personality measurement. He suggests that behavior is determined by many interacting variables, both in the person and situation, and that whereas this idea is certainly not new, the intent of the concept has only recently been translated into meaningful research methodology for the future. Person variables include the cognitive processes of attention, encoding, categorization of events, cognitive transformations, expectations of particular outcomes for certain responses, the value of potential outcomes, and the motivation behind individuals that influence the rate of behavior. Environment variables are factors that can be categorized in ways appropriate to the research. It is most important to consider those aspects of the environment that interact with persons to help explain behavior. Thus, his focus is on how qualities of the person interact with, influence, and are influenced by stimuli in the environment. The individual is viewed as an active participant in a setting that is changing. Mischel admits that this view of behavior is complex and difficult to derive generalizations from. However, he views multiple determinism and person–situation interaction as more accurate and as ultimately having greater practical use. Mischel's ideas are summarized in greater detail in the next section of this chapter. Consider, however, his words in light of what Bronfenbrenner stresses. The approach to research is very similar and underlies the suggested methodology for studying the effect of person–setting variables and interaction on behavior. Mischel (1977) asserts that

> The study of social interactions vividly reveals how each person continuously selects, changes, and generates conditions just as much as he or she is affected by them. The future of personality measurement will be brighter if we can move beyond our favorite pencil-and-paper and laboratory measures to include direct observation as well as unobtrusive, nonreactive measures to study lives where they are really lived and not merely where the researcher finds it convenient to look at them. In such studies, striking individual differences in preferred situations—in the contexts, environments, and activities different people prefer and select—are sure to be found [pp. 248–249].

Furthermore, another perspective on how to integrate person and environment variables has been offered by David Hunt (Hunt, 1975). Drawing on the work of Cronbach and Snow (1969), Shulman (1970), and others, Hunt reconceptualizes how the study of person–environment interactions can provide a reasonable research paradigm. He employs Kurt Lewin's formula, $B = f(P, E)$—behavior is a function of the person and the environment—as a model to organize and apply individual differences and instructional approaches to explain learning. Since he concentrates on the methods of teaching, or instruction, as the focus of "environment," his ideas are directed primarily to educational psychologists. He believes researchers have defined person–environment interactions too narrowly, resulting in the frustrating emphasis on finding Aptitude Treatment Interactions (ATI). He uses $B = f(P, E)$ as a philosophy, an admittingly self-evident yet complex approach, and suggests an alternative to the ATI interpretation in applying the formula to research in schools.

Hunt (1975) believes it is necessary to define person and environment variables that are compatible, describing persons in terms "that are directly translatable into specific forms of educational environments likely to be effective for the person's learning or development [p. 219]." He cites his own research on matching pupil conceptual levels (dependence on external standards, degree of responsibility to generate new concepts) with high or low structured instructional environments as an example of compatibility. Indeed, variables such as learning style, sensory modality preference, and locus of control have been studied recently in the context of different environments, with obvious implications for teachers. Furthermore, Hunt stresses the need for a developmental perspective, considering long-run changes in individual variables, to better accommodate environments, and much like Bronfenbrenner, he believes we must consider the effect of the individual on the environment. Finally, Hunt states the need for a practical approach, one that results in pragmatic application.

Although Hunt's suggestions are rather specific and oriented toward instructional procedures, his ideas provide yet another indication of the growing importance of person–situation interactions in the research on learning. Whereas this approach is certainly not new, only in the past several years have psychologists and educators developed research paradigms to utilize this perspective. Despite the different backgrounds represented, there is a significant overlap in the suggestions previously reviewed. However, there seems to be a clear emphasis on two fundamental ideas: (a) that human behavior is best understood and predicted as a function of individual-situation interaction; and (b) that new research methodologies may be needed to study behavior in this complex context. These propositions also form the basis for the social psychology of learning and research reviewed in this book. Social psychology has recognized the importance of person–environment interaction for many years, but stresses a particular aspect of the environment—social influences. Thus, we are assuming as a theoretical basis the notion that learning behavior is understood best by examining the variety of individual interaction with the social environment. This includes the perceptions, cognitive processes, needs, values, orientations, and other differences that individuals bring to a situation, which influence the nature and effect of social interactions.

The importance of the social environment in affecting behavior cannot be denied. Yet, there is a need for research and the synthesis of ideas that pull together the myriad aspects of social interactions most relevant in the influencing of academic learning behavior in schools. Moreover, how can one organize this approach in a concise, meaningful way that reflects the complexity of the process? A model to analyze those aspects of the person–social-environment interaction that seems to influence learning behavior most is developed later in this chapter. It is called a cognitive social-psychological concept of learning, which integrates and expands upon the work of several other models. It is simply a hypothesized procedure for systematically analyzing social interaction variables in pupil learning. As such, it concentrates on real-life learning behavior in schools. It does not represent a formal theory supported by specifically oriented research. Rather, it is a beginning, with some research that does support its conceptual framework. Before detailing the cognitive social-psychological conception of learning, it is useful to review briefly five related models, for each has contributed significantly to the paradigm developed especially for this book.

Getzels and Thelen

One of the first systematic applications of social psychology to teaching–learning situations was written by Getzels and Thelen in 1960. The model they developed is still useful in considering the factors that influence pupil learning behavior in classrooms. Their approach is based on examining individual behavior in the context of the group. They discuss the unique parameters of classroom groups, consisting of classroom goals, participants, leadership, and relationships to other groups, as a useful way to study how the classroom as a group influences behavior. Furthermore, these characteristics are developed to describe the classroom group as a "social system" consisting of factors that influence behavior. Two categories of these factors are identified—those ascribed by role requirements and those brought to the group by the individual. Getzels and Thelen conceive learning behavior to be a function of the relative influence of role demands or individual personality. In their words, "social behavior results as the individual attempts to cope with an environment composed of patterns of expectations for his behavior in ways consistent with his own independent pattern of needs [Getzels & Thelen, 1971, p. 16]."

They propose the following general equation to study these factors:

$$B = f(R \times P),$$

where B is observed behavior, R is the role expectation in a situation, and P is the personality of the individual defined by needs. They refer to the formation of role expectation as the nomothetic dimension of the social system. The institution a group functions in develops "roles" for positions within the institution. The roles define expected behavior, obligations, and responsibilities to carry out the objectives of the institution. Thus, the role of the teacher is to make sure students gain knowledge, and the student's role is to show evidence of learning. Individual personalities are referred to as the idiographic or personal dimension of the social system. Each individual brings particular needs to the situation that influence his or her behavior. Together, the individual needs and role expectations interact, each acting as a motive for behavior. It is, then, "personalistic propensities" and institutional obligations and requirements that determine behavior.

Getzels and Thelen describe how a classroom group may differ with respect to the relative influence of role-expectations or individual needs. They speculate about how incongruities between role expectations and individual dispositions will result in classroom conflict, and suggest that leadership styles can be either nomothetic—emphasizing role requirements—or idiographic, stressing individual personalities. They believe that if nomothetic and idiographic demands are understood and identified classroom groups can be more effective. Furthermore, they stress the need for the group to develop through "complexity, conflict and change."

The conceptualization developed by Getzels and Thelen is especially useful in organizing sociological influences of individual behavior in a classroom group. They indicate how "personalities" interact with institutional influences, but they do not develop in depth the individual characteristics that affect how institutional demands will be perceived or integrated with needs and desires to determine behavior. The strength of their model is its emphasis on a dynamic, changing social system that influences behavior, and the organization of many factors that contribute to this process. The next step in this analysis is to examine how certain organizational characteristics of a school influence role expectations, why individuals are more influenced by idiosyncratic elements than by expectations of others, and how the group climate or environment influences the type of role expectations and individual needs that are considered important by the student in determining behavior. These factors are considered in greater depth in later chapters.

Brookover

Wilbur Brookover (1955) and his associate Edsel Erickson (Brookover & Erickson, 1969, 1975) developed the first formal social-psychological conception of learning. Their theory is based on the premise that much of our learning is dependent on our decision to learn, and it is the social-psychological process of decision-making that forms the basis of the theory. Three propositions form the foundation of their theory:

1. Voluntary decision-making behavior is a function of the perceived probable outcomes of social acts.
2. The perceived probable outcomes of social acts are distinct from desired outcomes, as decision-making factors. Although aspirations and plans may at times be similar for an individual, these cognitive and affective constructs may be substantially different in their content and functions.
3. If voluntary behavior is a function of aspirations, these aspirations tend to function within the limits set by one's view of the possible alternatives and what might be expected to happen in the future.

Thus, decision-making is described as a cognitive process that anticipates the outcome of particular behaviors. As the individual perceives various outcomes in a particular situation, he will act on those behaviors that provide viable, realistic results—not dreams or long range goals. As a simple example, consider the student who expects to fail science class. As long as the student perceives the probable outcome to be failure, his or her "decision" will most likely be not to make any attempt to be successful in science, regardless of ultimate goals. Decision making, then, becomes a complex cognitive activity in which we construct a guide to our behavior based on what we perceive to be successful outcomes. Whereas Brookover and Erickson do not believe that the decisions of students totally determine their academic achievement, they believe that the intentions arrived at through decision-making contribute significantly to academic performance. Thus, if Johnny decides he cannot learn to read, it is unlikely that he will be a successful reader; if Susan decides she can and will learn math, chances are she will achieve in math. Based on the premise that decisions are crucial for learning, Brookover and Erickson turn to the factors that influence a student's decisions. In other words, what determines the perceptions of individuals, how is reality constructed, why are particular outcomes perceived as likely and others impossible, and what factors influence the decisions students make?

Brookover and Erickson maintain that the most important variable in determining decisions is the feedback individuals internalize from others. This notion is based on research and observation that suggest that other people, particularly those viewed with respect, credibility, and trust, are important in how we view ourselves. They stress that one's definition or perception of others, not the actual message or behavior, is the most crucial factor for understanding decision-making. Moreover, as an individual interacts with others who are important or significant, he or she learns "appropriate" behavior for certain situations. As others make evaluations of an individual, these evaluations are perceived as behaviors that can be expected. It becomes an expectation for behavior, and through these expectations the individual acquires a concept of self-ability. Thus, the individual's decision-making process, based on perceptions of what others expect of him or her—or on other information they provide, become related to learning behavior. As stated by Brookover and Erickson (1969), "a considerable proportion of what a student learns is dependent on his decisions to learn. These decisions are dependent on his conceptions of what is appropriate for self and what he thinks he is able to learn. In turn, the student's conceptions of self are acquired in interaction with others in his social system [p. 16]."

In analyzing the decision-making process, then, this theory relies heavily on interpersonal interaction and perceptions of one's self through this interaction. Decisions are based on how we perceive the responses and behaviors of others, and it is through this perceptual process that the theory constructs a paradigm by which to understand decision-making. To examine the perceptual process the authors integrate the work of Mead (1934), Sullivan (1953), Blumer (1969), and others identified as espousing a symbolic interactionist view of self-concept development. This perspective emphasizes internal communication and conversation within individuals to interpret the meaning of the environment to themselves. As such, "the actor selects, checks, suspends, regroups, and transforms the meanings in the light of the situation in which he is placed and the direction of his action [Blumer, 1969, p. 5]." Whereas this cognitive orientation is concerned most with self-concept in its broadest sense, Brookover and Erickson use these notions to explain academic behaviors. They derive an explanation for decision-making related to learning behavior from the principles of the symbolic interaction perspective. Moreover, they believe decision-making is based on conceptions of self, which, in turn, are developed through the process described by symbolic interactionists.

As individuals perceive responses from others that influence their behavior, a concept of "self" gradually develops. Self-concept, or the way we characterize ourselves and the attributes we use, is a term used by most educators to describe how and what students think about themselves. Unfortunately, many educators think of self-concept as a static condition; a student either has a "low" or "high" self-concept. Brookover, however, has conceptualized the "self" as a "defining behavioral process." As such, self-concept is not a trait or enduring characteristic; it is a cognitive process by which a person defines appropriate behavior in a particular situation. Thus, it is more accurate to say that William believes he will not benefit from working hard in his math class than to say that William has a low self-concept of math ability, or worse, that William has a low academic self-concept.

Brookover and Erickson identify four major factors that influence how interpersonal interaction shapes self-concept and, ultimately, the decision-making process that determines behavior. The first factor is the role require-ments for self. In most situations we develop a "role" to describe what behaviors others expect of us. For example, a student may take on the role of the class clown, or a teacher may define his or her role in the school as a disciplinarian. The expectations of others, which define role requirements, are influenced in turn by the "position" we occupy, as teacher, student or administrator. Each position has ascribed characteristics from the organiza-tion, community, or society at large. The precise ways in which organiza-tional characteristics of the school influence role development, as well as norms for behavior, will be explored in a later chapter. The role we develop for ourselves forms the foundation of the decision-making process. The second factor, self-concept of ability, refers to the person's perceived capa-bility to carry out the role requirements that have been defined. If an individual feels he is competent to succeed in the tasks that define the role, he will probably decide to carry out behaviors to be successful. However, a high self-concept of ability is not a sufficient condition to assure success-oriented behaviors. The third factor is the instrumental value to the self. This refers to "a person's cognitions or assessments of the rewards and costs to self associated with a given performance in a given role [Brookover & Erickson, 1975, p. 275]." That is, what is the payoff for being successful in a particular role? It is not uncommon for students who know they can suc-ceed, and who have a high self-concept of ability, to engage in inappropriate behavior. One likely reason is that these students see no benefit from successful achievement. The fourth factor is intrinsic value to the self. By this the authors mean the internal enjoyment or satisfaction of engaging in a behavior, regardless of social or economic consequences. Some students place a high value on reading, deriving positive feelings from the behavior itself, whereas others dislike or see no value in reading. The authors have provided evidence of a positive relationship between one of these factors, self-concept of academic ability, and academic performance. The effect of the other factors is theoretical, although supported by the writings of others (Rogers, 1951; Maslow, 1954; Combs & Snygg, 1959).

A crucial emphasis in the social-psychological conception of learning espoused by Brookover and Erickson is the influence of others in modifying student self-assessment. They believe that the selective perception of an individual to the reactions of others is crucial. They emphasize that the actual evaluations of an individual may not coincide with that individual's perception of the evaluation, and it is this perception which is most meaningful to the individual. They cite, for instance, the research on credibility as a means to assess the believability of others' responses, and they cite their own research, which points out the difference between parental and peer expectations in relationship to behavior. To assess perceptions of others, the authors simply asked students to name others who "are important in your life" and "concerned about how well you do in school." They developed an instrument, the School Social Environment Questionnaire, in which students were asked to indicate the expectations others held for them in school. The results showed, surprisingly, that in the area of academic behavior both junior and senior high school students viewed parents as more important than peers. They also found that most students' expectations were internalized from a wide variety of sources—neighbors and other adult groups— in addition to family and same-age friends. Furthermore, they found a significant positive correlation between perceived evaluations of others and academic performance, controlling for socioeconomic status, race, and other factors within a large population. Even though their research cannot claim the causal relationship suggested in the model, the evidence does provide some empirical support for their theory.

Since the evaluations and expectations of others are important, it is necessary to assess the conditions that affect this influence. Brookover and Erickson summarize how several factors can have an impact on how others affect self conceptions. These include (a) *the consequence of parental and peer expectations; (b)* expectations which differ because of social class; (c) involvement of parents, especially with children who have learning difficulties; (d) whether important others monitor our progress; (e) stability of the family; (f) teachers' expectations; (g) family assessment of teacher credibility; (h) membership and reference groups; and (i) present or past significant others. These influences are external to the individual, and individual traits and needs interact with these to shape the perceptual process. For instance, just as we have many "self-concepts," our perceived role in a given situation changes depending on the psychological needs we must attend to, the potential instrumental and intrinsic rewards, and the messages we perceive through those factors just listed. The process is complex because the external sources both shape our self-concepts and are selectively screened depending on our needs and other individual characteristics. Thus, it is possible that a student who has a strong need to achieve in English will attend to external sources, which tell him what is expected and what his ability is in relation to this role.

In summary, Brookover and Erickson's model organizes social psychological forces that affect learning behavior. Behavior is dependent on the cognitive process of decision-making. Moreover, these decisions are determined by the environment to the extent that important others influence the self-concepts of an individual in relation to a role. The self-concept then determines which behavior is most appropriate and desired. Other factors also affect the cognitions, such as the internal and external value of a particular behavior, societal demands for performance in a given role, and consistency of feedback from others. It is a dynamic interaction of internal and environmental forces, each related to social interaction, which finally determines the ultimate value or worth of a behavior to the individual. Alternatives are weighted and a decision is made. Once a particular behavior is engaged in, responses to the behavior are sought and, if these responses from others are appropriate, they reinforce the original perceptions that affected the decision. To a large extent, then, individuals will choose to learn what others define as appropriate and possible. These ideas form the basis of the cognitive social-psychological model of learning developed in this book, and these ideas are integrated with the material in each chapter. Several other authors, however, have developed other ideas about the impact of social-psychological processes on behavior, and each has an important contribution to the learning model presented later in this chapter.

Bandura

The well-known work of Bandura (1977, 1969) posits yet another interpretation of person–situation interactions. Bandura (1977) is associated with social-learning theory, an approach which examines behavior "in terms of continuous reciprocal interaction of person and environmental determinants [pp. 11–12]." The Lewinian formula, $B = f(P, E)$, is modified by Bandura to look like

$$[B \underset{\longleftrightarrow}{\overset{\nearrow P \nwarrow}{}} E].$$

He views behavior and personal and environmental factors as "interlocking determinants" of each other, rather than assuming that P and E function as independent causal variables of behavior. The relative influence of each factor varies in different settings for particular behaviors so that in some situations environmental factors are most influential, whereas in other situations personal traits regulate environmental events. Also called modeling or imitation theory, this view emphasizes the prominent role played by symbolic, vicarious, and self-regulatory processes. Thus, people can "learn" new behavior through the retention of images and other symbols attained by observing appropriate models.

Of particular interest is the process of social learning that Bandura and others have investigated. They have identified four categories of influences as determining the nature and effect of modeling phonemena. The first category involves attention, the extent to which modeled stimuli are observed or ignored. The selective perception of modeled behavior depends on such factors as others a person associates with regularly, interpersonal attraction, functional value of incentive conditions of modeled behavior, perceptual sets, the capacity to process information, and the salience and complexity of the modeled behaviors. A second category concerns the retentional activities of observed behavior. The nature of imaginal and verbal symbols that persons can recall will determine in part the effect of the observed behavior, and strategies such as organization, rehearsal, and labeling have been found to influence retention. The third component is concerned with how symbolic representations are converted to behavior. Several factors are important in this process including availability of component skills, support for correcting errors in initial behaviors, and feedback from others. Finally, the fourth category encompasses motivational and reinforcement factors. People are influenced by the consequences of observed behavior and by how the modeled behavior relates to the outcomes they value. Reinforcement variables also affect the behavior a person is likely to attend to. Thus, a person will probably be influenced most by observed behavior that elicits reinforcements they value.

Research in social learning has concentrated on three factors that influence the degree to which modeling affects behavior. The first factor encompasses certain characteristics of models that seem to be crucial. Those who have high status, competence, and power are most likely to be influential. This includes others who can meet our needs and provide rewards. In ambiguous situations, characteristics such as general appearance, speech, style and similarity to other models will determine the influential status of the model. A second factor concerns the types of people most responsive to modeling. Those individuals with low self-esteem, who lack confidence and are dependent, have been found to be influenced greatly by successful models, as have those whose goals are best reached by emulating others. In fact, bright and self-confident students seem to benefit more from modeling specific competency than do less bright and dependent students. Finally, the value of the modeled behavior is important. Modeled behavior is unlikely to be imitated if the response contingencies are unsatisfactory.

Social-learning theory provides the most extensive research base of all of the theories presented in this section of the chapter. This research is useful for specifying the conditions that determine interpersonal influence, and many of the factors may generalize to other forms of learning. For instance, variables that influence modeling, such as model status, behavior outcome reward, and attentional factors, may also be important in the process of expectation as developed by Brookover and Erickson. Modeling is certainly a theory of learning based on interpersonal dynamics, albeit only one aspect of social interaction, and must be considered in applying a social-psychological approach to pupil learning.

Rotter

Julian Rotter (1954) has combined two long-standing trends in psychology, stimulus–response (S–R) associationist theories and cognitive or field theories, to develop a social-learning theory of personality (as distinct from Bandura's social-learning theory). Perhaps better known for his work on internal–external locus of control, Rotter believes that several factors determine human social behavior. He believes that individual traits, needs, and habits interact with what the individual perceives in his or her meaningful environment. Situational parameters, and the way the individual interprets them, are just as important as individual characteristics. Thus, neither broad dispositional elements within people nor particular situational factors alone explain behavior very well. Not every person responds equally to the same situational cues, and overemphasis of situational variables will also be misleading. The theory examines different behaviors across situations that lead to similar rewards. Furthermore, this examination establishes a functional, purposeful relationship between goals and behaviors, and stresses the interrelationship among several experiences. For example, a student may exhibit several different behaviors, tapping his pencil, talking to other students, passing notes, to elicit the same outcome—attention from the teacher.

Rotter postulates that understanding and predicting behavior is best accomplished by examining three factors in the social environment that affect various choices of behavior available to the individual. These factors are expectancy, reinforcement value, and the psychological situation. Expectancy and reinforcement value are based on the notion that behavior is goal-directed, to attain or avoid particular outcomes, and that people will engage in behaviors for which they expect goals to be realized. Expectancy is defined by Rotter (1954) as the "probability held by the individual that a particular reinforcement will occur as a function of a specific behavior on his part in a specific situation or situations [p. 107]." That is, "behavior is determined by the degree to which people expect that their behavior will lead to goals [Phares, 1976, p. 13]." Expectancy is a subjective probability based on past success and failure experiences. If an individual has experienced a pattern of repeated failure in a task, an expectation of success is not likely, whereas the person who has been successful is more likely to develop an expectation that future similar behaviors will lead to the desired goal. Furthermore, expectancies can be general in a relatively novel situation, or specific, if the situation is very similar to past experiences. Reinforcement value is the degree of preference given to a stimulus that affects behavior. It indicates preference for a particular reinforcement, and is dependent on the "needs" of the individual at the time various reinforcements are available. A reinforcement will have a greater value if it can satisfy a "need," either physiological or psychological, such as those suggested by Rotter: recognition–status, protection–dependency, dominance–independence, love–affection, and physical comfort. The psychological situation refers to the environment in which the individual makes decisions. The situational cues —other people present, social interaction, time of day, familiarity—and other factors will help determine the impact of expectancies and reinforcers. Unfortunately, little research has been done on categorizing various kinds of situations and their impact. These three factors are interdependent and have been related by Rotter in the following formula:

$$BP_{x_1s_1,R_a} = f(E_{x,R_a,s_1} \ \& \ RV_{a_1s_1})$$

The formula is read: "The potential for Behavior x to occur, in Situation 1, in relation to Reinforcement a, is a function of the expectancy of the occurrence of Reinforcement a, following Behavior x in Situation 1, and the value of Reinforcement a in Situation 1 [Rotter, Chance, & Phares, 1972, p. 14]." In other words, a person's behavior is dependent on perceived expectancies that a particular behavior will lead to a reinforcement and on the value of that reinforcement to satisfy some need if attained.

The theory, which can be nicely applied to learning in schools, shows how simplified explanations of learning behavior are inappropriate. For example, when students are given an assignment to complete, they can work on the assignment or engage in several other behaviors. If they feel insecure and unwanted in the class, completing the assignment may have a low reinforcement value if it does not help satisfy this need. Or, they may have experienced failure in many related assignments so that the expectancy of receiving the reinforcement, even if valued, would be low. Thus, for students who have a combination of social needs that must be met and a history of failure with school assignments, it is likely that the pressure from parents and teachers and enticing external rewards for achievement will not be effective in promoting behaviors that demonstrate successful achievement. Another interesting implication is the utility of using experiences that are unfamiliar to students. Such situations avoid the negative influence of past failures and provide the opportunity for new expectations to develop. In any event, the social-learning theory developed by Rotter represents a meaningful way to think about the decision-making process, and when combined with other factors that influence decision-making, it provides a useful model to formalize the person and situational variables that affect the learning behaviors of pupils.

Mischel

Walter Mischel has proposed a cognitive social-learning theory of behavior, an approach that shifts the basic unit of study from individual traits to behavioral and cognitive activities in relation to particular situations. He integrates principles from cognitive and social psychology to conceptualize behavior in the context of person–situation interactions. More specifically, he suggests five major categories of person variables that define how persons perceive and incorporate stimuli in the environment (situation) and help to determine behavior:

1. *Construction competencies:* Ability to construct (generate) particular cognitions and behaviors. Related to measures of IQ, social and cognitive (mental) maturity and competence, ego development, social–intellectual achievements and skills. Refers to what the subject knows and can do.
2. *Encoding strategies and personal constructs:* Units for categorizing events and for self-descriptions.
3. *Behavior–outcome and stimulus–outcome expectancies in particular situations.*
4. *Subjective stimulus values:* Motivating and arousing stimuli, incentives, and aversions.
5. *Self-regulatory systems and plans:* Rules and self-actions for performance and for the organization of complex behavior sequences.

He admits that his list is open to augmentation and revision. Each of these factors will interact with the situation to influence behavior. The first factor, construction competencies, refers to the differences in prior learning that affect the perceived ability of an individual to perform the required response. Moreover, these perceptions are not viewed as an acquired set of cognitions and potential behaviors, but are actually actively processed information as the individual interacts with situations. Over a period of time, a generalized group of competencies is established, which defines the behavior the person believes he or she is capable of displaying. The second factor involves the field of information processing and stresses the importance of cognitive transformations on stimuli, such as selective attention, interpretation, and categorization. The expectations of a person that Behavior X will lead to Outcome Y are central to Mischel's theory. A set of contingencies is considered by the individual, influenced by previous behavior-outcome experiences in similar situations and the intentions of the motivating stimuli. Mischel cites the area of locus of control as an example of a trait that affects expectancies, but stresses the limited applicability of these personality characteristics across situations. The fourth factor affects behavior through the perceived value of the response-contingent outcome. Finally, self-regulatory systems, based on terminal goals, sequencing preferences, and consequences of achieving or failing to achieve the goals, will influence the decisions persons make about appropriate or needed behavior.

Despite the lack of empirical data to support the cognitive-social learning view of person–situation interactions, Mischel draws several interesting and reasonable implications that have relevance for pupil decision-making in schools. Based on his belief that the psychological environment affects behavior to the degree that person variables are influenced, Mischel examines conditions under which situations will have the greatest impact. Ambiguously structured situations, for which there are no clear expectations of appropriate behaviors, will be influenced to a greater degree by individual person variables. Conversely, when it is obvious that one particular response will be reinforced, or is otherwise appropriate, individual differences will have a minimal effect as compared to situational determinants. For example, the extent to which schools impose roles and rules for behavior influences the limits of behaviors and the degree to which individual variables are important. If behavior expectations and sanctions are rigidly imposed, there is little choice for the student—either conform if "competent" or devise strategies to withdraw psychologically. Covington and Beery (1976) have summarized several strategies that students use to withdraw when the school inappropriately imposes rigid standards and procedures. Finally, Mischel (1973) emphasizes the need to study behavior as the individual interacts with conditions in the environment. "Indeed, the conceptualization of behavior, whether psychologist defined (as in research) or subject defined (as in clinical, individually oriented assessment) must be embedded in relation to the specific conditions in which the behavior occurs [p. 278]." He views the situation as critical, but only to the extent that it provides information, which in turn is processed by the person to influence behavior.

A COGNITIVE
SOCIAL-PSYCHOLOGICAL VIEW
OF LEARNING

The cognitive social-psychological learning model is an integration of the work of Brookover, Rotter, Mischel, Bandura, and others who have suggested applications of person–situation interaction, with the conditions present in school learning. It represents a way of conceptualizing the social-psychological determinants of pupil behavior in schools. Whereas it is less than a formal theory, the model suggests how influences resulting from pupil–social interaction can be organized and analyzed to understand and predict the decision-making process of pupils that results in behavior. The perspective is social-psychological in assuming that a pupil's interactions with others is a primary determinant of behavior. Furthermore, it is cognitive in its emphasis on pupil perception, the meaning of stimuli to individuals and the unique way each person categorizes, transforms, and interprets social events.

The major factors in the model represent the essential aspects of each of the previously mentioned theories. To simplify the model as much as possible, and yet retain a sound theoretical basis, the areas of overlap and similarity between the theories are combined. There is some mention of individual characteristics in each of the theories. Brookover emphasizes "self-concept of ability," which is similar to Mischel's "construction competencies," what Rotter refers to as "expectancy," and is a factor Bandura considers as "availability of skills." Mischel extends individual characteristics by incorporating information processing variables, and though Bandura has also considered this area through the attention and retention factors in social learning, Mischel's contribution to understanding the cognitive process of decision-making is substantial. In addition, Schroder and Suedfeld (1971) present one of the few integrations of personality theory and information processing. By using such traits as cognitive style, locus of control, achievement motivation, meaningfulness of stimuli, and categorization of events, the process of perception and the importance of selected social interactions can be analyzed more accurately. Virtually every theory mentions reinforcement value of potential behaviors as an important factor. Brookover cites instrumental and intrinsic value, Mischel adds the value of long-range goals and plans, and certainly Bandura, as a behaviorist, believes reinforcement processes are crucial. In understanding and predicting behavior in a particular situation, however, it is more useful if the individual's needs, which determine "value," are considered rather than reinforcement. A "reinforcement" is often identified after the fact, whereas a psychological need is an antecedent condition that helps define the value of available reinforcements. The needs people bring with them also influence which stimuli in the environment are attended to. Thus, it seems more practical to think about pupil needs rather than reinforcement value. The final factor concerns the situation or environment. Assuming that social interactions are a crucial aspect of the situation one behaves within, it seems wise to follow Brookover's lead. He specifies one consequence of social interaction, feedback from important others, as a primary determinant of behavior. By broadening this notion slightly and incorporating the Getzels and Thelen model, a general factor can be identified: messages or information about "appropriate" behavior people assimilate. The information can come from "significant others" in the form of expectations, as stressed by Brookover and noted by Mischel, or come less explicitly through the norms for behavior established by the group or institution and roles that define acceptable behavior.

The cognitive social-psychological model can be represented by the following formula:

$$BP_s = f(IC_p, N_{ps}, F_s)$$

The equation states that the behavior (B) of a person (P) in a given situation (s) is a function of the individual characteristics of the person (IC_p), the needs of the person in that situation (N_{ps}), and the feedback the person receives regarding appropriate behavior in the situation (F_s). The model is formulated to account for significant factors which influence the decision to choose an action among potential behaviors. The model is expanded in Figure 1.1 to indicate factors in each of the three categories that pertain to pupil behavior decisions in schools.

The overall nature of the situation (s) can be conceptualized as ranging somewhere in a continuum from "familiar" to "unfamiliar." Familiar situations have characteristics the individual has been exposed to in the past whereas unfamiliar situations are new. Behavior in familiar situations is determined to a great extent by a person's past experiences in similar situations. As Mischel has pointed out, the individual traits of a person will probably not have much of an impact in such situations, since expectations and sanctions have been clearly delineated by past successes and failures of the person and by the establishment of environmental norms. This is quite evident in school, as students learn quickly what behaviors are "appropriate" and "inappropriate" in an environment that is relatively constant from teacher to teacher and year to year (Jackson, 1968). However, decisions by pupils to engage in learning behaviors occur in many unpredictable, specific situations, and many of these are "unfamiliar." For instance, a pupil engaged in library work may encounter an unforeseen circumstance that forces him to choose between completing his academic work or visiting with friends. Thus, we must analyze situations to the extent they are familiar or unfamiliar to the student. Other aspects of the situation, such as choice to be involved, relative importance of potential behaviors, and the overall nature of the situation as "crucial" or "trivial" may also be important.

The first factor in the model which influences behavior, individual characteristics, can be classified into constant or variable categories. Con-

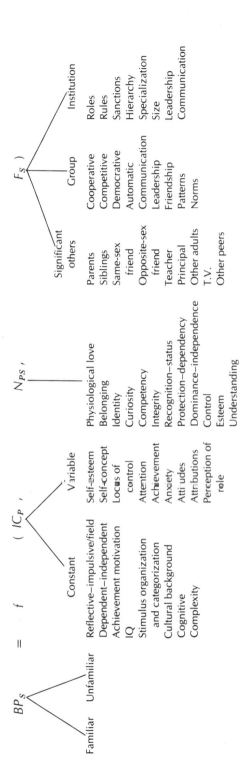

$$BP_S = f \quad (\quad IC_P , \quad N_{PS} , \quad F_S)$$

		Constant	Variable			
Familiar	Unfamiliar			Significant others	Group	Institution

Constant
Reflective–impulsive/field
Dependent–independent
Achievement motivation
IQ
Stimulus organization
and categorization
Cultural background
Cognitive
Complexity

Variable
Self-esteem
Self-concept
Locus of control
Attention
Achievement
Anxiety
Attitudes
Attributions
Perception of role

Physiological love
Belonging
Identity
Curiosity
Competency
Integrity
Recognition–status
Protection–dependency
Dominance–independence
Control
Esteem
Understanding

Significant others
Parents
Siblings
Same-sex friend
Opposite-sex friend
Teacher
Principal
Other adults
T.V.
Other peers

Group
Cooperative
Competitive
Democratic
Automatic
Communication
Leadership
Friendship
Patterns
Norms

Institution
Roles
Rules
Sanctions
Hierarchy
Specialization
Size
Leadership
Communication

Figure 1.1 This diagram represents the cognitive social-psychological model of learning developed in the chapter and lists examples of specific variables of each major component in the model. The major components are Behavior of a Person in a Situation (BP_s), Individual Characteristics of a Person (IC_p), Needs of a Person in a Situation (N_{PS}), and Feedback from Other Persons in a Situation (F_s).

stant characteristics are relatively stable across situations and include such traits as cognitive style, achievement motivation, and intelligence as defined by IQ scores. For instance, Covington and Beery (1976) have summarized the effect of achievement motivation on pupil behavior. Pupils with a need to avoid failure exhibit such strategies as: setting goals too high or too low, not trying, over achieving, and cheating to avoid feeling a sense of failure. Whereas students with a need to achieve success prefer situations in which there is some risk involved in attaining "success". Other individual characteristics are variable in the sense that they will change depending on the situation. Consider locus of control, an attribute that has received considerable attention over the past few years. Research in this area has demonstrated that the nature of the situation determines whether a person perceives himself to have an internal or external locus of control, that is, the same pupil can feel that he has no control over his achievement in science because of a biased teacher, but believe his performance in English is mostly up to him. Phares (1976) summarizes further research which suggests that internals concentrate on the content of communications in the context of previous experiences, whereas externals seem more likely to be affected by a prestigious source. Furthermore, internals are more independent than externals, and seem less susceptible to control by others. The implications of this research are significant to the model, since a pupil with an internal locus of control may be less willing to internalize the feedback received from others than a pupil with an external locus of control.

Other variable individual characteristics are well documented in educational research. The effect of anxiety on learning and transfer has been studied for many years, and self-concept of ability has been related empirically by Brookover to achievement. Brookover's conception of self-concept as a cognition related to appropriate behavior in a situation is relevant, since it stresses how the self-concept is multidemensional, not an enduring trait or characteristic. Research has also documented the motivational effects of appropriate prerequisite learning. Thus, the achievement level of skills and knowledge acquired before interactions in a situation will influence confidence, motivation, and competence of the individual.

It is well known that behavior is influenced by the second factor in the model, social and psychological needs of a person, and that needs and desires determine what constitutes a "reinforcement." Some theorists, such as Maslow (1954), Murray (1964), and Erickson (1968) have provided educators with meaningful categories of needs. Others, such as White (1959), Deci (1975), and Hunt (1971) have been given less attention. Their research of the need for humans to feel competent and self-determining by seeking out and resolving uncertainty or discrepant stimuli has definite implications. Murray's classification of needs related to students' interpersonal relationships is especially relevant for the cognitive social-psychological model. By examining such interpersonal needs as affiliation, nurturance, succorance, blame avoidance, deference, and similance, educators can better understand why students engage in certain behaviors.

The third factor of the model, feedback from others, is divided in three categories to emphasize the sources of evaluation that impinge on pupils. Most social scientists agree that feedback received from important others will determine what might be called "self-attitude" or "self-image," but these concepts are broad and difficult to define. The model examines specific feedback related to a given situation as a more accurate assessment of causal factors of a particular behavior. Of course, if feedback is consistent for many different situations over a long period of time, a more general view of appropriate behavior could be established, such as self-concept of academic achievement. In a given situation, though, information is sought from others, both in the present and from the past, to help us decide the behavior that will result in desired goals. The question in a particular situation is, however, whose behavior and responses will an individual attend to, believe, and incorporate to influence his decisions? Although sociologists have studied such characteristics of others as credibility, status, and trustworthiness, little research has extended these principles to pupil learning. It seems reasonable to postulate that the presence or absence of other people, real or vicarious, who are considered important or influential will affect the type of feedback an individual receives. In part, deciding who is "important" or "influential" will depend on the needs the individual must satisfy. A person could be viewed as important before giving feedback because of previous experiences or knowledge (the individual may be noted as an expert or respected by others) or may become an important person by providing relevant or needed information. The impact of the information given by a significant other may also depend on the intentions of the person providing the information. If the important person is perceived to be interested in the welfare of the individual, that information is more likely to be influential than cues received from a person who does not have the best interests of the individual in mind. It should be noted, also, that the popular field of expectancy and self-fulfilling prophecies is related to this category, yet there is no attempt to cover this area here since many sources already exist. However, certain research findings in expectancy are helpful in examining the conditions under which feedback and messages we perceive influence behavior. Such an approach is taken, for instance, by Jones (1977). Furthermore, under what circumstances do pupils view teachers as "significant others"?

The other two categories that provide sources of information are groups and the institutional and organizational characteristics of the environment.

Though more subtle, these factors may be more powerful than individual persons. Research on the effect of group processes in pupil learning is well documented, but the import of organizational properties of schools has been considered mostly in theoretical terms. With the exception of Barker and Gump's (1964) study of the effect of school size on behavior, there has not been much empirical study of this area. Moreover, research in group dynamics and organizational properties has not been analyzed with respect to individual decision-making and behavior.

The most intriguing aspect of the cognitive social-psychological model is the way the four causative factors are interrelated. As a person's needs vary from one situation to another, the stimuli from others that is perceived to be important will also vary, that is, a person with a strong need for affection will look for different cues from the environment than a person whose needs center around the establishment of a self-identity. A pupil who feels a need for affiliation with his peers is likely to perceive others as "important" if they provide information to help the pupil behave so others will like him. As persons strive to develop self-concepts in various domains, athletic, academic, social, sexual, etc., their perception of who is regarded as a significant other will differ. Thus, one general area of interaction would seem to involve the effect of individual needs on selective perception of feedback from others. Another interaction concerned with needs is the manner in which group processes and organizational characteristics satisfy certain needs and ignore or exacerbate others. An environment that does not develop a diverse pattern of potential interpersonal influence will probably be deficient in meeting pupil needs for belonging and status. A high school with rigid, ascribed, all-encompassing rules will do little to meet adolescent needs of responsibility and decision-making.

Another form of interaction is between individual characteristics of the group and the institutional nature of the school. The child who enters a competitive class with inferior skills will soon experience a need to feel competent. A child with a cultural background that stresses cooperation, not competition, may feel alienated and estranged, with conflicting messages from peers, parents, and teachers. Already noted is the effect of achievement motivation with resulting needs to feel competent, which are not met for children with a low need to achieve. At the other end of the spectrum, gifted and creative students are frustrated by the inability of a conforming school environment to meet their special needs.

The first step in analyzing potential behavior according to the cognitive social-psychological model is to understand individual characteristics of the student. This may seem at the outset like a difficult if not impossible task, given the list of possible traits, but salient characteristics are likely to have the greatest impact. It is not necessary to know all the individual characteristics, only those that affect behavior in a particular circumstance. Understanding individual characteristics is an important first step, since the effect of other factors is dependent on them. Second, the needs of the individual, at the time, must be assessed to determine the type of information needed to make decisions. Finally, an analysis of important others in the situation, the feedback from them, and information and messages from the group and organization will provide needed information about environmental influences.

It is difficult to specify how much each factor will influence behavior, although the relative impact of each variable is most dependent on the situation, the presence of significant others, and whether the potential behavior is public or private. The ambiguity and specific characteristics of the situation will determine if feedback received from others in the past is useful. The effect of important others depends on their presence or absence and the degree to which they are viewed as "significant" or role models. Therefore, it could be expected that "public" behavior, in which others in the situation are overtly effected, is more susceptible to the influence of significant others in the situation. Private behavior, on the other hand, may involve less direct interaction with others, so that decisions are based primarily on imitation and past experiences.

An example at this point is probably helpful. Consider the case of David, age 15, who is a highly intelligent student with a strong need to avoid failure. He maintains "success" in academic pursuits by *always* achieving A grades. Furthermore, David has been self-conscious for several years about his small stature. He is impulsive, and he tends to be anxious in performance situations. David was at his locker Wednesday morning when some friends asked him if he would like to meet them in the library next period, where they were planning to see some girls. David had planned to study for a chemistry test he had that day, but this was an opportunity to be part of the "group" and meet some girls. The "big" dance was scheduled for the weekend and David did not have a date yet. His decision is a difficult one: By going to the library he may not get an A on the test, but by not going he may not have a date for the dance. The cognitive social-psychological theory of behavior suggests the following analysis:

1. David's individual characteristics imply a strong need to do whatever is necessary to attain an A on the test.
2. David's social and sexual needs have not been adequately satisfied recently. If these needs were met, he would probably choose to study, not go to the library.
3. The situation is a new one; he has few past experiences to help him.
4. Several others who intend to go to the library are perceived by David as

successful in social and sexual concerns. Thus, he views their behavior and feedback as important in these circumstances.
5. The decision is public, which increases the pressure for David to go along with his peers.

Since David's decision presents a dilemma, it seems likely that he would question his friends further about who will be at the library and what, specifically, they will do there. In doing this, he is trying to determine the expectancy of reinforcement (eventually getting a date and satisfying social needs) if he made the decision to go to the library. Considering David's pervasive need to avoid failure and his concern about his size, he would probably have to be well convinced that going to the library would fulfill his expectancies.

Another example is Susan, who is in the third grade. Susan is a poor student in reading, and because of her performance she tends to withdraw from reading groups. She has a strong need to avoid failure and an external locus of control with respect to reading. She also has a need to feel competent, but the competitive nature of the class and stress on achieving competency skills seems to heighten her anxiety and withdrawal. She is secure socially, quiet, and unassuming. To improve her reading, the teacher has decided to try peer tutoring, and has asked a sixth grade student to work with Susan. The teacher has also made a point to create a "new" reading situation for Susan by emphasizing the acceptability of reading at a different level from others in the class. Further, the teacher ascribed status to the tutor by asking Susan's friends to respond favorably to the tutor. Hopefully, the tutor will become a significant other for Susan and help provide realistic, positive expectations and a supportive, cooperative setting in which mistakes are viewed as feedback to improve, not as an indication of poor knowledge. By changing the situation to adapt better to Susan's individual characteristics, the teacher is successful in improving her reading performance.

In summary, the cognitive social-psychological model of learning is not intended to specifically predict behavior but to organize person–environment factors that influence the choice of behavior. The factors fall into three categories, individual characteristics (constant and variable), needs, and feedback received regarding appropriate behavior (significant others, groups, organizational characteristics). The situation in which decisions are made, defined as familiar or unfamiliar, is also important. While there has not been any research done that demonstrates the usefulness of the model, data can be integrated into various parts of the model to provide empirical justification. A portion of each of the chapters in this book considers the model with respect to current research and implications in a social-psychological area. As such, the model provides a point of departure and organization for each chapter. Rather than study the various social-psychological topics in isolation from each other, which has been common in other writings, the intent is to adapt the philosophy of person–situation interaction and integrate the areas through the model. This integration of areas represents a realistic and useful way to view the learning process, which accounts for the complex interaction of individual differences and social environment.

OVERVIEW OF THE CHAPTERS

Chapter 2, by Irene Frieze, considers causal attributions; the beliefs students have about the causes of success and failure. This is an area of study that has been investigated intently by social psychologists over the past several years, and represents an important link in understanding how events in school (success or failure) are interpreted by students to influence subsequent behavior. Frieze begins her chapter with a summary of research, which has resulted in a theoretical conception of typical causal attributions given by students. She further summarizes the effect of various attributions on student expectations of future performance and the affects associated with the success of failure. She stresses, however, the limitations of this research, which has largely been done with college students under artificial conditions.

In examining the implications of the present research for elementary and secondary pupils, Frieze suggests that many variables may influence how causal attributions are formed and how they influence expectancies and affects. Individual differences such as age, self-esteem, achievement motivation, sex, race, and past experiences, probably influence the nature of real-life attributions. She also suggests that the perceptions of others' expectancies and comparisons with other individuals in the same situation may be important determinants.

While there is a need for more real-life, classroom-oriented research, the implications of this area of study seem clear. As an individual characteristic of the cognitive social-psychological model of learning, attributions mediate between social-psychological factors such as expectations, groups and institutional characteristics, and behavior. Furthermore, as we more fully understand how these beliefs are formed and the extent of their impact, we will be better able to structure feedback and social interaction to develop healthy and positive pupil perceptions. This chapter effectively integrates attributions with the larger environmental context of schooling in the analyses of laboratory and applied studies, and suggests directions for future research in school settings.

In Chapter 3, Tom Good analyzes recent applied research in the area of teacher expectations and relates this research to teacher–student interactions. He indicates why expectation is an important variable of teacher–pupil interactions, how teachers form and communicate expectations, and postulates the consequences of expectations for both teachers and students.

By carefully examining research methods and results in this area, he is able to suggest many worthwhile recommendations for future research. Much of this research will depend on ethnographic techniques to analyze systematically the nature and consequences of teacher–student interaction. As a form of feedback teachers give to students, expectancies represent the process of cognitive social-psychological learning. Furthermore, this chapter focuses on how this process is translated to student behavior. Chapters 4 and 5 summarize social interaction variables that influence the nature of this process, whereas Chapter 2 has identified student perception factors that affect how information is utilized by the student in determining behavior.

In Chapter 4, David Johnson discusses the nature of student–student relationships in the classroom. He summarizes research that indicates how peer relationships influence the cognitive and social outcomes of schooling, and describes how the structure of learning goals affects student interaction. By viewing student learning as a result of group processes, Johnson is expanding one dimension of the cognitive social-psychological model—the nature of feedback we receive as influenced by the nature of the group. As the classroom group develops norms and patterns of interactions, each individual is influenced by expected and rewarded forms of communications with each other. Group processes, then, affect learning directly by the type of feedback students give each other, and indirectly, through structural influences. This chapter summarizes a wealth of recent research which, when combined with Chapter 3, suggests many important factors that determine student behavior and learning.

Chapter 5, by Richard Schmuck, is concerned with the school as a societal institution, an organization that influences student learning in less overt but no less significant ways. Schmuck develops the perspective that organization characteristics—structures, norms, roles, procedures—impart the way in which students think and feel about themselves. By analyzing the context of the school (neighborhood and school size), the formal structure (complexity, roles, hierarchy of positions), and the informal structure of the school (trust, openness, morale), Schmuck discusses how student learning is affected through structural demands and staff and teacher expectations. This chapter provides a macro analysis of social-psychological influence and focuses on one part of the social-psychological model of learning. Thus, this chapter, along with Chapter 4, completes the perspective of the book by emphasizing determinants of social interaction, whereas Chapters 2 and 3 are mostly concerned with the specific process of interpersonal interaction.

In some ways, Chapter 6 would be better presented as parts of each of the other chapters. The study of attitudes has been a focal point of social-psychological inquiry and remains an important factor in school learning. The development of student attitudes is examined in the context of social psychological variables both as an outcome of student learning that is affected by social interactions and as a factor that determines the perceptions of others, communication, and the nature of interactions. Since attitudes are constructs that have been difficult to assess, suggestions for the measurement of attitudes are summarized. A social-psychological perspective implies affective learning outcomes, but an objective study of affect depends on sensitive and accurate instruments.

SUMMARY

This chapter has introduced a social-psychological perspective in student learning. By stressing the importance of interpersonal and person–situation interaction, the material has been organized to provide the reader with a framework for considering more specific research that is summarized in subsequent chapters. This included an overview of the social psychology of education as a field of study. Whereas social psychology has definite implications for education, there has not been much attention to research in this area. Most of the applications continue to have weak external validity. Several models of social-psychological learning were presented to organize interaction variables that affect learning based on the need for ecological, ethnographic, and anthropological research methods which can capture social interaction. These included Getzel and Thelen's $B = f(R \times P)$, Brookover's social-psychological concept of learning, Bandura's social learning, Rotter's social-learning theory, and Mischel's integration of cognitive and social psychology.

A cognitive social-psychological view of learning was presented to combine and integrate several other models. This paradigm organizes pupil social interaction variables and relates them to help explain student learning. The model is based on the assumption that a pupil's interaction with others is a primary determinant of behavior and that each pupil's perceptions and meanings should be accounted for. The model summarizes behavior as a function of individual characteristics of the student, the needs of the student in a particular situation, and the feedback the student receives from others regarding appropriate behavior in the situation. Moreover, feedback from others is further divided into significant others, groups, and organizational characteristics, since each of these factors determines the types of responses the student will incorporate. Examples of how the model might be used to analyze student learning are also summarized.

An overview of each of the remaining chapters is presented. The material in each chapter can be thought of as an extension of parts of the cognitive social-psychological model of learning. Attribution is concerned with individual differences and the importance of student perceptions of school outcomes on expectations for future behavior and affect. Teacher–student relations and the process of expectancy are examined in Chapter 3, whereas student–student relationships are the focus of Chapter 4. Each of these chapters discusses antecedents and consequences of student interaction with the immediate social environment. Chapter 5 suggests the general ways in which the organizational character of the school affects the nature of social interactions, and Chapter 6 reviews pupil attitude development as an individual characteristic and an important outcome of school, influenced by social interaction. Together, the emphasis is on how the individual interacts with the social environment, and the relationship between this interaction and student behavior.

REFERENCES

Backman, C. B., & Secord, P. F. *A social psychological view of education*. New York: Harcourt, 1968.

Bandura, A. Social learning theory of identificatory processes. In D. A. Goslin (Ed.), *Handbook of socialization theory and research*. Chicago: Rand-McNally, 1969, 213–262.

Bandura, A. *Social learning theory*. Englewood Cliffs, New Jersey: Prentice-Hall, 1977.

Bany, M. A., & Johnson, L. V. *Educational social psychology*. New York: Macmillan, 1975.

Barker, R., & Gump, P. *Big school, small school: High school size and student behavior*. Stanford: Stanford University Press, 1964.

Bar-Tal, D., & Saxe, L. *Social psychology of education: Theory and research*. New York: Halsted, 1978.

Berliner, D. C., & Gage, N. L. The psychology of teaching methods. In N. L. Gage (Ed.), *The psychology of teaching methods*. Chicago: National Society for the Study of Schools, 1976.

Bidwell, C. Schools as a formal organization. In J. C. March (Ed.), *Handbook of Organizations*. Chicago: Rand-McNally, 1965.

Blumer, H. *Symbolic interactionism: Perspective and method*. Englewood Cliffs, New Jersey: Prentice-Hall, 1969.

Bracht, G. H., & Glass, G. V. The external validity of experiments. *Review of Educational Research*, 1968, *5*, 437–474.

Bronfenbrenner, V. The experimental ecology of education. *Educational Researcher*, 1976, *5*(9), 5–15.

Brookover, W. B. *A sociology of education*. New York: American Book Company, 1955.

Brookover, W. B., & Erickson, E. L. *Society, schools, and learning.* Boston: Allyn & Bacon, 1969.

Brookover, W. B., & Erickson, E. L. *Sociology of education.* Homewood, Illinois: The Dorsey Press, 1975.

Brophy, J. E., & Good, T. L. *Teacher–student relationships: Causes and consequences.* New York: Holt, Rinehart & Winston, 1974.

Charters, W. W. Social psychology and education: An essay. Review of Lindzey-Aronson, *American Educational Research Journal,* 1973, *10*(1), 69–78.

Charters, W. W., Jr., & Gage, N. L. (Eds.). *Readings in the social psychology of education.* Boston: Allyn & Bacon, 1963.

Combs, A. W., & Snygg, D. *Individual behavior.* New York: Harper, 1959.

Covington, M. V., & Beery, R. G. *Self worth and school learning.* New York: Holt, Rinehart & Winston, 1976.

Cronbach, L. J. Beyond the two disciplines of scientific psychology. *American Psychologist,* 1975, *30*, 116–127.

Cronbach, L. J., & Snow, R. E. Individual differences in learning ability as a function of instructional variables. Final report, U.S. Office of Education. Palo Alto, California: Stanford University, School of Education, 1969 (ERIC No. ED 029001).

Cronbach, L. J., & Snow, R. E. *Aptitudes and instructional methods: A handbook for research on interactions.* New York: Irvington, 1977.

Deci, E. L. *Intrinsic motivation.* New York: Plenum Press, 1975.

Erickson, E. *Identity: Youth and crises.* New York: Norton, 1968.

Getzels, J. W. A social psychology of education. In G. Lindzey & E. Aronson (Eds.), *The handbook of social psychology* (2nd ed.), Vol. 5. Reading, Massachusetts: Addison-Wesley, 1969.

Getzels, J. W., & Thelen, H. A. The classroom group as a unique social system. In A. H. Yee (Ed.), *Social interactions in educational settings.* Englewood Cliffs, New Jersey: Prentice-Hall, 1971, 25–60.

Guskin, A. E., & Guskin, S. L. *A social psychology of education.* Reading, Massachusetts: Addison-Wesley, 1970.

Hunt, D. E. Person–environment interaction: A challenge found wanting before it was tried. *Review of Educational Research,* 1975, *45*(2), 209–230.

Hunt, J. McV. Intrinsic motivation and psychological development. In H. M. Schroder & P. Suedfeld (Eds.), *Personality theory and information processing.* New York: Ronald Press, 1971, 85–117.

Hunt, J. McV. Toward a history of intrinsic motivation. In H. I. Day, D. E. Berlyne, & D. E. Hunt (Eds.), *Intrinsic motivation: A new direction in education.* Toronto: Holt, Rinehart & Winston, 1971, 1–32.

Johnson, D. W. *The social psychology of education.* New York: Holt, Rinehart & Winston, 1970.

Johnson, D. W., & Johnson, R. T. *Learning together and alone: Cooperation, competition, and individualization.* Englewood Cliffs, New Jersey: Prentice-Hall, 1975.

Jones, R. A. *Self-fulfilling prophecies: Social, psychological, and physiological effects of expectancies.* Hillsdale, New Jersey: Lawrence Erlbaum Associates, 1977.

Lewin, K., Lippitt, R., & White, R. Patterns of aggressive behavior in experimentally created 'social climates'. *Journal of Social Psychology,* 1939, *10*, 271–299.

Magnusson, D., & Endler, N. S. (Eds.). *Personality at the crossroads: Current issues in interactional psychology.* Hillsdale, New Jersey: Lawrence Erlbaum Associates, 1977.

Magoon, A. J. Constructivist approaches in educational research. *Review of Educational Research,* 1977, *47*(4), 651–693.

Maslow, A. *Motivation and learning.* New York: Harper, 1954.

McMillan, J. H. The social psychology of education: New field of study or just educational psychology? *Educational Psychologist,* 1978, *12*(3), 345–354.

Mead, G. H. *Mind, self and society.* Chicago: Chicago University Press, 1934.

Miles, M. B., & Charters, W. W. Jr. (Eds.). *Learning in social settings: New readings in social psychology of education.* Boston, Mass.: Allyn & Bacon, 1970.

Mischel, W. Toward a cognitive social learning reconceptualization of personality. *Psychological Review,* 1973, *80,* 252–283.

Mischel, W. On the future of personality measurement. *American Psychologist,* 1977, *32*(4), 246–254.

Murray, E. *Motivation and emotion.* Englewood Cliffs, New Jersey: Prentice-Hall, 1964.

Phares, E. J. *Locus of control in personality.* Morristown, New Jersey: General Learning Press, 1976.

Rogers, C. *Client and centered therapy.* Boston: Houghton Mifflin, 1951.

Rotter, J. B. *Social learning and clinical psychology.* Englewood Cliffs, New Jersey: Prentice-Hall, 1954.

Rotter, J. B., Chance, J., & Phares, E. J. (Eds.). *Applications of a social learning theory of personality.* New York: Holt, Rinehart & Winston, 1972.

Schmuck, R. A., & Miles, M. *Organizational development in the schools.* Palo Alto, California: National Press Books, 1975.

Schmuck, R. A., & Schmuck, P. A. *Group processes in the classroom.* (2nd ed.). Dubuque, Iowa: William C. Brown, 1975.

Schroder, H. H., & Suedfeld, P. (Eds.). *Personality theory and information processing.* New York: Ronald Press, 1971.

Shulman, L. S. Reconstruction of educational research. *Review of Educational Research,* 1970, *40,* 371–396.

Stephens, J. M. *The process of schooling.* New York: Holt, Rinehart & Winston, 1967.

Sullivan, H. S. *The interpersonal theory of psychiatry.* New York: Norton, 1953.

White, R. W. Motivation reconsidered: The concept of competence. *Psychological Review,* 1959, *66,* 297–333.

Wilson, S. The use of ethnographic technique in educational research. *Review of Educational Research,* 1977, *47*(1), 245–265.

Yinger, J. M. Research implications of a field view of personality. In S. P. Spitzer (Ed.), *The sociology of personality.* New York: Van Nostrand Reinhold, 1969, 168–188.

chapter 2

Beliefs about Success and Failure in the Classroom

IRENE HANSON FRIEZE

INTRODUCTION

A great number of social-psychological variables affect classroom performance and interactions in the classroom and in the larger school environment. This chapter will focus on a particular set of variables related to students' beliefs about why they do well or poorly on various school-related activities.

In any social system, the members of that system have a set of shared beliefs about how that system operates (Lancy, 1978). Members of the school environment (students, teachers, administrators, parents, educational researchers, and local politicians) have ideas about the factors leading to high student achievement in the classroom and about the importance of schooling. To some extent, they probably all agree upon what the relevant variables are, although they may disagree on the relative importance of these variables. Furthermore, they have shared ideas about how these various factors may interrelate.

As will be shown in this chapter, people tend to have similar ideas about why students do well in reading, arithmetic, art, sports events, and other school activities. Within each of these areas, there are also some differences in the degree to which one factor or another is stressed, especially in reference to a particular student. As shown in Figure 2.1, various participants may have quite different views about why a student received a particular grade, even though they all agree that success is a function of hard work, ability, the difficulty of the test, and the quality of teaching.

39

THE SOCIAL PSYCHOLOGY
OF SCHOOL LEARNING

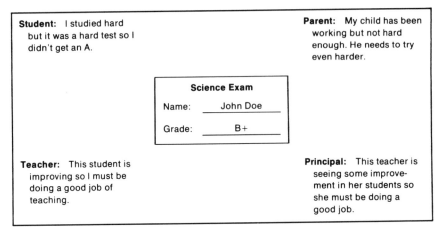

Student: I studied hard but it was a hard test so I didn't get an A.

Parent: My child has been working but not hard enough. He needs to try even harder.

Science Exam

Name: _____John Doe_____

Grade: _____B+_____

Teacher: This student is improving so I must be doing a good job of teaching.

Principal: This teacher is seeing some improvement in her students so she must be doing a good job.

Figure 2.1. Differential beliefs about the causes of a grade on a science exam.

These beliefs about the causes of success and failure are known as causal attributions. Research based on understanding the types of causal attributions people make and the implications of various attributions has indicated that the individual's belief about why a particular success or failure occurs is an important predictor of the individual's reactions to that event. In a school setting, the causal attribution will have an affect upon how happy and proud students feel about their exam grades. It will also effect the students' expectancies for how well they will do on the next exam in this subject and how hard they will try in preparing for the next test.

This process of making a causal attribution about a particular event and then having this attribution mediate the emotional and cognitive reactions to the situation is known as the attribution process. It is generally assumed that this attribution process operates in most, if not all, real-life situations involving achievement activities. However, much of the research that has been done to develop this model has been done in laboratory settings with college students as subjects; yet some tests of the model have been done with children, and others have directly observed children and adults in actual classroom settings. These latter types of studies have shown us more about how the basic theoretical model works in actual situations, and they have also raised some questions about the model. This chapter will look at both types of studies. First, the basic theoretical model will be reviewed. Next, work in classroom settings, in which an attempt is made to apply the theoretical model, will be reviewed. Taken together, these two research areas will help us to elaborate the theoretical attribution model and to look at areas for future research.

THE THEORETICAL ATTRIBUTION PROCESS

In 1971, Weiner, Frieze, Kukla, Reed, Rest, and Rosenbaum proposed an attributional theory of motivation. This model proposed a framework for looking at one's affective and cognitive reactions to a success or failure on an achievement task as a function of the causal attributions used to explain why a particular outcome had occurred. For example, if individuals attributed their failures to lack of effort, they would feel some shame about doing poorly, but they would also be motivated to try harder in the future. If a young girl attributed her good performance on an arithmetic task to good luck, she would lack the pride of someone else who felt that they had succeeded because of high ability or trying hard. She would also have low expectancies for her performances on future tests of this type, since people do not expect luck to continue. Other causal attributions were hypothesized to relate in systematic ways to these and other affective reactions and expectancies for the future. These variables were in turn believed to affect future achievement behavior.

The Weiner attribution model, then, conceptualizes the achievement process as a multi-stage process involving an achievement event, which is interpreted as a success or failure, followed by a causal explanation or attribution made for why this success or failure occurred. This causal attribution has subsequent consequences for affect and for future expectancies, which then together determine achievement orientation and behavior in a new situation. This model is diagrammed in Figure 2.2.

Causal Attributions

One of the central variables in the attribution process model is the causal attributions themselves. Attribution theorists assume that people are constantly forming causal explanations for why various events occur in their lives (Frieze & Bar-Tal, 1979; Weiner, 1979). Weiner (1979) suggests that these "why" questions are most asked for unpleasant and unexpected events, but that they probably occur most of the time, often below a level of immediate awareness.

Following an achievement event, such as a test or examination, any of a number of causal explanations might be used to account for the exam's outcome. For instance, success on the exam might be attributed to the person's ability in that subject, his or her trying hard, the exam's being easy, or good luck. Similarly, if the person failed, it might be attributed to lack of ability, lack of effort, the difficulty of the exam, or to bad luck. Failure may

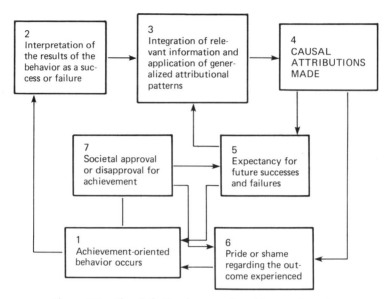

Figure 2.2. The attributional process for achievement events.

also be attributed to a variety of other factors including stable effort; a consistent pattern of diligence or laziness; other people, such as the teacher or other students who may aid or interfere with performance on a task; mood, fatigue or sickness; having a good or bad personality; and physical appearance (Elig & Frieze, 1975; Frieze, 1976a; Weiner, 1974).

Within an academic-achievement situation, these seem to be the causes most often cited. When Frieze (1976a) asked college students why someone might do well or poorly on a hypothetical exam, she found that effort, ability, the test difficulty, and the teacher were the most often cited causes. Other studies report similar findings although the labels used may vary (e.g., Bar-Tal & Darom, 1979; Bar-Tal, Ravgad, & Zilberman, 1978; Cooper & Burger, 1978; Frieze & Snyder, 1980). For example, Bar-Tal and Darom (1979) divide overall effort into effort during the test and preparation at home before the test. In recent research interest is typically separated from effect (Bar-Tal & Darom, 1979; Elig & Frieze, 1979). Cooper and Burger (1978) separate "ability" into academic ability, physical and emotional ability, and previous experience. They also include ability-like factors such as habits, attitudes, and maturity.

These differences in the labeling of similar causes present one of the difficulties with free-response data. Since the data is unstructured, it must be coded into a workable system of categories. Definitions of the categories vary among the different systems and across coders using any particular system. Furthermore, since the data is categorial rather than scaled, it presents problems for complex statistical analysis. However, these free-response studies do appear to give us the best indications of what causes people actually use in deciding why a particular success or failure occurred. We know, though, that subjects will use other causes if they are provided by the experimenter. For example, luck is rarely cited in free-response data as a cause of an academic success or failure, but this cause is often provided for subjects as one of a number of causes to rate as potential contributors to a particular outcome.[1] When provided, subjects do use luck and other causes in meaningful ways. Thus, the specific format used (free response versus scales for rating a list of causes) should depend upon the goals of the study. If a list is used, it should reflect the causal factors shown to be relevant to the situation on the basis of free-response pretesting (Elig & Frieze, 1979). Furthermore, attributions have been shown to vary greatly across situations (Frieze & Snyder, 1980) and across cultural groups (Barrett & Nicholls, 1978; Triandis, 1972).

Causal Dimensions

Many of the interesting predictions derived from attribution theory are related not to the specific causal categories themselves but to the underlying dimensions of the various causal categories. Causal categories can be analyzed in various ways (see Weiner, 1979). We have found that the most useful categorization system is based upon three dimensions: internality, stability, and intentionality. Each of these dimensions is assumed to be independent as shown in Table 2.1. Furthermore, although often concep-tualized as dichotomies, each is more accurately described as a continuum. For example, the first dimension, internality, has to do with whether the cause of an event is associated with the primary actor in the situation and is thus internal, or whether the cause is external to this person. Thus a person may succeed on an exam because of the *internal* causes of ability, trying hard, feeling good, or background. He may also succeed because of *external* factors: easy test, someone else's help, or a good teacher. These would represent the internal–external extremes. Other causes, such as doing well on an exam because of studying together with another student or getting a

[1] There are at least two reasons for the frequent use of luck as a causal category. First, much of the locus of control work that predated the achievement attribution work was concerned with comparing people using luck to those who attributed events to ability (e.g., Rotter, 1966). Secondly, the original Weiner et al. (1971) framework was based upon four causes: ability, effort, luck, and task difficulty; and much of the original theorizing was based upon these four. Many researchers still use only these four causes in spite of evidence that other causes may be of more importance.

Table 2.1

A THREE-DIMENSIONAL MODEL FOR CLASSIFYING CAUSAL ATTRIBUTIONS FOR THE
SUCCESS AND FAILURE OF OTHERS[a]

Causal attribution	Stable	Unstable
INTERNAL		
Intentional	Stable effort of actor (diligence or laziness)	Unstable effort of actor (trying or not trying hard)
Unintentional	Ability of actor	Fatigue of actor
	Knowledge or background of actor	Mood of actor
	Personality of actor	
EXTERNAL		
Intentional	Others always help or interfere	Others help or interfere with this event
Unintentional	Task difficulty or ease	Task difficulty or ease (task changes)
	Personality of others	Luck or unique circumstances
		Others accidentally help or interfere

[a]Modified from Elig and Frieze (1975).

high grade on a group project because everyone tried hard, would be intermediate between internal and external causes. Thus, when coding free-response data, it is often more useful to use a 3-point scale rather than a dichotomy for internality and for other dimensions (Elig & Frieze, 1975).

Related to the internality dimension, and sometimes confused with it, is the third dimension of intentionality.[2] If the actor has control over the internal cause it is intentional (see Elig & Frieze, 1975; or Rosenbaum, 1972). Thus, effort is internal and intentional, whereas ability and mood are unintentional, although still internal. This assumes that individuals can control their efforts, but that they have little control over their natural ability level or moods. If one knew that people making these causal attributions had other assumptions, the causes would be assigned a location upon the intentionality dimension consistent with their beliefs. However, since it is typically not possible to find out how people would assign their own causal beliefs along this and other dimensions, the causes are usually classified on the basis of the coder's understanding of the context and the logical definitions of the dimensions (see Elig & Frieze, 1975). Empirical studies based on multidimensional scaling of a large number of causes tend to yield both

[2] Weiner (1979) now calls this a controllability dimension since people presumably do not intend to fail but they may fail because of not doing something they had control over (such as studying).

an internality and an intentionality dimension similar to those described here, so there is also empirical evidence to support this logically derived classification system (Passer, 1977; Weiner, 1979).

Depending upon the needs of the particular study, one can also consider certain external causes as intentional. For example, if another person is responsible for the outcome, it may make a great deal of difference if that person was seen as intentionally causing something good or bad to happen as compared to a situation where the other person was accidentally responsible. The former case would be considered intentional whereas the latter would be unintentional.

Another dimension that is extremely important for classifying causal attributions is stability. Ability, background, and unchanging environmental factors are stable and change relatively little over time, whereas effort and mood are unstable and are highly changeable. Stability involves a relatively unchanging cause during the time period and across the situations one wishes to generalize to. Although the difficulty of the achievement task has typically been classified as stable, one would have to consider whether the *same* task would be repeated or if a future task would be similar but not the same. Only in the former case is the task truly stable (Valle & Frieze, 1976; Weiner, Russell, & Lerman, 1978). If the situation is taking an exam in a class, the test difficulty would generally be considered unstable, since the next exam could be harder or easier. However, one exception to this would occur if a particular teacher had a reputation for always giving easy or difficult exams. Thus, in this situation, exam difficulty, if it were in accord with this reputation, would be a stable causal factor. As well as being stable over time, one must also consider if the attribution is stable over situations (Elig & Frieze, 1975). If a student gets a poor grade on a social studies test and attributes this to his low ability in this subject area, this low ability attribution would not be stable if he or she were considering how well he or she might do on his or her next arithmetic test. However, it would be stable if the individual wanted to generalize to another social studies class. Thus, stability must always be considered within the context one wishes to generalize to.

A similar distinction has been proposed by Abramson, Seligman, and Teasdale (1978). They limit the concept of stability to stability for the same situation over time and use the concept of *globality* to define the generalizability of the cause over other related situations. Abramson et al. suggest that attributing a negative situation to both stable and global causes leads to depression and feelings of helplessness. Stable causes alone produce helpless feelings in regard to the particular situation, but since the negative outcome may not generalize if it is *situational* rather than global, there is less depression.

Expectancies

The theoretical achievement attribution model makes certain predictions about the consequences of causal attribution for future expectancy. It has been proposed and supported by several studies that changes in expectancy are related to the stability of the causal attribution made to explain the outcome (e.g., Fontaine, 1974; McMahan, 1973; Valle & Frieze, 1976; Weiner, Nierenberg, & Goldstein, 1976). Attributions to relatively stable causes, such as ability or the difficulty of an on-going task, produce expectancies that outcomes will continue to be the same, whereas more unstable attributions, such as luck, effort, and mood, produce expectancy shifts away from the outcome. For example, a student attributing failure on an exam to lack of ability (relatively stable) should continue to expect to do poorly on the next test, whereas if the failure were attributed to lack of effort in studying (unstable), the person may expect to get a good grade the next time by trying harder. Unstable causes, by definition, suggest that there is more possibility for change in the future, whereas stable causes imply that the future will resemble the past. This stability effect is especially true for global attributions.

Expectancies are related in another way to the stability of the causal explanation. If a high grade on an exam is attributed to high ability in the subject matter (a stable causal attribution), the expectancy for doing well on the next exam (which is sometimes labeled the posttest or future expectancy) will be high. The pretest expectancy, in turn, helps to determine how stable the causal attribution will be. If someone expects to do well on an exam (has a high pretest expectancy), and then in fact does do well, it is likely that the person will attribute the outcome to stable factors. However, if this person gets an unexpectedly low score, he or she will probably attribute it to some unstable factor such as not trying hard enough or being in a bad mood that day. In general, unexpected outcomes, or outcomes that vary widely from initial expectancy, tend to be attributed to unstable causes such as luck, whereas expected outcomes are attributed to more stable factors such as ability (e.g., Feather & Simon, 1971a, 1971b; Valle & Frieze, 1976).

Taken together, these two relationships imply that once an expectancy for success has been developed for a particular task, this expectancy is difficult to change. An expected outcome is attributed to stable factors (Simon & Feather, 1973; Valle & Frieze, 1976) which in turn lead to the expectancy for future outcomes to continue at the same level. If the outcome is unexpectedly high or low, an attribution will be made to unstable factors. Since unstable causes lead to the belief that this particular outcome was unusual and will not continue, there is little change in the future expectation from the initial pretest expectancy (Valle & Frieze, 1976). This leads to a self-fulfilling prophecy where those who expect to do well will continue to have high expectations, and those who have low expectations will maintain them regardless of how they actually perform. Furthermore, this effect seems to occur both for the individual and for someone else making attributions about another person (such as a teacher having expectations for a particular student). This model is outlined in Table 2.2.

This self-fulfilling prophecy model may have numerous implications for explaining low student performances and for the expectancy effect observed in teachers (see Chapter 3). However, since most of the tests of this model are laboratory studies with college students, we are not sure how this model works in actual classroom settings. One major question is how long this effect lasts. Presumably, a student who continually does poorly cannot keep attributing his low performance to unstable factors. At some point the student would have to conclude that he or she had low ability or that some other stable factor was working. However, we still do not understand when or how this transition would take place.

Affective Reactions

Along with the formation of expectations for the future, the attribution model also predicts certain affective or emotional reactions to success or failure that are mediated by the type of causal attribution made for the outcome. Common sense as well as empirical evidence tells us that people feel good or happy when succeeding and bad or unhappy when failing, regardless of the causal attribution made (e.g., Nicholls, 1975; Ruble, Parsons, & Ross, 1976). Beyond this overall main effect, there is a general tendency for outcomes attributed to internal factors to produce stronger affective reactions than those attributed to external factors (e.g., Reimer, 1975; Weiner, 1974). Thus, successes attributed to ability or effort produce

Table 2.2
SELF-FULFILLING PROPHECIES FOR ACHIEVEMENT EXPECTANCIES[a]

Initial expectancy	Performance level	Causal attribution	Final expectancy
High	High	Ability or other stable internal factors	Higher
High	Low	Bad luck or lack of effort or other unstable factors	High
Low	High	Good luck, special effort or other unstable factors	Low
Low	Low	Lack of ability or other stable, internal factors	Lower

[a]Modified from V. A. Valle and I. H. Frieze. The stability of causal attributions as a mediator in changing expectations for success. *Journal of Personality and Social Psychology*, 1976, 33, 579–587. Copyright 1976 by the American Psychological Association. Reprinted by permission.

more pride than those attributed to luck, the teacher, or the ease of the task. Similarly, failures attributed to internal factors produce more shame. Effort attributions (which are always internal *and intentional*) tend to produce especially high rewards (Nicholls, 1976; Weiner, Heckhausen, Meyer, & Cook, 1972; Weiner et al., 1978). Effort is also most strongly associated with self-reward (Weiner et al., 1972).

More recent research has further clarified the relationship between affective reactions and causal attributions. As implied by the earlier findings, not only internality, but intentionality as well, seem to be related to stronger affective reactions in general. In addition, external causes that are seen as intentional may also generate stronger feelings than those attributed to external factors. For example, if someone believes that a teacher purposefully gave a difficult exam so that everyone would get a low grade, that person will have more hostility toward the teacher than if the teacher's behavior was not seen as intentional (Baron, 1977). Angry and hostile reactions are mediated by the perceived intentionality of the person causing a negative outcome. Intentionality may, in fact, be a stronger predictor of affective reactions than internality, but this hypothesis has not received adequate empirical testing to be certain.

Weiner, Russell, and Lerman (1978) have done a number of studies to show the specific affective reactions that are associated with various causal attributions. Happiness and pride are seen as common affective reactions to any type of success (although there is much less pride if the outcome is believed to be caused by other people or by luck). Attributing an event to one's abilities leads to feelings of competence and confidence, whereas attributions to effort produce feelings of relief and satisfaction. Furthermore, feelings of gratefulness are especially strong when a good event is attributed to other people and luck produces feelings of surprise, relief, and guilt.

Attributions for failure were also associated with specific emotional reactions, along with the overriding negative feelings. Lack of ability attributions lead to feelings of incompetence and resignation; lack of effort is associated with guilt; bad luck again leads to surprise.

Summarizing these findings, Weiner (1979) suggests that there are three sources of affect about a success or failure. First, there is the basic good or bad feeling depending upon whether the outcome was a success or failure. Weiner further suggests that these basic emotions are the strongest ones and are directly related to the outcome experienced and are not mediated by the causal attribution made. Second, there are the specific reactions discussed earlier (such as surprise) being generated by luck and confidence from ability attributions associated with the causal attribution. Finally, there is the mediation of the internality dimension upon feelings associated with self-esteem. Thus, feelings of competence and pride and shame are greater when an internal attribution is made.

As mentioned earlier, the stability dimension also affects emotional reactions. Failures attributed to stable, global causes lead to depression and helpless resignation (Abramson et al., 1978). Arkin and Maruyama (1979) have also shown that attributing success to unstable causes leads to more anxiety and that attributions of failure to stable causes leads to more fear, especially for less successful students.

Forming Causal Attributions

Attribution researchers working with achievement attributions as well as with other types of causal attributions have devoted a good deal of attention to the question of how various sources of information are combined to form a causal attribution. However, we still know very little about the actual ways in which information is processed. We do know what types of information are relevant and the final resulting attribution for various information cue combinations. These relationships between patterns of information and resulting attributions for success and failure are reviewed in the following sections of this chapter. After that, some attention is given to the question of what actually goes on in people's heads as they process this information.

Informational Cues

As discussed earlier in this chapter, individuals' initial expectations for how well they will do on an exam or other achievement task affect the causal attribution that will be made once the outcome is known. If the outcome is the expected one, the attribution is more likely to be stable, whereas if it is unexpected, more unstable attributions are made. There are also many other sources of information that are utilized in making a causal attribution.

One important source of information is the outcome itself. Successful outcomes are more attributed to internal factors than failing outcomes (Arkin & Maruyama, 1979; Frieze & Weiner, 1971; Gilmore & Reid, 1979; Luginbuhl, Crowe, & Kahan, 1975; Miller, 1976). It appears that subjects show this tendency to take responsibility for success across a wide variety of situations (e.g., Miller & Ross, 1975), probably because people are motivated to make themselves look good (Miller, 1976). However, it is also possible that this attributional "bias" is a rational approach to the available information (Miller & Ross, 1975). Miller and Ross argue that since people generally expect success and they are more likely to take responsibility for an expected event, they would logically take more responsibility for success. They also discuss the fact that people are more likely to see how their actions have led to success than they are to see how they have caused failure. Other informational explanations are also suggested. However, Miller's (1976) study gives more credibility to the motivational explanation than to these informational explanations.

It should also be noted that although people tend to be more internal for success than for failure, they are generally still internal to some degree for failure. It is common to blame failure on the lack of effort or ability as well as on task difficulty or bad luck (Frieze & Weiner, 1971; Luginbuhl, Crowe, & Kahan, 1975; Miller & Ross, 1975). This means that the motivational bias of attributing good things to oneself seems to apply much more to success, and that people do not deny all responsibility for failure.

In addition to the outcome itself, people seem to use a variety of other informational cues in forming causal judgments. When asked what information they would like to have to form a causal judgment, people request the following types of information (Frieze, 1976b):

- Specific information about the *task* or type of exam being analyzed
- Incentives the person had to do well
- The ability level of the person or his past history of successes
- The skills or abilities of other people who have attempted the same task
- The amount of effort exerted by the actor
- Information about the instructor of the course if success or failure on an exam is being evaluated
- The mood or state of mind of the person
- Detailed information about the exact outcome or the exact items missed on an exam
- General information about the type of person the actor is
- Information about other people who may have affected the outcome by cheating or other means
- Information about whether the actor cheated
- The presence of luck in the situation

Typically, people asked for two or three types of information to explain each event they were asked to evaluate. Other research has shown that people only ask for two or three bits of information, but they are able to use as many as five informational cues if they are given the information in a structured format (Frieze & Weiner, 1971). In addition our own unpublished research has indicated that people will tend to use whatever information they are given, even if it appears to be irrelevant or is not something they would have requested themselves.

Other research has shown that there are specific relationships between the types of information available to help explain a particular success or failure and the type of causal attribution made. In a typical study, the subject is provided with a number of informational cues in all possible combinations and is asked to rate why each of the events described by a particular combination of informational cues might have occurred. A sample situation would be: "A student got a high score on an exam, he has done very well on past exams, most of the other students did not do as well as he did, and he was very motivated to do well on this exam since it would allow him to pass out of the course. Why did he do well on this exam?" The typical response would be that he did well because of high ability and trying hard. These types of studies have been highly consistent in showing the relationships between information and attributions.

When the available information signifies that the present outcome is consistent with the outcomes of the person over time (the person does well and has consistently done well in the past, or does poorly and has tended to do poorly in the past), there is a strong tendency to attribute the current outcome to the person's ability (Chaikin, 1971; Feather & Simon, 1971a,b; Frieze & Weiner, 1971; Ryan, 1978). Ability attributions are also commonly made for outcomes that are unique to the person (for example, a student who does poorly on an exam in which everyone else did well is considered to have low ability) or when the person's outcome is the same as that of other people who are highly similar (Fontaine, 1974).

Effort attributions result from situations in which the person does better or worse than everyone else, when his or her outcomes are inconsistent with past performance, and when the outcome is consistent with the motivation or incentive the person had to perform at a high level (Fontaine, 1974; Frieze, 1976b; Frieze & Weiner, 1971; Ryan, 1978). If one does well on something that he or she considers important, or does poorly when the task is considered unimportant, the attribution is commonly to high and/or low effort, respectively.

Luck and mood attributions and attributions to the unique circumstances of the situation seem to be made when the information is inconsistent with some of the patterns mentioned earlier. If the present outcome is inconsistent with the past or is unique to the individual, especially if the past history is also up and down, there is more attribution to these unstable factors (Bane & Brown, 1977; Fontaine, 1974; Frieze & Weiner, 1971; McArthur, 1972; Orvis, Cunningham, & Kelley, 1975).

Antecedents of task attributions are the person being in a situation where everyone else experiences the same thing, where the immediate outcome is consistent with how the person has performed on this task in the past, and when the person fails after working a long time on the task

(Fontaine, 1974; Frieze & Weiner, 1971; Orvis, Cunningham, & Kelley, 1975).

The pattern of past successes and failures also has a significant impact on the attribution made, especially when a person is making an attribution about someone else's success or failure. As mentioned earlier, a consistent pattern of successes or failures is most frequently attributed to ability. A consistent increase in the level of success experienced by the person is attributed to increasing effort; a decreasing level of performance is attributed to decreasing effort, but such a person is also seen as having high ability. In the latter case, the belief may be that the person is bored and not trying as hard as he or she might (Beckman, 1970; Jones, Rock, Shaver, Goethals, & Ward, 1968; Ryan, 1978).

To summarize these findings, it might be noted that stable attributions are more commonly made for situations that are consistent with the past (as might be expected), and internal attributions are more common when the actor in the situation experiences something different from what others do. Events that are inconsistent with the past are attributed to unstable factors, and outcomes shared with others are attributed to the task or to some other aspect of the situation (Frieze, 1976b).

Along with looking at the effects of individual informational cues, there is also research that attempts to specify how various cues will interact in producing a causal attribution. For example, Kun and Weiner (1978) demonstrated that people feel success can be achieved on an easy task with high effort or with high ability, whereas for a difficult task both are needed. Kelley (1972) has labeled the example typified by the easy task as a *multiple sufficient schemata*. When both factors are needed, as in the case of the difficult task, the situation is described by a *multiple necessary schemata*. In general, events of greater magnitude or more extreme outcomes tend to elicit multiple necessary schema whereas those of lesser magnitude elicit the multiple sufficient schema (Cunningham & Kelley, 1975). Other schema are additive—the more factors that are operating, the greater the effect (Kelley, 1972). However, there is as yet little research outlining the specific schema relevant in school settings.

Information Processing

In order to understand how various causal attributions are formed we must know what types of information are relevant. However, once this is understood, the next step is to see how people actually process this information in forming their causal judgments. Much research is now being done in an attempt to describe this process more fully. At the present time, we probably know more about the questions that need to be answered than we

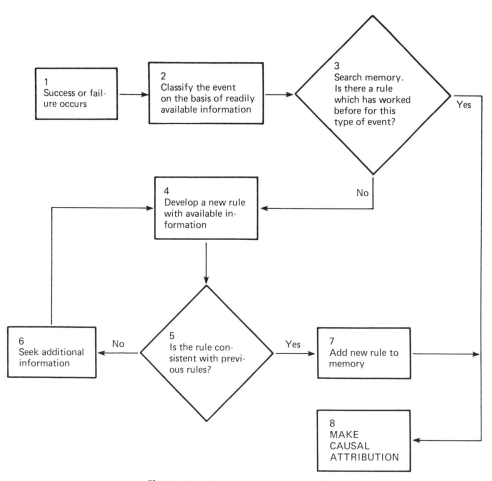

Figure 2.3. Forming a causal attribution.

do about the process itself. However, we will briefly review the findings of some of this research.

First, the information is probably processed in a way that is at least somewhat like that described in Figure 2.3. This model suggests that the attribution can be formed in two basic ways. In situations similar to those experienced in the past, the person may classify the situation as a familiar one (Boxes 2 and 3) and then form an immediate causal attribution (Box 8). For example, if an excellent student gets another high grade, he or she may quickly conclude that this latest success is due to ability and diligence in doing homework. A failing student could as easily conclude that he or she just does not have the ability to do well, without even noticing that any other people did poorly on this exam also.

There is evidence that these rapidly formed attributions may be based on other factors as well as on past experiences. Langer (1978) suggests that people often make attributions "off the top of their heads" with little thought. However, these situations may well be learned ones. They may also represent situations in which there is one obvious salient bit of information that could have plausibly caused the event to happen (e.g., Taylor & Fiske, 1978). Smith and Miller (1978) further suggest that people appear to use a subtraction method for forming causal attributions where they consider a small list of possible causes and eliminate those that seem superfluous or incorrect. Of course, this small list could be based upon past experience in a real-life situation where people are not given a list of possible causes by the experimenter.

As discussed earlier, there are a number of patterns of information that seem to lead immediately to a particular attribution (Frieze, 1976b; Orvis, Cunningham, & Kelley, 1975). For example, if one succeeds again after consistently succeeding in the past, nearly everyone quickly makes an attribution to ability. Or, if a person who is highly motivated to do well succeeds on an exam, his or her high score is typically attributed to effort. Such patterns may be examples of causal schemata or scripts. Kelley (1972) has outlined a number of schemata, or abstractions of situations, which lead to a particular type of attribution. Schemata are believed to exist in memory and appear to be commonly held within our culture. Schemata may also be considered as abstractions of the more general concept of scripts. Abelson (1976) suggests that people have ideas about certain types of people or events that are somewhat like stories. For example, "John is an average student, but he works very hard. He gets good grades because of studying so hard, no matter what class he takes. If he does poorly, it must be a particularly hard teacher or else there is something wrong." Such a script might be applied to explain the successes of someone else known to do well in spite of not being particularly bright. Abelson suggests that we have a large array of such scripts and that we try to find one which fits the information we have in making a judgment about a new situation or person. They may be based upon logic or upon past learning. Many of them may be widely shared by members of a particular cultural group.

The script provides a good deal of other information upon which a judgment can be made. Empirically, we know that script processing operates in making decisions about admitting candidates to graduate school. If an application shows average scores, good recommendations, and a candidate with a special interest in applications of psychology to business, such an application may remind members of the admission committee of another student with a very similar background and interest profile. If the other student did well in the program, the committee would be more likely to admit the new student, since they will assume his or her performance will resemble that of the other student. Another example of script processing within an academic environment might be our conception of the athlete. Typically, such a person is not expected to be a serious student, and reactions to this person are often based on this and other associations we have of athletes that form our athlete script.

For self attributions, scripts about situations are probably more relevant than those about people, since we already have a good deal of information about ourselves. For example, an upcoming test in science may bring to mind our ideas about science being a very difficult subject area for which doing the homework regularly is essential for getting a good grade. In such a situation, if the person did get a good grade, he or she would more likely attribute this success to ability and effort rather than to the ease of the subject area.

The ideas of script or schema processing appear to be important concepts for understanding the attribution process, but as yet they have been little studied. Even less studied is the situation in which no readily available rule or attribution presents itself to explain a particular success or failure. As diagrammed in Figure 2.3, we assume that in such a case, the person attempts to develop a new rule (Box 4) by systematically analyzing the available information. Kelley (1967) and others (see Jones & Davis, 1967) have attempted to outline how this type of systematic evaluation might take place, but more current thought suggests that these rules are too complex for people to actually do, at least in most cases (Carroll, Payne, Frieze, & Girard, 1976). However, proceeding with our model, after such a rule were developed, it would have to be checked for consistency with previous judgment rules, schema, or scripts (Box 5). If this test were passed, then the new rule could be added to the set of others in memory so that it would be available if a similar situation presented itself again (Box 7), and the attribution could be formed. If the rule were inconsistent, it is hypothesized that new information would be sought (Box 6), so that another new rule could be developed.

A final consideration in looking at how people process information in making causal judgments is the consistent differences people show in their preferences for different causal attributions (see Bar-Tal, Raviv, Raviv, & Bar-Tal, 1978; Ruble & Boggiano, in press). The next section will explore this issue in more detail.

Implications of Various Attributional Patterns

Self-Esteem

Using the theoretical attribution framework described earlier, one can easily derive certain implications of making one type of attribution or another. One should feel the greatest degree of pride and security about the future if one makes a stable, internal, intentional attribution for success (such as seeing success as due to one's consistent pattern of diligence). Ability attributions should also be quite positive. For failure, one would feel best if the failure was attributed to external, unstable factors. The external attribution would be less threatening to feelings of competence and the instability of the causal factor would provide more confidence that success could be achieved in the future. This would imply that bad luck would be an ideal attribution for failure, as would an attribution to the difficulty of the particular situation at that time. Individuals with a consistent pattern of making these types of positive attributions should have high self-esteem and high confidence in their academic abilities (see Figure 2.3). Fitch (1970) supported these hypotheses with data that males with high self-esteem attributed success more to internal causes than those with low self-esteem. The low self-esteem group also made more attributions to internal factors for failure. Ames (1978) reported similar results with children. High self-concept children rated their abilities higher after success than low self-concept children. The high self-concept group also rewarded themselves more after success, as would be predicted from their more internal attributions. Shrauger and Terbovic (1976) also found that high self esteem subjects rated their performances higher than low self-esteem subjects, even though the actual outcomes did not differ.

Achievement Motivation

Other consistent attributional patterns are associated with high achievement motivation or a high desire for achievement success (see Atkinson, 1964). High achievement motivation in men appears to be associated with a tendency to attribute successes to ability, and effort and failures to lack of effort (Kukla, 1972). These high motivation subjects also have higher estimates of their overall abilities (Bar-Tal & Frieze, 1977; Kukla, 1972). The low achievement motivated men are less likely to attribute their successes to internal factors, and they attribute their failures more to their low ability (Weiner & Kukla, 1970; Weiner & Potepan, 1970). These attributional patterns support other findings that the high achievement motivated person feels more pride in success and is motivated by failure to work harder than the low motivated group (Atkinson, 1964; Weiner, 1970). High achievement motivated women tend to show similar patterns of attributions, although they have less confidence in their abilities and make more use of effort attributions for success as compared to comparably motivated men (Bar-Tal & Frieze, 1977; Frieze, Fisher, Hanusa, McHugh, & Valle, 1978).

Although these predictions for the relationship between achievement motivation and causal attribution patterns appear to be supported by at least a few studies, others have found conflicting results (e.g., Latta, 1976). Since there is also a continuing discussion about how best to measure achievement motivation, it has also been suggested that these attributional findings are dependent upon the particular motivational measure used (deCharms & Muir, 1978). Therefore, there is still some question about the relationship between achievement motivation and causal attributions. This is especially true for females, since so few studies deal with female achievement motivation and causal attributions.

Sex Differences

Along with differences in attributions as a function of various personality measures, differing patterns of causal attributions for success and failure have been reported for males as compared to females and for blacks as compared to whites. The sex difference work is much more extensive and will be discussed first.

One of the differences between males and females, which most clearly emerges when reviewing the literature on achievement related attributions, is the highly consistent finding for females of all ages to have lower initial expectancies for success than males (e.g., Crandall, 1969; 1978a; Cole, King, & Newcomb, 1977; Frieze et al., 1978; Gjesme, 1973). Beginning at preschool ages, when girls are asked to estimate how well they will do on an unfamiliar task, they tend to underestimate the performance level they will later achieve. Boys, on the other hand, are more likely to overestimate their eventual performance. This occurs for intellectual tasks as well as for artistic tasks and for tasks involving physical skills (Crandall, 1978a). These findings replicate for all ages of students—girls and young women consistently demonstrate lower expectations for success than boys and young men. Even male college students give higher estimates for the grades they will receive than women, although for college students, both sexes overestimate their actual performance levels to some degree. College men's estimates are very high, whereas women's are only slightly higher than what they will actually receive (Cole, King, & Newcomb, 1977). College women still underestimate performance on other tasks (Gjesme, 1973).

As discussed earlier, having low expectations can be debilitating in a number of ways. One may be less likely to attempt difficult tasks if one continually underestimates how well one will do (Crandall, 1978b; Frieze et *al.*, 1978). The fact that adolescent girls continue to have lower educational aspirations than boys (Marini & Greenberger, 1978) may be an example of this phenomenon. Low initial expectations also create a self-fulfilling prophecy since they lead to perpetuating causal attributions (Jackaway, 1974). Indirect evidence for this is seen in the fact that boys tend to be more optimistic after failure than girls (Dweck & Gilliard, 1975). More directly relevant data indicate that females of all ages are more likely than males to attribute their successes to unstable and external factors such as luck and task ease. Furthermore, females are less likely to see their successes as the result of ability, but they make more attributions to their lack of ability and bad luck for failure (e.g., Bar-Tal & Frieze, 1977; Dweck & Repucci, 1973; Feather, 1969; Feather & Simon, 1975; McMahan, 1973, Nicholls, 1975; Wiegers & Frieze, 1977).

The self-fulfilling prophecy model shown in Table 2.2 suggests that females, who have lower initial expectations for success, should attribute their successes more to unstable factors and their failures more to stable, internal factors. The attribution studies indicating sex differences only partially support this model, since they also show females making more external attributions (task and luck) for success and unstable attributions (bad luck) for failure as well as the predicted relationships. However, these additional findings are clearly as debilitating for success since the greater use of external attributions would result in less pleasure from doing well at achievement tasks for females. The more frequent use of luck to explain failure (which is a greater relative use—there is still little absolute use of luck as a causal explanation even in females) may be a defensive attribution. Moreover, using luck as a causal explanation will also keep girls who do experience failure from trying harder. Frieze et al. (1978) have suggested that the greater externality of females is a symptom of their withdrawing from achievement tasks where they feel doomed to failure or where they anticipate few rewards for accomplishment.

Commonly held stereotypes about the personalities of men and women include the idea that men are basically more competent than women in handling a variety of achievement tasks (e.g., Broverman et al., 1972). Other more specific research further indicates that for a number of different types of achievement tasks, males are expected by others to outperform females, even on tasks commonly defined as female-related (see reviews by Frieze et al., 1978; O'Leary & Hansen, 1979). Given these general beliefs, it is not too surprising that girls and women have lower achievement expectations for themselves than do males. Success may be seen as unfeminine, especially in a field such as mathematics, which is seen as an especially strong male domain. Girls who are successful may see themselves as tomboys or in other ways that make them different from other girls. Many girls still consider it a compliment to be told, "Gee, you did that just as good as a boy." Other, equally competent girls may simply direct their skills in other areas than traditionally defined academic achievement, especially as they reach adolescence.

Race Differences

Just as our stereotypes tend to see females as less competent than males, racial stereotypes include the idea that blacks are less intelligent and less motivated to do well in school than whites (Freedman, 1972; Karlins et al., 1969). It would be reasonable to assume that blacks also have lower expectations for themselves than whites although we know of no studies directly testing this hypothesis.

Looking more directly at causal attributions, there is a good deal of evidence that blacks in general make more external attributions for success and failure than whites. Blacks are especially likely to attribute their outcomes to good or bad luck (e.g., Friend & Neale, 1972; Lefcourt, 1970; Murray & Mednick, 1975). In a study of college students, Murray and Mednick (1975) further found that black females with high achievement motivation made attributions similar to whites with high achievement motivation, with the exception of the black females using luck attributions more than whites, in addition to making high use of ability and effort as causal explanations. In this same study, black males did not differ from whites in their attributions as a function of achievement motivation.

Although the results are sketchy and more research is clearly needed, the existing data indicate that blacks, too, suffer from the low expectation cycle of self-fulfilling prophecies. This appears to be especially true for black males.

The Influence of Other People upon the Attribution Process

The theoretical attribution model presented thus far has been primarily concerned with internal attribution processes—how the individual forms a causal attribution to explain a particular achievement event and the consequences of that attribution for the person. Other people have been peripheral to this process. However, there are a number of ways in which others do influence this process. On a simple level, one can attribute their outcomes to other people. The teacher is mentioned as a cause of success or failure by some students when asked why they succeeded or failed on an exam (e.g., Frieze, 1976a). The interference of other students (who cheated or otherwise obstructed one's performance) is also a spontaneously mentioned attribution, although neither of these is especially common for academic achievement settings (e.g., Frieze, 1976b; Frieze & Snyder, 1980). As discussed earlier, another person can be perceived as intentionally influencing one's outcomes or as inadvertently or accidentally doing so. Attributions can also be made to stable features in the other person (he or she is a naturally good teacher) or to a particular behavior (he or she tried hard to make the test very fair). In all of these cases, the outside person is seen as a central factor in determining one's performance.

Other people also enter into the attribution process as standards with whom one can compare oneself. If a student does well, but everyone else does too, the attribution is made to task ease, whereas discrepant outcomes are more frequently attributed to internal factors. The use of information about other people has been extensively studied as a general phenomenon known as social comparison processes. Although this has not been directly tied to the achievement attribution process to the degree to which it could potentially be, a brief examination of this literature is clearly relevant.

Comparing Oneself with Others

Popular knowledge suggests that students are well aware of how well other students in their classes are doing. In college the comparison process is made explicit through the instructor making the grade distribution for various exams publicly available. In younger grades, students also make it a point to find out how well their classmates are doing, even in settings that are designed to minimize ability comparisons and grade competition (Levine, 1979). Levine and Snyder (1978) found that first and second graders were able to give reasonably accurate evaluations of the reading and math ability of their fellow students. These students were in an individualized instruction setting where each child worked independently and was not in competition with any other student.

The question then arises as to why students are so anxious to compare themselves with others even when discouraged from doing so by the classroom environment. Festinger (1954) suggested that there is a basic drive in humans to compare themselves with others in order to gain an accurate assessment of their abilities. Others have continued to view the social comparison process as a basic human response and have clarified some of the variables affecting this behavior (see Suls, 1977). Although there are a number of variables that may affect the choice of comparison persons (e.g., Gruder, 1977; Miller & Suls, 1977), it appears that the individual is most interested in comparing him or herself with others who are believed to be similar in attributes that are predictive of performance levels for the ability in question (Goethals & Darley, 1977). For the child in school, relevant variables would usually include age, grade level, sex, and, possibly, race. In one test of this idea, Suls, Gastorf, and Lawhon (1978) found that after giving high school students possible comparison persons of the same sex or a different sex and the same age or older or younger for evaluating performance on an "unusual uses test", students choose a same-age-same-sex person with whom to compare their score. As a second choice, someone of the same age, but of the other sex, was chosen. These results indicated that subjects choose the most similar person they could for comparison purposes. It is hypothesized that such a choice gives people the maximum amount of information about their own ability levels.

Levine further points out that the desire to engage in social comparison behavior is affected by the cognitive maturity of the person and by various situational variables. Children must be a certain age before they will even use social comparison information given to them, and they become more interested in such information during their early school years (Ruble & Boggiano, in press). Data from several studies indicate that children must be at least second graders before they readily use social comparison information for self-evaluation (Ruble & Boggiano, in press). Along with these maturational factors, the use of social comparison information also depends upon the situation. Social comparison information is more sought after and utilized in competitive situations, important situations, and situations in which one is unsure of ability. In many ways the school setting is one in which the desire for social comparison information is maximized (Levine, 1979).

The use of social comparison information affects the attribution process in various ways. As already noted, this information determines whether an ability attribution or a task ease or difficulty attribution is made for a particular success or failure. Even primary school children have been shown to use such information in making causal attributions (Frieze & Bar-Tal, 1980). Knowledge about how well others with similar characteristics to oneself have done on a particular task will also determine one's own expectations for success on the task. Moreover, this influence is especially salient for unfamiliar tasks and for tasks where others' performances are attributed to their abilities (Fontaine, 1974).

Achievement Expectations of Other People

Other people can affect the attribution process in yet another way. In most real-life achievement situations, there are other people who know about an individual's performance and who have prior expectations of how the individual will do. These expectations may be based on knowledge about how well the person has done in the past or on other prior experience, or they may result from generalizations based upon stereotypes about the group to which the individual belongs. In either case, the individual is often aware of these expectations, and they may well influence performance.

Having others rooting for you and expecting you to do well is often cited as a factor in sports success (e.g., Frieze, McHugh, & Duquin, 1976). Data also indicate that children with high achievement motivation have parents who are supportive of their accomplishments and who expect them to do well in achievement tasks (e.g., Hoffman, 1972). Teacher expectations have also been shown to influence student performance (Rosenthal & Jacobson, 1968; Chapter 3).

Along with these subtle, indirect influences of others expectations upon performance, the expectations and attributions others make for the performance of a particular student can have very direct effects upon the experiences of that student. Teachers, counselors, and parents make many decisions about the types of classes and special training programs to which the student will be exposed. There will be a wider range of these for the students seen as having high abilities and who are seen as doing well because of their efforts and abilities. Rewards given by these significant others will also depend upon the attributions made for performance (which are in turn at least partially determined by the initial expectations for success for the individual). Some of our own unpublished data show that grades are highly correlated with teacher ratings of student effort. Students who are not expected to perform well in school may have numerous hurdles to overcome before they are seen as competent, even if they perform at a relatively high level. This is especially unfortunate if the low expectations are falsely based upon negative stereotypes.

The negative effects of stereotypes upon attributions and performance can be seen for girls and blacks, as mentioned earlier. They can also be devastating for the mentally retarded. The unreasonably low expectations held for retarded students may result in these students having very low views of their own abilities and a resulting inability to approach even quite simple tasks. Attributional retraining of these students and of their trainers can have surprising results for their performance (Gold & Ryan, 1979).

LABORATORY ATTRIBUTION RESEARCH
AND CLASSROOM DATA

The conception of the achievement attribution process outlined above is based largely on laboratory studies where college students' did artificial tasks that had little, if any, relevance to these students' lives. Successes and failures were typically manipulated by the experimenter through false norms for performance. Although the basic model is well supported under these conditions, certain modifications appear to be necessary when attributional studies are done in less rigid settings such as the classroom (see Frieze, 1977).

Defining the Event:
Subjective Definitions of Success

One of the questions that has been raised by attribution research in classroom settings is how students come to decide that a particular grade or score on a test is a success or a failure. In much attribution research, subjects are told how well they have done on a task and then are asked to state why they performed at this level. Typically, subjects have been told whether they should consider their performance a success or failure either by direct labeling (e.g., Riemer, 1975) or on the basis of (false) college student norms (e.g., Bar-Tal & Frieze, 1976). Even when such a procedure is used, subjects do not always accept this experimenter evaluation (Elig & Frieze, 1979).

One of the difficulties with this type of approach is that defining an event as a success or failure appears to be a highly complex process and different people appear to use various criteria in making such a judgment. On an intuitive level, we all know that a B+ grade on an exam might be responded to with joy and a clear feeling of success by one student, whereas another will be quite disappointed and will feel that he or she has failed. Empirically, we now know that even when students are assigned to a "success" group and given feedback that indicates that their performance level is quite high in comparison to other students, some will accept this information whereas others will reject it and still feel that they have failed. Similarly for failure, when some students are told that they did much worse than other students, they accept this as a failure for themselves, whereas others still rate themselves as successful (e.g., Elig & Frieze, 1979). Thus, defining a performance as successful seems to involve as complex a process as that of determining why a particular success or failure occurred.

In one of the few studies that has been done to investigate subjective success evaluations and their relationship to causal attributions, Frieze, Snyder, and Fontaine (1978) asked fifth graders to evaluate their performances on either a social studies or a mathematics exam. These ratings were compared to their actual scores. Other attributional measures were also taken before and after the exam. When correlations were done between the students' actual scores and their subjective ratings of how successful they were, the correlation between the two was .74. Although this is clearly significant, it also suggests that these subjective evaluations are influenced by a variety of other factors in addition to actual outcome.

In order to explore the relationship between subjective and objective success more fully, a series of stepwise multiple regressions were done. Looking first at the variables impinging upon the subject before he is told the exam score, it was found that variables predicting subjective outcome and objective outcome (actual score) were quite different. Students who actually performed well were seen as trying hard by their teachers and themselves.

Teachers also saw them as having high ability. This may indicate that teachers believe that school success is dependent upon both ability and effort. Students who felt they had done well (independent of their actual score) were seen by the teacher as trying hard. They felt that doing well was important for them and for their teacher. They also felt that they were relatively bright.

Aside from suggesting that subjective evaluations of outcome are indeed different psychologically from the actual performance levels; these data also demonstrate the importance of a subject's perceptions of others' expectations for him or her.

The predictors of subjective evaluation of performance were further explored with stepwise multiple regression equations that allowed all variables as potential predictors. It was found that students who rated their performances most successful also felt happier and did better. Similar regressions done for actual scores showed that those who performed at a higher level evaluated their performance higher, were rated as brighter by teachers, and were happier with their scores.

These results suggest that subjective success is more important in predicting affective reactions than objective success. However, they also indicate that for fifth graders the two are closely linked. College students, in a similar study, showed a tendency for actual scores to be related to a pattern of general confidence, whereas subjective success was more related to a kind of affective reaction and a feeling of having done well on a difficult task (Frieze, Snyder, & Fontaine, 1977).

Other researchers have suggested that a number of variables may be related to more positive affect about one's performance and, therefore, presumably to greater feelings of subjective success. House and Perney (1974) found that doing better than expected led to more positive affect in an achievement setting for college students. Crandall (1978b) suggested that the degree of improvement over one's minimal standards for performance is a major determinant of positive affect (also see Crandall, Katkovsky, & Preston, 1960). Other important factors may include how well other students do (e.g., Festinger, 1954) and doing better than one has in the past.

Another important factor in deciding the degree of success is the value one attaches to doing well within a particular domain. Failure in a sex-appropriate task creates more negative affect than failure in an area typically associated with the other sex (Kipnis & Kidder, 1978). Parsons and Goff (1978) discuss how the incentive value for successful performance may vary as a function of one's motives. In general, women are seen as having more social motives and goals whereas men are more motivated by competition (Parsons & Goff, 1978). Astin (1978) cites evidence for this distinction in a study of career aspirations of college students. She found that women choose jobs that relate to their basic interests and give them an opportunity to contribute to society, to work with ideas and people, to be helpful to others, and to express their identity. Men, on the other hand, want jobs with an opportunity for high salaries, high prestige, rapid advancement, and a stable future. This means that men and women probably define job success very differently. Other research shows that college women are most likely to define general success in terms of personal life satisfaction (being happy) and interpersonal relationships (Jenkins, 1979). Achievement motivated men would attach more importance to career success and achieving money and status (e.g., Atkinson, 1964).

Success values in children have not yet been systematically studied. Therefore research is needed to better understand how boys and girls view success in various subject areas and when the sex differences found in college students begin to occur in younger people. There may well be race differences in success values as well as class and other ethnic differences, and all of these differences may be an important key to helping us to better understand differences in the achievement patterns of various types of students.

Subject Matter Differences

One of the areas in which sex differences may be maximized is in mathematics classes. Mathematics is typically stereotyped as a "masculine" subject area where boys and men are expected by others (and by themselves) to be better than girls and women (e.g., Broverman et al., 1972; Sherman & Fennema, 1977). Girls who do very well in math may be seen as unfeminine or otherwise disliked. One study of fifth and sixth graders showed that boys who did well in mathematics were liked more than girls who did well (Mokros & Koff, 1978). Older girls and women may well fear being seen as unfeminine if they do too well in mathematics. They may also devalue achievement in mathematics and may fail to see its relevance to their own success goals.

Even though girls may do better in mathematics than boys in the early years of school, their performance advantage disappears in the later years (Hilton & Berglund, 1974). We suspect that the relative decline in girls' performances begins in the early years of school when differential views of mathematics begin. Since mathematics is seen as a difficult subject area, especially for students in later grade levels (Husen, 1967), the attributions and expectancies formed in the early years may well affect how the child reacts to his first failure in mathematics. More difficult tasks in general tend to produce more ability attributions for success and failure (e.g., Cunningham & Kelley,1975; Frieze & Snyder, 1980). Therefore, it is expected that there will be a relatively high level of ability attributions used for mathematics success. Furthermore, since females are more likely to make ability attributions for failure than males, this tendency may be further exaggerated in mathematics where females already expect to do poorly.

Classroom Attributions

Research specifically dealing with classroom attributions has shown that academic successes and failures are attributed primarily to effort or lack of effort when students are asked to simply state *why* they did well or poorly in their own words. Frieze (1976) found that college students cited effort 84% of the time as the primary cause of success on a hypothetical exam and 75% of the time as the major cause of failure. Frieze and Snyder (in press) reported similar results in a study using children as young as first graders who were asked to say why another student succeeded or failed. When college students were asked about an actual grade on an exam, 69% said that effort was the major cause of their performance (Frieze, Snyder, & Fontaine, 1977). Similar data were found for fifth graders taking an actual classroom exam (Frieze, Snyder, & Fontaine, 1978).

The frequent use of effort as a causal explanation for exam performance appears to be found primarily for academic achievement situations and when students are asked to state the causal factors for performance in their own words. Causal attributions clearly differ across situations (Frieze, 1977; Teglasi, 1977). Frieze and Snyder (1980) found quite different patterns of attributions for various types of classroom achievement situations. For an art project, success or failure was attributed most often to ability (34%) and secondly to effort (27%). There were also a substantial number of interest attributions (18%). For sports, effort, ability, and being better than the other team were the most common attributions. Being successful at catching frogs, a common activity for these children, was most attributed to the frogs, an external factor.

Frieze, Snyder, and Fontaine (1978) also found differences in the attributions made for social studies exams as compared to math exams for fifth graders as shown in Table 2.3. For success, relatively more use of effort was made for social studies, whereas ability-task interaction (being good at mathematics) was more often cited for math success. However, there were few differences for failure.

As mentioned earlier, this frequent use of effort attributions as an explanation for exam performance is most often found when using open-ended data. When students were asked to rate each of a number of potential causes for how much they contributed to the outcome or for how prevalent that factor was, results were quite different. Bailey, Helm, and Gladstone (1975) asked students to choose the major cause of their performance on an

Table 2.3
OPEN-ENDED CAUSAL ATTRIBUTIONS FOR SUCCESS AND FAILURE[a]

Causal category	Success (%)			Failure (%)		
	Overall	Math	Social science	Overall	Math	Social science
Ability	2	4	0	1	0	1
Effort	69	53	84	65	65	65
Stable effort	1	1	1	0	0	0
Mood	0	0	0	1	1	0
Interest	1	1	1	1	1	0
Ability–task interaction	18	29	8	28	28	28
Task difficulty	6	7	2	4	4	4
Luck	1	1	1	1	0	1
Other people	1	3	0	0	0	0
Outside activities	0	0	0	1	0	0

[a]From Frieze, Snyder, & Fontaine (1978).

actual exam from a list containing ability, effort, luck, and task ease as possible causes. They found high use of all of these causes except luck. Using independent rating scales for each of a list of causes (ability, preparation, and task difficulty), Simon and Feather's (1973) college student subjects rated ability highest and luck lowest. Arkin and Maruyama (1979), again using rating scales for ability, effort, luck, and task ease, found the most frequent use of effort, followed by ability, task and luck for success. For failure, the ordering was task, effort, ability and luck. These studies, taken together, do not support the very high use of effort attributions found in open-ended studies, although effort remains as one of several important factors. Luck is rarely used in either type of study. Reasons for these discrepancies are not clear, but one explanation is that students are reluctant to mention ability as a factor in open-ended data, but seeing it on a list of possible causes removes any social constraints associated with claiming high ability.

Actual exams differ from the typical laboratory achievement task in a number of ways. The exam is probably more important than the laboratory task. Miller (1976) found in a laboratory study that high involvement in the task led to greater use of ability and task attributions. Luginbuhl, Crowe, and Kahan (1975) also found more use of ability attributions relative to effort attributions in situations in which continued success beyond the particular event is important. Once again, continued success is important in classroom situations. Continued success and importance being high in the classroom may, then, be another reason for the relatively high use of ability and task attributions.

Predicted Consequences of Attributions in the Classroom

Just as causal attributions may be affected by the type of situation, the predicted effects of causal attributions upon future expectancies and affective reactions may also differ from those found in laboratory experiments. The classroom is a complex environment with many variables which might potentially influence affect and expectancies. For example, Bailey et al. (1975) found that affect was most related to outcome (with students who did well feeling good and those who did poorly feeling bad) as predicted by earlier experimental work. However, they further found that luck attributions produced the most happiness or discontent. This contradicts the theoretically predicted relationship between internal attributions and affect. Similar relationships between affect and violations of expectancies (typically attributed to luck) were reported by House and Perney (1974). They reported that subjects were most satisfied with unexpected success and most dissatisfied with unexpected failure.

Using a slightly different attribution measure, Frieze, Snyder, and Fontaine (1977, 1978) had students who had just taken an exam in the classroom rate their ability, luck, and the difficulty of the exam. Results of two studies (one with college students and the other with fifth graders) indicated that students felt more pride for success when they made higher ratings for their efforts and their abilities. Moreover, feeling lucky was somewhat related to affect for the fifth graders but not for the college students. These results are more consistent with previous research and support the idea that ability is especially important in situations where continued success is important (Nicholls, 1976). Further research is needed, though, to clarify the relationship between affect and attributions in the classroom.

Expectancies for the future after receiving an exam grade may also differ from those predicted by the theoretical attribution model presented earlier in this chapter. Although Simon and Feather (1973) found that unexpected outcomes in an exam situation were more frequently attributed to unstable causes as predicted, they also found that task attributions were higher for unexpected outcomes. Also, Bailey et al. (1975) reported that regardless of their causal attribution, all students expected to do better on the next exam. They interpreted this finding as evidence of students' learning the cultural belief in our society that improvement is always possible. Similar patterns of optimism were reported by Frieze, Snyder, and Fontaine (1977, 1978).

Valle and Frieze (1976) found in a laboratory study that stable attributions led to higher future expectations whereas unstable attributions were correlated with lower expectations. Parallel correlations for these data were computed by Frieze, Snyder, and Fontaine (1977, 1978). Their classroom data strongly supported this relationship, especially for stable attributions. Valle and Frieze also reported more support for predictions relating to stable attributions, so this is consistent. The classroom data suggest, though, that high ratings of ability are most strongly related to high future expectations so that the theoretical predictions may need more refinement.

Other expectancy predictions involve difference scores among initial expectancies, actual exam score, and future expectancies. These predictions were in general not well supported by Frieze, Snyder, and Fontaine's classroom studies, possibly because of a ceiling effect caused by the uniformly high initial and future expectancies. Once again, more research is needed in classroom settings to clarify and extend the theoretical models developed in the laboratory.

Developmental Changes and Causal Attributions

In applying attribution research based on studies with college students to a classroom situation, one must take into account not only the complexity of the school environment, but also the fact that the subjects will generally be children. Developmental factors undoubtedly interact with various phases of the attribution model. As Ruble (1978) points out, developmental influences can be seen in children's concepts of the various constructs important for achievement and in the ways in which these constructs are processed or integrated. Some of the constructs in which developmental changes have been noted include the concepts of ability and effort and the concepts of success and failure. Nicholls (1978) has shown that a developmental process is involved in children's understanding that more difficult tasks require more ability for successful completion. Furthermore, several studies have demonstrated changes as children mature in their inferences about relative levels of ability and effort as they relate to task performance (e.g., Kun, 1977; Kun, Parsons, & Ruble, 1974; Nicholls, 1978).

Ruble (1978) discusses another developmental change—the increasing sense of personal responsibility for their outcomes seen as children get older, although the exact ages involved in this change and the process by which it occurs are not well understood. Veroff (1969) feels that children evolve from defining success in terms of one's own past history to definitions based upon social comparison. The latter basis is seen as occurring after the child enters school (see Ruble, 1978, for a review of this literature).

Along with these definitional differences, children also show differences in processing achievement information as they develop cognitively. As mentioned earlier, although children as young as fourth graders can use information to form causal judgments in the same ways as adults (Frieze & Bar-Tal, 1980), they are more systematic and can make finer discriminations as they get older (Frieze & Bar-Tal, 1980; Ruble, 1978; Shaklee, 1976).

Attributions in the Classroom

The existing data showing how attributions are formed and how they affect actual classroom settings are generally supportive of the theoretical attribution model developed with laboratory studies, but this support is better in some areas than others. Many of the linkages in the model have not yet been adequately tested. A comprehensive classroom model will have to consider how success and failure judgments are made rather than to assume that the objective grade is equivalent to internal feelings of success. It may also have to explore in more detail how initial expectancies for performance are formed since these expectancies appear to be so important in determining causal attributions. Other little-investigated factors that may also be of importance include the importance of doing well to the student and the effects of other people upon success judgments as well as upon the attributions made. The effects of causal attributions upon future expectations and emotional reactions also need more study within a school situation, and all of these factors need to be looked at within a developmental perspective.

Other variables, which may well become major factors in future studies of the attribution process, are subject matter differences and the effects of different types of classroom structures upon the attribution process. The role of the teacher in attribution training and reinforcement also needs to be more fully analyzed along with studies of parents and other socializing agents.

SUMMARY AND CONCLUSIONS

This chapter has reviewed the research dealing with people's beliefs about the causes of events, specifically about why they believe a particular success or failure has occurred. A theoretical model developed by Weiner and his associates was reviewed, which was originally based on the idea that attributions to ability, effort, luck, and the ease or difficulty of the task were significant mediators of affective and cognitive reactions to the success or failure experienced after doing an achievement task. Much of the research supporting this basic model has been done in laboratory settings with college students as subjects.

After reviewing the basic Weiner achievement attribution model, some modifications have been made as it has been applied to non-laboratory settings, and more specifically to actual classroom environments. As is so often the case, the model has become increasingly more complex as it has been adapted to new situations. The list of important causes has been greatly expanded. In classroom and school settings, effort is of great importance as a causal explanation for success and failure. Other important attributions include the teacher, ability–task interactions ("math is difficult for me") and interest in the task or subject matter. There is strong evidence that each type of situation has its own set of relevant attributions, so that the pattern of attributions used may even differ from a mathematics to a social studies class.

Another important addition to the basic theoretical model has been the definition of the event about which the causal attributions are made. Rather than assuming that the decision about whether the outcome is a success or failure is straightforward and similar for everyone, it has been found that people's subjective appraisals of their outcomes may be quite different even given the same level of objective performance. Preliminary research has shown that the process of evaluating an outcome and determining if it is a success or failure for the person is a highly complex process. A related question is what information people really use in making an attribution after they decide the outcome is a success or failure. We know about important types of information for laboratory studies—the past history of the individual, how important it was for him or her to do well, and how well others working on the same task did—but little research has been done in real-life settings to see how much people rely upon these informational cues in making attributional judgments.

Finally, another area in which we need to know more is in the affective and cognitive consequences of various attributions in actual classrooms. One finding is that students seem to be eternally optimistic about doing better in the future, regardless of what they attributed their last exam grade to. However, attributions do have some effect upon this optimism, with more stable attributions, especially ability attributions, leading to more positive expectations. Moreover, affective reactions are even more complex, and there seem to be specific reactions associated with different causal attributions. Behavioral effects of different attributions are yet even more complex and have not been systematically dealt with by attribution theorists.

Overall, the attributional perspective provides educators with an intuitively appealing and experimentally supportive way of viewing events in the classroom. It can be used to explain sources of disagreement between teachers and students or partners and teachers (or between any two groups). Providing a model that relates behavior to belief systems, the attributions theory may also provide us with a way of improving school performance and self-esteem of students by working with and modifying causal attributions.

ACKNOWLEDGMENTS

I would like to thank Daniel Bar-Tal and Theodore A. Chandler for comments on an earlier version of this chapter.

REFERENCES

Abelson, R. P. Script processing in attitude formation and decision-making. In. J. S. Carroll and J. W. Payne (Eds.), *Cognition and social behavior*. Hillsdale, New Jersey: Lawrence Erlbaum Associates, 1976.

Abramson, L. Y., Seligman, M. E. P., & Teasdale, J. D. Learned helplessness in humans: Critique and reformulation. *Journal of Abnornal Psychology*, 1978, *87*, 49–74.

Ames, C. Children's achievement attributions and self-reinforcement: Effects of self-concept and competitive reward structure. *Journal of Educational Psychology*, 1978, *70*, 345–355.

Arkin, R. M., & Maruyama, G. M. Attribution, affect, and college exam performance. *Journal of Educational Psychology*, 1979, *71*, 85–93.

Astin, H. Women and work. In J. Sherman and F. Denmark (Eds.), *Psychology of women: Future directions of research*. New York: Psychological Dimensions, 1978.

Atkinson, J. W. *An introduction to motivation*. Princeton, New Jersey: Van Nostrand, 1964.

Bailey, R. C., Helm, B., & Gladstone, R. The effects of success and failure in a real-life setting: Performance, attribution, affect, and expectancy. *The Journal of Psychology*, 1975, *89*, 137–147.

Bane, A. L., & Brown, E. R. Causal attributions for success and failure: Heuristic processing of sequential information. Paper presented at the annual meeting of the Midwestern Psychological Association, Chicago, 1977.

Baron, R. A. *Human aggression*. New York: Plenum, 1977.

Barrett, C. A., & Nicholls, J. Motivational factors in the intelligence test performance of Maori and Pakeha children. *Journal of Cross-Cultural Psychology*, 1978, *9*, 349–357.

Bar-Tal, D., & Darom, E. Pupils' attributions for success and failure. *Child Development*, 1979, *50*, 264–267.

Bar-Tal, D., & Frieze, I. H. Attributions of success and failure for actors and observers. *Journal of Research in Personality*, 1976, *10*, 256–265.

Bar-Tal, D., & Frieze, I. H. Achievement motivation for males and females as a determinant of attributions for success and failure. *Sex Roles*, 1977, *3*, 301–313.

Bar-Tal, D., Ravgad, N., & Zilberman, D. Development of causal perception of success and failure. Unpublished manuscript, Tel-Aviv University, 1978.

Bar-Tal, D., Raviv, A., Raviv, A., & Bar-Tal, Y. Consistency of pupils' attributions regarding success and failure. Unpublished manuscript, Tel-Aviv University, 1978.

Beckman, L. Effects of students' performance on teachers' and observers' attributions of causality. *Journal of Educational Psychology*, 1970, *61*, 76–82.

Broverman, I. K., Vogel, S. R., Broverman, D. M., Clarkson, F. E., & Rosenkrantz, P. S. Sex role stereotypes: A current appraisal. *Journal of Social Issues,* 1972, *28,* 59–78.

Carroll, J. S., Payne, J. W., Frieze, I. H., & Girard, D. Attribution theory: An information processing approach. Unpublished manuscript, Carnegie-Mellon University, 1976.

Chaikin, A. L. The effects of four outcome schedules on persistence, liking for the task, and attributions of causality. *Journal of Personality,* 1971, *39,* 512–526.

Cole, D., King, K., & Newcomb, A. Grade expectations as a function of sex, academic discipline, and sex of instructor. *Psychology of Women Quarterly,* 1977, *1*(4), 380–385.

Cooper, H. M., & Burger, J. M. Internality, stability, and personal efficacy: A categorization of free response academic attributions. Unpublished manuscript, University of Missouri—Columbia, 1978.

Crandall, V. C. Sex differences in expectancy, intellectual and academic reinforcement. In C. P. Smith (Ed.), *Achievement-related motives in children.* New York: Russell Sage, 1969.

Crandall, V. C. Expecting sex differences and sex differences in expectancies: A developmental analysis. Paper presented at the annual meeting of the American Psychological Association, Toronto, 1978. (a)

Crandall, V. C. Toward a cognitive-learning model of achievement behavior and development. Paper presented at the annual meeting of the Motivation and Education Group, Ann Arbor, 1978. (b)

Crandall, V. J., Katkovsky, W., & Preston, A. Conceptual formulation for some research on children's achievement development. *Child Development,* 1960, *31,* 787–797.

Cunningham, J. D., & Kelley, H. H. Causal attributions for interpersonal events of varying magnitude. *Journal of Personality,* 1975, *43,* 74–93.

deCharms, R., & Muir, M. S. Motivation: Social approaches. *Annual Psychological Review,* 1978, *29,* 91–113.

Dweck, C. S., & Gilliard, D. Expectancy statements as determinants of reactions to failure: Sex differences in persistence and expectancy change. *Journal of Personality and Social Psychology,* 1975, *25,* 109–116.

Dweck, D. S., & Repucci, N. D. Learned helplessness and reinforcement responsibility in children. *Journal of Personality and Social Psychology,* 1973, *25,* 109–116.

Elig, T., & Frieze, I. H. A multi-dimensional scheme for coding and interpreting perceived causality for success and failure events: The coding scheme of perceived causality (CSPC). *JSAS: Catalog of Selected Documents in Psychology,* 1975, *5,* 313.

Elig, T., & Frieze, I. H. Measuring causal attributions for success and failure. *Journal of Personality and Social Psychology,* 1979, *37,* 621–634.

Feather, N. T. Attribution of responsibility and valence of success and failure in relation to initial confidence and task performance. *Journal of Personality and Social Psychology,* 1969, *13,* 129–144.

Feather, N. T., & Simon, J. G. Attribution of responsibility and valence of outcome in relation to initial confidence and success and failure of self and other. *Journal of Personality and Social Psychology,* 1971, *18,* 173–188. (a)

Feather, N. T., & Simon, J. G. Causal attributions for success and failure in relation to expectations of success based upon selective or manipulative control. *Journal of Personality,* 1971, *37,* 527–541. (b)

Feather, N. T., & Simon, J. G. Reactions to male and female success and failure in sex-linked occupations: Impressions of personality, causal attributions, and perceived likelihood of different consequences. *Journal of Personality and Social Psychology,* 1975, *31,* 20–31.

Festinger, L. A theory of social comparison processes. *Human Relations,* 1954, *7,* 117–140.

Fitch, G. Effects of self-esteem, perceived performance and choice on causal attributions. *Journal of Personality and Social Psychology,* 1970, *16,* 311–315.

Fontaine, G. Social comparison and some determinants of expected personal control and expected performance in a novel task situation. *Journal of Personality and Social Psychology,* 1974, *29,* 487–496.

Freedman, J. Stimulus characteristics and subject prejudice as determinants of stereotype attribution. *Journal of Personality and Social Psychology,* 1972, *21,* 218–228.

Friend, R. M., & Neale, J. M. Children's perceptions of success and failure: An attributional analysis of the effects of race and social class. *Developmental Psychology,* 1972, *7,* 124–128.

Frieze, I. H. Causal attribution and information seeking to explain success and failure. *Journal of Research in Personality,* 1976, *10,* 298–305. (a)

Frieze, I. H. The role of information processing in making causal attributions for success and failure. In J. S. Carroll and J. W. Payne (Eds.), *Cognition and social behavior.* Hillsdale, New Jersey: Lawrence Erlbaum Associates, 1976. (b)

Frieze, I. H. Causal attributions for success and failure: Advances in theory and applications. Invited paper presented at the annual meeting of the Midwestern Psychological Association, Chicago, 1977.

Frieze, I. H., & Bar-Tal, D. Attribution theory: Past and present. In I. H. Frieze, D. Bar-Tal, and J. S. Carroll (Eds.), *New approaches to social problems: Applications of attribution theory.* San Francisco: Jossey-Bass, 1979.

Frieze, I. H., & Bar-Tal, D. Developmental trends in cue utilization for attributional judgments. *Journal of Applied Developmental Psychology,* 1980, *1,* 83–94.

Frieze, I. H., Fisher, J., Hanusa, B., McHugh, M. C., & Valle, V. A. Attributions of the causes of success and failure as internal and external barriers to achievement in women. In J. Sherman and F. Denmark (Eds.), *Psychology of women: Future directions of research.* New York: Psychological Dimensions, 1978.

Frieze, I. H., McHugh, M., & Duquin, M. Causal attributions for women and men and sports participation. Paper presented at the annual meeting of the American Psychological Association, Washington, D.C., 1976.

Frieze, I. H., & Snyder, H. N. Children's beliefs about the causes of success and failure in school settings. *Journal of Educational Psychology,* 1980, *72,* 186–196.

Frieze, I. H., Snyder, H. N., & Fontaine, C. M. Student attributions and the attribution process during an actual examination. Paper presented at the annual meeting of the American Psychological Association, San Francisco, 1977.

Frieze, I. H., Snyder, H. N., & Fontaine, C. M. Fifth grader's attributions and the attribution model during an actual examination. Unpublished manuscript, Learning Research and Development Center, University of Pittsburgh, 1978.

Frieze, I. H., & Weiner, B. Cue utilization and attributional judgments for success and failure. *Journal of Personality,* 1971, *39,* 591–606.

Gilmore, T. M., & Reid, D. W. Locus of control and causal attribution for positive and negative outcomes on university exams. *Journal of Research in Personality,* 1979, *13,* 154–160.

Gjesme, T. Achievement-related motives and school performance for girls. *Journal of Personality and Social Psychology,* 1973, *26,* 131–136.

Goethals, G. R., & Darley, J. M. Social comparison theory: An attributional approach. In J. M. Suls and R. L. Miller (Eds.), *Social comparison processes.* Washington, D.C.: Hemisphere, 1977.

Gold, M. W., & Ryan, K. M. Vocational training for the mentally retarded. In I. H. Frieze, D. Bar-Tal, and J. S. Carroll (Eds.), *New approaches to social problems: Applications of attribution theory.* San Francisco: Jossey-Bass, 1979.

Gruder, C. L. Choice of comparison persons in evaluating oneself. In J. M. Suls and R. L. Miller (Eds.), *Social comparison processes.* Washington, D.C.: Hemisphere, 1977.

Hilton, T. L., & Berglund, G. W. Sex differences in mathematics achievement: A longitudinal study. *Journal of Educational Research*, 1974, *67*, 231–237.

Hoffman, L. W. Early childhood experiences and women's achievement motives. *Journal of Social Issues*, 1972, *28*, 129–155.

House, W. C., & Perney, V. Valence of expected and unexpected outcomes as a function of locus of goal and type of expectancy. *Journal of Personality and Social Psychology*, 1974, *29*, 454–463.

Husen, T. (Ed.) *International study of achievement in mathematics*. Vols. 1 and 2. New York: Wiley, 1967.

Jackaway, R. Sex differences in achievement motivation, behavior, and attributions about success and failure. Unpublished Ph.D. dissertation, State University of New York at Albany, 1974.

Jenkins, S. R. "And what do you mean by success?": Fear of success and personal success goals. Paper presented at the annual meeting of the Eastern Psychological Association, Philadelphia, 1979.

Jones, E. E., & Davis, K. E. From acts to dispositions: The attribution process in person perception. In L. Berkowitz (Ed.), *Advances in Experimental Social Psychology*. Vol. 2. New York: Academic Press, 1967.

Jones, E. E., & Harris, V. The attribution of attitudes. *Journal of Experimental Social Psychology*, 1967, *3*, 1–24.

Jones, E. E., Rock, L., Shaver, K. G., Goethals, G. R., & Ward, L. M. Pattern of performance and ability attribution: An unexpected primacy effect. *Journal of Personality and Social Psychology*, 1968, *10*, 317–340.

Karlins, M., Coffman, T., & Walters, G. On the fading of social stereotypes: Studies in three generations of college students. *Journal of Personality and Social Psychology*, 1969, *13*, 1–16.

Kelley, H. H. Attribution theory in social psychology. In *Nebraska symposium on motivation*. Lincoln: University of Nebraska Press, 1967.

Kelley, H. H. *Causal schemata and the attribution process*. Morristown, New Jersey: General Learning Press, 1972.

Kipnis, D. M., & Kidder, L. H. How failure strikes men and women. Paper presented at the annual meeting of the American Psychological Association, Toronto, 1978.

Kukla, A. Attributional determinants of achievement-related behavior. *Journal of Personality and Social Psychology*, 1972, *21*, 166–174.

Kun, A. Development of the magnitude-covariation and compensation schemata in ability and effort attributions of performance. *Child Development*, 1977, *48*, 862–873.

Kun, A., Parsons, J. E., & Ruble, D. N. Development of integration processes using ability and effort information to predict outcome. *Developmental Psychology*, 1974, *10*(5), 721–732.

Kun, A., & Weiner, B. Necessary versus sufficient causal schemata for success and failure. *Journal of Research in Personality*, 1978, *7*, 197–207.

Lancy, D. G. The classroom as phenomenon. In D. Bar-Tal and L. Saxe (Eds.), *Social psychology of education*. Washington, D.C.: Hemisphere, 1978.

Langer, E. J. Rethinking the role of thought in social interaction. In J. H. Harvey, W. J. Ickes, and R. E. Kidd (Eds.), *New directions in attribution research*. Vol. 2. Hillsdale, New Jersey: Lawrence Erlbaum Associates, 1978.

Latta, R. M. Differential tests of two cognitive theories of performance: Weiner vs. Kukla. *Journal of Personality and Social Psychology*, 1976, *34*, 295–304.

Lefcourt, H. M. Recent developments in the study of locus of control. In B. A. Maher (Ed.), *Progress in experimental personality research*. New York: Academic Press, 1970.

Levine, J. M. Social comparison: A review and integration with special relevance to education.

Unpublished manuscript, Learning Research and Development Center, University of Pittsburgh, 1979.

Levine, J. M., & Snyder, H. N. Perceived peer ability and liking in the classroom. Unpublished manuscript. Learning Research and Development Center, University of Pittsburgh, Pittsburgh, 1978.

Luginbuhl, J., Crowe, D., & Kahan, J. Causal attributions for success and failure. *Journal of Personality and Social Psychology,* 1975, *31,* 86–93.

Marini, M. M., & Greenberger, E. Sex differences in educational aspirations and expectations. *American Educational Research Journal,* 1978, *15,* 67–79.

McArthur, L. The how and what of why: Some determinants of consequences of causal attribution. *Journal of Personality and Social Psychology,* 1972, *22,* 171–193.

McMahan, I. D. Relationships between causal attributions and expectancy of success. *Journal of Personality and Social Psychology,* 1973, *28,* 108–114.

Miller, D. T. Ego involvement and attributions for success and failure. *Journal of Personality and Social Psychology,* 1976, *34,* 901–906.

Miller, D. T., & Ross, M. Self-serving biases in the attribution of causality: Fact or fiction? *Psychological Bulletin,* 1975, *82,* 213–225.

Miller, R. L., & Suls, J. M. Affiliation preferences as a function of attitude and ability similarity. In J. M. Suls and R. L. Miller (Eds.), *Social comparison processes.* Washington, D.C.: Hemisphere, 1977.

Mokros, J. R., & Koff, E. Sex-stereotyping of children's success in mathematics and reading. *Psychological Reports,* 1978, *42,* 1287–1293.

Murray, S. R., & Mednick, M. T. S. Perceiving the causes of success and failure in achievement: Sex, race and motivational comparisons. *Journal of Consulting and Clinical Psychology,* 1975, *43,* 881–885.

Nicholls, J. G. Causal attributions and other achievement-related cognitions: Effects of task outcome, attainment value, and sex. *Journal of Personality and Social Psychology,* 1975, *31,* 379–389.

Nicholls, J. G. Effort is virtuous, but it's better to have ability: Evaluative responses to perceptions of effort and ability. *Journal of Research in Personality,* 1976, *10,* 306–315.

Nicholls, J. G. The development of the concepts of effort and ability, perception of academic attainment, and the understanding that difficult tasks require more ability. *Child Development,* 1978, *49,* 800–814.

O'Leary, V. E., & Hansen, R. D. Sex-determined attributions. Paper presented at the annual meeting of the Eastern Psychological Association, Philadelphia, 1979.

O'Leary, V. E., & Repucci, N. D. Learned helplessness and reinforcement responsibility in children. *Journal of Personality and Social Psychology,* 1973, *25,* 109–116.

Orvis, B. R., Cunningham, J. D., & Kelley, H. H. A closer examination of causal inference: The role of consensus, distinctiveness and consistency information. *Journal of Personality and Social Psychology,* 1975, *32,* 605–616.

Parsons, J., & Goff, S. Sex differences in achievement motivation: The influences of values, goals, and orientation. Paper presented at the annual meeting of the Motivation and Education Group, Ann Arbor, Michigan, 1978.

Passer, M. W. Perceiving the causes of success and failure revisited: A multidimensional scaling approach. Unpublished doctoral dissertation, University of California, Los Angeles, 1977.

Riemer, B. S. The influence of causal beliefs on affect and expectancy. *Journal of Personality and Social Psychology,* 1975, *31,* 1163–1167.

Rosenbaum, R. M. A dimensional analysis of the perceived causes of success and failure. Unpublished doctoral dissertation. University of California, Los Angeles, 1972.

Rosenthal, R., & Jacobson, L. *Pygmalion in the classroom.* New York: Holt, Rinehart & Winston, 1968.

Ruble, D. N. A developmental perspective of theories of achievement motivation. Paper presented at the conference on Motivation and Education, University of Michigan, Ann Arbor, October, 1978.

Ruble, D. N., & Boggiano, A. K. Optimizing motivation in an achievement context. In B. Keogh (Ed.), *Advances in special education.* Vol. 1. Greenwich, Connecticut: JAI Press, in press.

Ruble, D. N., Parsons, J. E., & Ross, J. Self-evaluative responses of children in an achievement setting. *Child Development,* 1976, *47,* 990–997.

Ryan, K. M. Impact of academic performance pattern on predicted performance and assigned grade. Unpublished masters thesis, University of Pittsburgh, 1978.

Shaklee, H. Development in inferences of ability and task difficulty. *Child Development,* 1976, *47,* 1051–1057.

Sherman, J., & Fennema, E. The study of mathematics by high school girls and boys: Related variables. *American Educational Research Journal,* 1977, *14,* 159–168.

Shrauger, J. S., & Terbovic, M. L. Self-evaluation and assessments of performance by self and others. *Journal of Consulting and Clinical Psychology,* 1976, *44,* 564–572.

Simon, J. G., & Feather, N. T. Causal attributions for success and failure at university examinations. *Journal of Educational Psychology,* 1973, *64,* 46–56.

Smith, E. R., & Miller, F. D. Reaction time measures of attribution processes. Paper presented at the annual meeting of the American Psychological Association, Toronto, 1978.

Suls, J. M. Social comparison theory and research: An overview from 1954. In J. M. Suls and R. L. Miller (Eds.), *Social comparison processes.* Washington, D.C.: Hemisphere, 1977.

Suls, J. M., Gastorf, J., & Lawhon, J. Social comparison choices for evaluating a sex- and age-related ability. *Personality and Social Psychology Bulletin,* 1978, *4,* 102–105.

Taylor, S., & Fiske, S. Salience, attention, and attribution: Top of the head phenomena. In L. Berkowitz (Ed.), *Advances in Experimental Social Psychology,* New York: Academic Press, 1978.

Teglasi, H. Influence of situational factors on causal attributions of college females. *Psychological Reports,* 1977, *41,* 495–502.

Triandis, H. *The analysis of subjective culture.* New York: Wiley-Interscience, 1972.

Valle, V. A., & Frieze, I. H. The stability of causal attributions as a mediator in changing expectations for success. *Journal of Personality and Social Psychology,* 1976, *33,* 579–587.

Veroff, J. Social comparison and the development of achievement motivation. In C. P. Smith (Ed.), *Achievement-related motives in children.* New York: Russell Sage Foundation, 1969.

Weigers, R. M., & Frieze, I. H. Gender, female traditionality, achievement level and cognitions of success and failure. *Psychology of Women Quarterly,* 1977, *2,* 125–137.

Weiner, B. A theory of motivation for some classroom experiences. *Journal of Educational Psychology,* 1979, *71,* 3–25.

Weiner, B. Achievement motivation as conceptualized by an attribution theorist. In B. Weiner (Ed.), *Achievement motivation and attribution theory.* Morristown, New Jersey: General Learning Press, 1974.

Weiner, B. New conceptions in the study of achievement motivation. In B. Maher (Ed.), *Progress in experimental personality research.* Vol. 5. New York: Academic Press, 1970.

Weiner, B., Frieze, I., Kukla, A., Reed, L., Rest, S., & Rosenbaum, R. M. *Perceiving the causes of success and failure.* New York: General Learning Press, 1971.

Weiner, B., Heckhausen, H., Meyer, W., & Cook, R. E. Causal aspirations and achievement behavior: Conceptual analysis of effort and reanalysis of locus of control. *Journal of Personality and Social Psychology,* 1972, *21,* 239–248.

Weiner, B., & Kukla, A. An attributional analysis of achievement motivation. *Journal of Personality and Social Psychology,* 1970, *15,* 1–20.

Weiner, B., Nierenberg, R., & Goldstein, M. Social learning (locus of control) versus attributional (causal stability) interpretations of expectancy of success. *Journal of Personality, 1976, 44,* 52–68.

Weiner, B., & Potepan, P. A. Personality correlates and affective reactions toward exams of succeeding and failing college students. *Journal of Educational Psychology, 1970, 61,* 144–151.

Weiner, B., Russell, D., & Lerman, D. Affective consequences of causal ascriptions. In J. H. Harvery, W. J. Ickes, and R. F. Kidd (Eds.), *New directions in attribution research.* Vol. 2. Hillsdale, New Jersey: Lawrence Erlbaum Associates, 1978.

chapter 3

Classroom Expectations: Teacher–Pupil Interactions[1]

THOMAS L. GOOD

INTRODUCTION

The influence of teachers' expectations on student performance has been, and continues to be, a very active research area. The attractiveness of this research lies in its clear implications for classroom application if linkages between teacher attitudes and student performance can be identified. Attempts to change teacher behavior are relatively inexpensive compared to the construction of new buildings or the development of new curricula. Hence, educators continue to be interested in the possibility that the educational decline of certain students could be altered by making teachers more aware of their behavior and its consequences for students.

In this chapter a variety of issues will be explored. Some of the questions that will be raised include: What is a self-fulfilling prophecy? Why might teachers be susceptible to self-fulfilling acts? What research evidence supports the expectation hypothesis? How do teachers form and communicate expectations? How do students internalize and/or respond to the influence of teachers' expectations? To what extent do pupils determine teacher expectations? What other expectations (other than those that teachers hold toward individual pupils) also help to determine the specific form of pupil-

[1] The author would like to acknowledge the support received at the center for Research in Social Behavior, University of Missouri, Columbia, Missouri. The development of this paper was also partially and indirectly supported by Grant NIE-G-77-0003 from the National Institute of Education. However, opinions expressed here do not necessarily reflect the position or policy of the National Institute of Education.

teacher interaction and students' opportunity for achievement generally? What research seems important now?

SELF-FULFILLING PROPHECY

The term *self-fulfilling prophecy* implies that a possible event becomes a reality because of the belief that it will occur. That is, once an expectation is developed, a person tends to act as if the belief was true, and eventually his or her action causes it to be fulfilled. Popular writers and scientists have often discussed the possible linkage between beliefs and behaviors. For example, George Bernard Shaw noted (on his 90th birthday), "Remember, our conduct is influenced not by our experience but by our expectations." Similarly, Thomas and Thomas (1928) wrote, "If men define situations as real, they are real in their consequences." The premise, simply stated, is that actively held beliefs tend to mobilize both behavior and perceptions in a way that is consistent with the beliefs. For instance, if we *believe* someone likes us (or will like us), then we are likely to operate in a way consistent with that belief. We may call the person when we have interesting news to share (gossip, a good investment, a bargain sale). Gradually, the other person may begin to reciprocate and seek us out for friendly and useful exchanges such that in time friendship may develop. Such reciprocal behavior fulfills the original prophecy.

The expectation that a person likes us may control how we act toward that person. Also, our expectation may influence how we *interpret* another's behavior. For example, if a "friend" calls to inquire about the illness of a family member, the call may be interpreted as a courteous gesture. However, if a "nonfriend" calls (using the same tonal expression, raising the same questions, expressing the same degree of concern, etc.), the behavior may be interpreted as an unwanted intrusion and the person may be suspected of having surplus motivations (he'll call me for a favor next week).

Hence, our expectations control both our behavior and how we interpret the behavior of others. Jones (1977), among others, has argued that interpersonal expectations have been found to influence both the person holding the expectation and the behavior for whom the expectation is held. He writes, "Studies of the influence of the examiner play a significant role in determining the outcomes of testing. . . . Different examiners both see different cues in the same patient and use the same cue to infer different things [p. 86]."

It is easy to understand how self-fulfilling prophecies might operate in certain conditions. For example, if a person is making a decision on the basis of written information describing numerous people (e.g., which 5 out of 300 applicants to interview for a job) or when the initial contact is brief (e.g., at an initial fraternity or sorority rush party), expectations may make the selection process easier. Under such circumstances somewhat superficial or indirect criteria may be used to fulfill one's expectations (e.g., applicants from large state universities make better employees; students who have participated in certain activities make better "Greeks" than those who haven't). Obviously such beliefs (whether accurate or not) tend to fulfill themselves in direct ways that are not difficult to understand.

At another level, expectations may be self-serving or self-protecting rather than simply prejudiced. Jones (1977) describes an interesting example of how differently he and faculty colleagues reacted to potential faculty members who were interviewing for a position. Jones noted that when he and colleagues discussed an applicant it was frequently the case that vastly different opinions had been reached about a candidate. In retrospect, Jones concluded that certain beliefs influenced or moderated the reactions to job candidates. Namely, he felt that all faculty members wanted to recruit a productive faculty member, but younger faculty members wanted to recruit an older person, whereas older faculty wanted to recruit a younger faculty member. Everybody wanted a "superstar" but nobody wanted to compete with a superstar as a peer.

It would be possible to continue to list examples of how expectations affect our behavior toward others or our behaviors toward ourselves (e.g., placebo effects), but the illustrations just given are probably sufficient to suggest that expectations may exert motivational pressure to fulfill them. However, why should self-fulfilling prophecies occur in classrooms, given that most teachers are motivated to develop the abilities of all students?

Why Might Self-Fulfilling Prophecies Operate in the Classroom?

Why would a motivated, well-meaning teacher act in a manner that fulfills a low expectation (e.g., Sally will have a hard time learning to read)?[2] The basic rationale lies in the fact that classrooms are very busy places. Jackson (1968) has pointed out that a single teacher may engage in more than one thousand interpersonal exchanges a day with students. If, as Jones (1977) has noted, trained examiners can see different cues in the same person during individual testing sessions, therefore it is easy to see how

---

[2] If one does not assume positive motivation on the part of the teacher, there are many other ways to explain differential teacher behavior. For example, some teachers may be more interested in their own satisfaction and comfort when dealing with students and relatively less concerned about what happens to students. That is, such teachers may tend to call on students who fulfill their comfort needs.

teachers' expectations in a complex classroom setting might be fulfilled. The fast pace of the classroom almost guarantees that teachers can spend little time with individuals. Hence, once an expectation is formed, there is little basis or occasion for it to be altered.

A second factor supporting the possibility of an expectation influence is the *selective attention* of teachers. Since the classroom is a complex environment, teachers cannot monitor all aspects of classroom life, and they therefore have to decide what to pay attention to. If teachers are looking for signs of success they are more likely to find them than if they are looking for failure. For example, the teacher, after asking a difficult question, may instinctively look in the direction of a better student. Although several students may be able to answer the question, the teacher focuses attention upon only a few students because of the belief that the question is difficult and only a few are capable of answering it.

Similarly, a teacher who hears a disturbance in the classroom may instinctively look for a student whom he or she expects to be a behavior problem. Since the teacher looks (because of the expectation) for a particular student to be a behavior problem, the student is likely to be criticized when the situation is ambiguous. Similarly, if the student is engaged in one of several minor discussions that are operating in the classroom, the student and his or her group are likely to be criticized and other students will escape undetected because the teacher did not look their way initially.

The selective attention problem that teachers have is made more complex by the self-presentation strategies of students. Spencer-Hall (1976) found that some students behave differently on stage (when the teacher is watching) than off stage. One subgroup of such students was found not to work any harder or misbehave less frequently than other students, but were thought of more highly by teachers because they were seldom seen off-task or misbehaving. Hence, these students were successful in obtaining the "fruits" of off-task behavior (a brief and fun catharsis) but without damaging their image in the eyes of the teacher. Student behavior can be an important factor in creating and/or sustaining teacher expectations.

A third factor that would allow self-fulfilling prophecies to occur is the need for rapid *interpretation*. In a complex setting that has to be monitored selectively, interpretations must be made quickly. The argument here is that much classroom behavior is ambiguous and has no meaning independent of how the teacher processes available information. For example, the teacher asks a question and the student raises an eyebrow. The raised eyebrow has no meaning independent of the teacher's interpretation. It is conceivable that the raised eyebrow of a student from whom the teacher expects good performance may be interpreted as meaning, "The student is thinking; I'll wait longer for an answer."

Similarly, the raised eyebrow of a student from whom the teacher expects poor performance may lead the teacher to conclude, "The student is hopelessly lost. I had better call on someone else." Obviously, such *differential* teacher conclusions to the same stimuli (e.g., a raised eyebrow) are consistent with a self-fulfilling prophecy hypothesis. The teacher expecting good performance interprets the cue in a favorable way and provides the student with additional time to respond.

In contrast, the teacher expecting poor performance interprets the same cue differently and ends the response opportunity for the student. If this *differential* behavior is consistent over time, then it is conceivable that students' expectations and behaviors will become different as time goes on. Students receiving additional time may become more relaxed in future response situations and their expectations for success will increase. Students perceived unfavorably may become more tense in academic interactions, and their expectations may be lowered. Once a student is labeled as a good or bad student, it is difficult to alter this expectation, because even neutral stimuli are likely to be interpreted in a way consistent with the teacher's existing expectation.

There are other factors that are consistent with a self-fulfilling prophecy, but these variables are more pertinent to a discussion of individual differences among teachers (why some teachers are more susceptible to self-fulfilling prophecies than are others) and will not be dealt with here. It is argued, then, that three factors—classroom complexity, the need for selective attention, and the interpretation problem—make the possibility of classroom self-fulfilling prophecies real.

Support for the fact that teachers are susceptible to expectation influences can be drawn from the fact that most people, at least in some situations, are influenced by their own expectations. Tversky and Kahneman (1971) have noted that there is a tendency for people (even scientists!) to interpret small samples of behavior as if they were highly representative. There is also research to show that initial (whether accurate or erroneous) reactions bias subsequent observations such that future observations tend to be seen as consistent with initial observations (Hayden & Mischel, 1973). Hence, the student who misbehaves early in the school year on one or two occasions may be seen as a behavior problem, and subsequent ambiguous behavior may then be seen as misbehavior.

The complexity and rapid pace of the classroom make it a unique setting that is ripe for the quick formation of expectations, but one in which there are considerable role constraints against the expression of negative expectations by teachers. Hence it is likely to be much more difficult to find consistent ways in which low expectations are fulfilled in the classroom than in a business or social setting.

A MODEL OF TEACHER
EXPECTATIONS

A general model describing how teachers' expectations may be fulfilled in the classroom has been advanced by Brophy and Good, 1970; Good and Brophy (1973, 1977, 1978). The model has five steps.

Step 1. The teacher expects specific behavior and achievement from particular students.

Step 2. Because of these different expectations, the teacher behaves differently toward different students.

Step 3. This treatment tells the student what behavior and achievement the teacher expects from them, and affects their self-concepts, achievement motivation, and levels of aspiration.

Step 4. If this treatment is consistent over time, and if the students do not resist or change it in some way, it will shape their achievement and behavior. High-expectation students will be led to achieve at high levels, whereas the achievement of low expectation students will decline.

Step 5. With time, students' achievement and behavior will conform more and more closely to the behavior originally expected of them.

The model clearly shows that teacher expectations are not automatically self-fulfilling. To become so, they must be translated into behavior that will communicate expectations to the students and will shape their behavior toward expected patterns. This does not always happen. The teacher may not have clear-cut expectations about every student, or some expectations may continually change. Even when the expectations remain consistent, the teacher may not communicate them to the students consistently. In this case, the expectation would not be self-fulfilling even if it turned out to be correct. Finally, the student alone might prevent expectations from becoming self-fulfilling by overcoming them or by resisting them in a way that made the teacher change them. A teacher expectation requires more than its own mere existence in order to become self-fulfilling. It must lead to teacher *behavior* that will *communicate* the expectation to the student, and this behavior must cause the student to behave in the manner that is expected.

All aspects of the model do not have to be present for a self-fulfilling prophecy to be operative. Teachers' differential behavior (Step 2), such as allowing certain students less time to read, might lead directly to Step 5 (differential achievement) without the indirect erosion of student motivation occurring (Step 3). Once Step 3 does occur, however, the effects of a particular teacher are apt to influence a student's achievement not only in that class but also in subsequent classes. The model does *not* assume that the differential behavior mechanisms will be *constant* across teachers (the model can be fulfilled in many different ways) or that the same teacher behavior will be interpreted by students in a uniform way. Students have to interpret teacher behavior and doubtlessly attend to teacher stimuli in a selective fashion. In brief, students are not passive recipients but *active interpreters* of teacher behavior.

Pygmalion in the Classroom

Although the possibility of self-fulfilling effects has long been discussed in social-psychological literature, it has only recently become an educational issue. The initial classroom study that created the interest was Rosenthal and Jacobson's *Pygmalion in the Classroom* (1968). These investigators attempted to manipulate teachers' expectations for student performance and to see if these expectations would be fulfilled. The research took place in a single elementary school in San Francisco. An attempt was made to increase teacher expectations by claiming that a test (that was actually a general achievement test) had been developed to identify late intellectual bloomers. The teachers were told that this test would select children who were about to bloom intellectually and, therefore, could be expected to show unusually large achievement gains during the coming school year. A few children in each classroom were identified to the teachers as late bloomers, yet they actually had been selected randomly, not on the basis of any test. Thus, there was no real reason to expect unusual gains from them. The investigator had attempted to create a favorable but erroneous bias toward the target students.

Achievement test data from the end of the school year offered evidence that these children as a group did show better performance (although the effects were confined mostly to the first two grades). Rosenthal and Jacobson explained their results in terms of the self-fulfilling prophecy effects of teacher expectations. They reasoned that the expectations they created about these special children somehow caused the teachers to treat them differently, so that they really did do better by the end of the year. Unfortunately, no classroom observations were made so it was not possible to verify the differential behavior hypothesis.

Controversy has raged over this topic ever since. The findings of *Pygmalion in the Classroom* were widely publicized and discussed, and for a time were accepted enthusiastically. Later, however, after critics (e.g., Snow, 1969) had attacked the Rosenthal and Jacobson study, and after a replication failed to produce the same results (Claiborn, 1969), the idea that teacher expectations could easily function as self-fulfilling prophecies began to be rejected. (For a critical analysis of teacher expectation research, see Brophy

& Good, 1974; Braun, 1976; Dusek, 1975; Rosenthal, 1974; West & Anderson, 1976; and Cooper, 1979.)

To understand the form of research that followed this initial study, it is important to recognize the historical context in which the data were collected. These findings came at a time when massive amounts of money were being spent on education and social programs designed to improve the plight of the disadvantaged student. But this was also a time in which some of the research was beginning to cast doubt upon the efficacy of such spending. Perhaps the most influential of such reports was that of Coleman et al. (1966), which concluded that the quality of schooling as estimated by such indices as money spent and the availability of curriculum materials did not make a difference in student achievement.

At a time when more resources were beginning to be placed in public education, the apparent news that school resources made no difference was disappointing, to say the least. For those who wanted to believe that schooling was important and the existing system modifiable, teacher expectations became an important focus. Hence, the timing of the Rosenthal–Jacobson study could not have been better for capturing interest and stimulating research activities. Sociologists, psychologists, and educators began to speculate that perhaps the key to educational progress was how teachers used resources (including textbooks, equipment, time, psychological rewards), and not their availability per se.

The expectation hypothesis was thus believable to social scientists in general and the resultant impact was to encourage research that attempted to verify either the initial study (create teacher expectation and look for differences in student achievement) or to see if teachers, as a function of their own beliefs, did treat high and low potential students differently. Unfortunately, there was little interest in systematically examining all aspects of the self-fulfilling prophecy hypothesis: How do teachers form expectations, how do teachers communicate their expectations, what is the impact of teacher expectations upon student achievement, what are the individual characteristics of students, teachers, and particular educational contexts that make expectation effects more or less likely to occur?

As has been noted elsewhere (Brophy & Good, 1974), it is important to distinguish between naturalistic and induced teacher expectations when evaluating the research evidence. Induced expectations refer to situations in which someone attempts to manipulate or to create expectations for teachers (as in the Rosenthal–Jacobson study mentioned previously). In general, attempts to induce expectations have not been very successful, partly because teachers simply do not believe the information they are given or they know that the expectation is not true.

One study is particularly instructive on this point. Schrank (1970) manipulated teachers' expectations for the mathematics classes they were working with. All classes were of equal ability; the Air Force mathematics instructors were told that they would have classes with high or low learning potential. In each case the classes that had been described as having high potential outperformed those described as having low potential. In a followup study Schrank asked teachers to instruct students as if they had been tracked by ability. In this study no instructional differences were found. The teachers' knowledge of how groups had been formed prevented the self-fulfilling prophecy (i.e., teachers did not have the expectation that the students would learn).

One of the difficulties in obtaining results in induced expectation studies is that teachers may not believe the expectation and/or may realize that an attempt is being made to manipulate them. Presumably, it is a personally formed or accepted belief that propels behavior, and it is difficult to fabricate such a belief. After all, given the considerable publicity that the Pygmalion study has received, it may prove very difficult to find a group of uninformed teachers on whom to test the hypothesis.

Naturalistic expectations are those formed by teachers on their own (through interaction with students, examination of school records, knowledge of older siblings, etc.). Studies of naturalistically formed expectations have regularly found relationships between teacher expectations and behavior (Brophy & Good, 1974; Rosenthal, 1974; Braun, 1976). That is, teachers often treat differently students who are perceived to possess high and low potentials.

How Do Teachers Communicate Expectations?

The purpose of this section is to describe some of the ways in which teachers have been found to behave less favorably toward students perceived as possessing low potentials. Presumably it is through classroom behavior that teachers communicate and fulfill their expectations. However, the design of the naturalistic studies that have been used to collect information about teacher behavior toward high and low students varies somewhat from study to study. Typically, though, teachers were asked to rank their students in terms of demonstrated achievement and observers then noted how teachers interacted with students who were high and low on the list. Information about the particular studies that produced these findings can be found elsewhere (Rosenthal, 1974; Brophy & Good, 1974; Good & Brophy, 1978; Braun, 1976; Dusek, 1975). Behaviors that are sometimes found to reflect how teachers differentially treat high and low achievers are:

1. Seating low students farther from the teacher and/or seating lows in a group

2. Paying less attention to lows in academic situations (smile less often and maintain less eye contact)
3. Calling on lows less often to answer classroom questions or to make public demonstrations
4. Waiting less time for lows to answer questions
5. Not staying with lows in failure situations
6. Criticizing lows more frequently than highs for incorrect public responses
7. Praising lows less frequently than highs after successful public responses
8. Praising lows more frequently than highs for marginal or inadequate public responses
9. Providing low achieving students with less accurate and less detailed feedback than highs
10. Failing to provide lows with feedback about their responses more frequently than highs
11. Demanding less work and effort from lows than from highs

Behaviors that have been found to describe the way in which teacher interactions differs with high and low potential students seem consistent with the process model presented earlier and with the rationale explaining why a self-fulfilling prophecy might work in the classroom. To begin with, there are differences in where high and low students sit in the classroom. Given that at least some lows may process information more slowly and that some of them would be hesitant to seek out adult authority figures, their placement in the rear of the room would appear to make contact with the teacher more difficult, thereby lowering their opportunities for achievement.

When lows are seated as a group in the classroom, it would seem to make it easier for the teacher to ignore them during public questioning and to treat lows as a group (rather than reacting to their unique differences). Moreover, if highs and lows are dispersed throughout the classroom, then the behavior of the highs (waving their hands for a response opportunity) can influence lows directly (e.g., as a role model) and indirectly (inadvertently calling teacher attention to lows).

Paying less attention to lows in academic situations via eye contact and affect (e.g., smiling) would seem to limit the lows' chances for response opportunities, feedback, and to lower their task involvement. Furthermore, physical seating arrangements can make it more or less difficult to monitor the behavior of lows. When they are placed in the rear of the room, it is probably more difficult, or at least more unlikely, that teachers will establish eye contact with them.

Infrequent opportunity to answer classroom questions seems to have direct effects on young students. On the one hand, students who are called upon have the chance to practice answers, to receive corrective feedback and/or affective support, and to develop communication skills. On the other hand, it is possible that students learn as much by listening to teachers' interchanges with other students as they do from direct interaction with the teacher. Thus, it can be contended that nonparticipating students are rewarded vicariously when other students receive teacher approval. However, this argument would seem to be weak for low achieving students with poor academic self-concepts, since such students probably do not view themselves as being capable of responding to the question correctly.[3]

Waiting less time for lows to answer a question would appear to have the potential for self-fulfilling effects both in direct and indirect ways. The direct effect occurs when, by waiting less time for lows to answer (before giving them the answer or before calling on another student), teachers limit the number of questions that a student has a chance to respond to and the chance for useful feedback. Given that low achievers may need more time to process information and to rehearse answers, the fact that they are given less time to respond is startling.

The perceived need to maintain control of the classroom and to keep things moving is probably a concomitant cause of such teacher behavior. That is, the silence (coupled with the anticipation that the student will respond incorrectly or perhaps in a disruptive way) "compels" the teacher to wait less time for lows.

If teachers consistently wait less time for low students to respond, they may be indirectly communicating that they are not *serious* about obtaining a response from them. Some lows therefore may not even think about the question because they realize that the teacher will quickly call on someone else or give them the correct answer. To clarify this and related issues, it would seem important to attempt to collect data from students in future studies that describe *their thoughts* and strategies during public questioning.

Some research has also indicated that after low students respond incorrectly, teachers tend to spend less time with them than with high students. Thus, in addition to the fact that they are called upon less often and given less time to respond, lows are quickly given up on (the teacher provides the answer or calls on another student) when they attempt unsuccessfully to respond or when they fail to respond. Lows are also more likely than highs to be criticized for incorrect responses and to be praised less for correct responses than are highs. Thus, in addition to limited access to public response opportunities, lows also receive less reinforcing feedback.

[3] For a related discussion see the research on patterned reading turns (Brophy & Evertson, 1976).

It is important to note that some of the research on praise and criticism is based upon proportions. That is, even though low achieving students give fewer correct answers (in an absolute sense), they are provided with less praise per correct answer (in a relative sense) than are high achieving students. Those teachers that do offer proportionately less praise and more criticism provide a dramatic demonstration of the fact that expectations can affect teachers' perceptions and reactions to similar responses (correct answers) from students perceived to be dissimilar. However, it is important to note that the disproportionate provision of teacher praise and criticism is not a typical finding (some teachers exhibit the behavior; other ones do not).

In contrast to the fact that certain teachers criticize low achievers proportionately more frequently than highs for incorrect responses, other teachers have been found to praise low students more frequently for marginal and even incorrect responses! These two findings appear to reflect two *different types* of teachers. Teachers who criticize lows for incorrect responses are apt to be basically intolerant of them. They are irritated because they perceive the amount of time that it takes for a low to respond to be excessive and/or they are intolerant of their poor answers. Teachers who reward very marginal or erroneous answers appear to be inappropriately (i.e., excessively) sympathetic to lows and unnecessarily protective of them. As has been noted elsewhere (Good & Brophy, 1980), both types of teachers appear to be teaching students that *effort* and *outcome* are not related. If students come to accept this expectation, then it is unlikely that they will apply themselves fully to classroom tasks.

When teachers fail to give lows feedback about their responses, lows have to determine whether or not an answer is adequate. Unfortunately, there is some tendency (at least in laboratory studies) for individuals to interpret ambiguous feedback or the absence of feedback as confirmation of poor performance if these individuals have experienced much failure. Similarly, ambiguous feedback is apt to be perceived as confirmation of success in individuals who typically experience success (see, for example, Crandall, 1963). It seems reasonable to conclude that if students are given less specific feedback about their performance they are less likely to know how to improve or less likely to understand why their response was adequate.

Demanding less of lows directly reduces the opportunity for these students to learn. If students are aware of such differential standards, it is likely that their motivation for learning will be reduced as well. Unfortunately, the expectation literature has focused on Step 2 of the model proposed by Brophy and Good (1970), and there is little literature linking differential teacher behavior to different motivational states of students. Presumably, one way in which the teacher might depress student achievement is by influencing the attributions that students make about their classroom behavior. Does differential teaching behavior lead some students to credit themselves for success and other students to believe that external factors are largely the reason for their success? For example, Dweck et al. (1978) argue that teachers tend to give girls more noncontingent praise than they provide for boys. As Frieze has noted in Chapter 2, when students do develop stable internal explanations for failure (e.g., I'm dumb), then they are less likely to exert as much personal effort as they would if they felt they were capable of responding to classroom challenges.

Not All Teachers Treat Highs and Lows Differently

It is important to state that not all teachers show a *consistent* pattern of sharply differentiated interaction toward high and low potential students. One estimate based on several studies that were gathered over a number of years suggested that roughly one-third of the teachers observed acted in a way that appeared to exaggerate the initial deficiencies of low achievers Good & Brophy, 1980). That is, the teachers appeared to "cause" the students to decline by providing them with less educational opportunity and by teaching them less. These teachers were described as being *overreactive* because they overreacted to the learning deficiencies of lows in ways that reduced both the opportunity and motivation for learning.

A second group of teachers were described as *reactive*. These teachers also allowed high students to dominate the class, but not to the extent that overreactive teachers did. In these classrooms, high students received more opportunity, but they did so because they raised their hands more or sought out the teacher more frequently. But it was possible to find another group of teachers who did not allow their expectations for low-achieving students to interfere with their attempts to teach them. This group of teachers were designated as *proactive*. The term proactive was used because these teachers built a classroom structure in which they could meet the needs of low achievers with increased time and attention but yet not ignore the instructional needs of other students. That is, these teachers appeared to anticipate the needs of different students and to plan in such a way that diverse student needs could be satisfied in the classroom.

These descriptions of teachers are oversimplified, yet they characterize some differences in basic teacher styles that were evident in observational studies. Clearly, the extent to which teachers express differential behavior toward high and low students is an "individual difference variable" (Brophy & Good, 1974). This topic will be discussed again later on in the chapter.

The eleven variables presented earlier are not the only ways that teachers have been found to differ in their behavior toward high and low students. They do, however, reflect some common (replicated in separate studies) ways in which expectations have been communicated. Other interesting differences have also been reported. It is beyond the scope of this chapter to characterize all of the variables that have been discussed, but a few examples will illustrate other types of variables that have been explored.

Weinstein (1976), in a thorough study of reading groups in three first-grade classrooms, found that the reading group to which the student was assigned contributed a significant increment (25%) to the prediction of mid-year achievement over and above the student's initial readiness score. She did *not* find differences in teaching behavior toward high and low reading groups that would account for the differential effects of being assigned to a high or low group, despite the fact that the gap in achievement widened between high and low groups as the year progressed. Group placement may thus represent an expectation effect that influences student behavior indirectly (by decreasing motivation) or directly (by exposing students to poor or good reading models). Rist (1970), in a longitudinal study of a group of students, also noticed that differences in high and low students expanded over time in ways that could be attributed to teacher treatment and group placement.

Weinstein did identify one potential mechanism through which performance measures may have been communicated to students. She noted anecdotally that teacher statements to the entire class about particular reading groups often reflected differential performance expectations. She suggested that statements such as "Joey's group has all of this to do because they are very smart and this is more difficult" may have a detrimental motivational effect on at least some students. In visits to public school classrooms, I too have been amazed by the statements some teachers make about low-achieving individuals and groups. Such comments are well meant, but have a devastating effect on student motivation. Rist (1970) also reports that teachers' pejorative public statements seem to communicate teacher expectation.

It would seem useful to attempt to account for the frequency and the effects of attributions that teachers express publicly about the characteristics that students possess or the reasons for their classroom success (Cooper, 1979). Fortunately, some coding systems that could be adapted for this purpose already exist but have not been used to code classroom dialogue (Frieze, 1976; Cooper & Burger, 1978).

In contrast to Weinstein's findings, other researchers who have examined teacher behavior toward high and low reading groups have reported teaching differences. McDermott (1977) describes how children who were already good readers were able to spend more time reading to the teacher than children who were poor readers. He argued that the reason for such differential opportunity was *not* simply teacher bias but rather it was due to a complex circle of teacher and student influence. Interestingly, he notes that lows received less practice time for reading, despite an apparent attempt on the teacher's part to divide time equally among reading groups.

How, then, did the bias occur? First, the low reading group was frequently interrupted by requests to the teacher from students not in the reading group. Such interruptions did not occur when the teacher was working with the high group. Another, and more serious, problem from McDermott's point of view was that much time was wasted because the teacher did not move around the low group in sequence as she did with the high group. Rather than attend to the story line, low students spent time attempting to get teacher attention so that they could read. In contrast, the teacher allowed students in the high group to read in order and thereby reduced the need for students to spend time negotiating with the teacher for a turn.

Thus, as a result of the interruptions by other classmates and the time spent competing with other group members for a reading turn, lows received less time to practice reading than did highs. Given the extra time that highs received, it seems probable that the gap between their reading ability and that of the lows will widen with time.

The cause of this difference is only partly a function of teacher expectations. The teacher does monitor the activity (who is capable of reading this page or paragraph) and presumably it is the attempt to match task difficulty and student ability that leads the teacher not to call on low students in turn. But the lows' lack of confidence that they will get a turn and the initiative of other students also contribute to the problem. Clearly, student and teacher influences are tightly intertwined.

McDermott suggests that highs are interrupted infrequently because they maintain "reading posture" even when no one is reading. Lows are interrupted more frequently because their projected involvement often suggests that their group work is "interruptable." It seems possible that other teacher and student expectations may be associated with reading group behavior. For example, it is acceptable to interrupt a reading group to get new assignments, but not to clarify an initial assignment (i.e., if lows had not been criticized or "rationalized" away earlier in the year it is highly unlikely that they would be interrupting the teacher during the highs' reading time).

The research on teacher expectations has produced some conflicting results. However, there are several ways to explain these differences. For example, if Weinstein had coded the amount of involved time as opposed to the amount of reading time per se, perhaps her results would have been more similar to McDermott's. Some differences, however, cannot be resolved. For example, the fact that some teachers praise low students more and others criticize them more following failure flatly represents a difference in the ways in which teachers express expectations. Given the diversity of teacher attitudes (some like to teach, some like children, others do not like either) and teacher abilities (some know a lot about the subject matter, some are good managers, others are inadequate in terms of both) it would seem *unreasonable to expect* a single set of differences to represent the way in which teachers differ in their behavior toward high and low achievers.

To illustrate the futility of trying to find a simple set of behaviors, it is only necessary to cite additional research that has focused on reading group behavior. Hunter (1978) examined teacher behavior toward high, middle, and low reading groups in seven second-grade classrooms. Her results support certain aspects of earlier research efforts but do not directly replicate the findings of Weinstein or McDermott. In five of the seven classrooms she found that reading lasted longer for the high group than for the low group. These results differ from those obtained by Weinstein (1976) and by Brophy and Good (1970). However, the differences in reading time between highs and lows were large in only two cases (but in those cases substantial differences were found: 11.83 minutes versus 6.83 minutes; and 14.5 minutes versus 24.33 minutes).

She did find that low reading groups were interrupted more than high groups in six of the seven classes. This finding is somewhat similar to McDermott's, but Hunter's data do not support his characterization that the reading period for highs is interruption-free. The observed differences in the number of interruptions between high and low groups are minor in Hunter's study (but still, such differences may over time sufficiently lessen practice time for lows, so that their reading achievement would suffer to some degree as a consequence).

Several comments about discrepancies in research findings are relevant. First, to bring about a self-fulfilling prophecy, it would *not* appear necessary for teachers to exhibit all, or even many, of the variables cited previously as indices of "low expectations." If teachers assign lows a considerably lower amount of matterial than they can handle, that variable alone could reduce student learning (even if teachers call on lows frequently, etc.). Similarly, if teachers give low students less time to practice reading (or allow allocated time to be frequently interrupted) this could be a sufficient condition for reducing student achievement. Third, some of the teaching differences identified by the observational research collected in the attempt to verify self-fulfilling effects seem to be illogical and/or inappropriate (e.g., less reading time for lows, noncontingent praise) whether or not the occurrence of the behavior is due to teacher expectations. Fourth, naturalistic studies prohibit inferences about causality, but the teacher expectation construct, at a minimum, provides a rich conceptual heuristic for looking at classroom behavior by both practitioners and researchers.

In answer, then, to the question, do teachers' expectations influence their behavior toward high and low students, the best answer *at present* is an evasive sometimes yes, sometimes no. More specifically, it has been estimated from a large pool of observational studies of elementary school teachers that roughly one-third of the teachers acted in ways that seemed to exaggerate differences between high and low students unnecessarily. Unfortunately, all of these teachers were drawn from a single geographical area and hence this estimate may not accurately represent the number of teachers who behave differently toward high and low students in American elementary schools.

Too few studies have been performed at the secondary level to allow for even unformed speculation about the number of teachers who reflect self-fulfilling behaviors in their teaching. However, it may be the case that different expectation variables are operative in secondary schools.

TEACHER EXPECTATIONS AND STUDENT ACHIEVEMENT

We have seen then that some teachers behave differently toward high- and low-achieving students, but is there any evidence that such behavior lowers or enhances achievement? Unfortunately, there is very little research that has examined the teacher-expectation–classroom-behavior–student-achievement linkages in the same design. There is some evidence, however, and some of it will be presented in the following discussion.

Perhaps the most comprehensive attempt to examine teacher expectations and their relationship with student outcome variables was the Texas Teacher Effectiveness Research Project (Brophy & Evertson, 1976). Brophy and Evertson identified, from a large sample, teachers who had consistently outperformed other teachers teaching similar students under similar circumstances. They also administered a complex set of interviews and written questions to assess teachers' beliefs and expectations about a wide variety of teaching issues. Brophy and Evertson found that the belief that most consistently separated high and low effective teachers was the extent to which they considered themselves as important contributors to the students' mastery of academic material. Simply put, teachers who were obtaining good student performance were those who had a high sense of *personal efficacy*. That is, they felt they could teach effectively.

Unfortunately, these data were collected in a correlational study.

Perhaps it was because teachers were successful that they developed the expectation that they could influence student performance. Still, it seems that the teacher belief, "I can make a difference," would at least *sustain* teacher efforts to instruct. If teachers do not actively believe that they can make a difference, it seems they would be unlikely models for teaching students that appropriate effort is associated with positive outcomes. These results suggest that a personal expectation for teaching success covaries with student achievement.

Another attempt to relate teacher expectations and student achievement was made by McDonald and Elias (1976). They found that teacher expectations contributed to the variance in students' academic growth (in second- and fifth-grade classrooms) more than the students' sex or race. They noted that in some instances high teacher expectations appeared to increase the achievement of the average student as much as one standard deviation when compared to similar students for whom teachers held low expectations. Again we see that teacher expectations co-occur, and the data suggest that it is plausible (but not necessary) to conclude that teacher expectations "cause" student achievement.

There are also some experimental data to suggest that changes in teacher behavior can improve student achievement. For example, general ideas about the effects of teacher expectations presented in *Looking in Classrooms* (Good & Brophy, 1973) were expanded and field-tested by Mary Martin and Sam Kerman (Martin, 1973). The study was a 3-year program, carried out in elementary schools in Los Angeles. This project attempted to increase teachers' awareness of the consequences of their behavior toward lows and to present teachers with new skills for teaching lows. Project teachers received information about teacher expectation effects, suggestions about how to interact with lows, and were also trained to use a coding system for recording behavior related to teacher expectation effects. Participating teachers had the chance to be observed and to code the classroom behavior of fellow teachers teaching at the same grade level.

The classroom observational records demonstrated that teachers did change their behavior as a function of the training program. More important, the attitudes and reading achievement of low expectancy students in the experimental group showed improvement in contrast to those of low expectancy students in the control group. Such data illustrate that teacher expectations and behaviors can be altered and that such changes can lead to improved achievement.

Cooper (1978), in a small study of six teachers, has also shown that presenting teachers with information about expectation effects and requesting behavioral changes can result in classroom improvements. His study also suggested an individual difference variable that may be associated with the extent to which teachers communicate expectations in their behavior. He found that the performance expectations could be predicted much more easily for some teachers than for other teachers. Cooper described these teachers as "unalterable," and reasoned that it would be more difficult to change the behavior of these teachers. In contrast, the three teachers whose rankings showed less correspondence with student sex and IQ he called "alterable," and he hypothesized that the behavior of these teachers could be modified more easily than that of "unalterable" teachers.

He then presented all six teachers with information about the potential effects of teacher expectations on teacher behavior and student performance. Next he requested that teachers change their behavior toward certain students (i.e., reduce criticism toward lows when they initiate academic interactions in public settings). Cooper collected data on the students' perception of the relationship between personal effort and classroom outcomes before and after the intervention with teachers, as well as information about students' actual achievement.

He reported that at the beginning of the year, the perceived effort-outcome relationships of high and low students did not differ significantly. But at the end of the year (despite his presentation of information about expectation effects), students classified as high expectation by their teachers had relatively greater effort-outcome covariation gains (as estimated by residual change scores) than did low expectation students in "unalterable" teachers' classrooms. He also noted that students with "alterable" teachers made better reading achievement gains than students with "unalterable" teachers. Furthermore, there was less spread in achievement between high and low expectation students in "alterable" classrooms.

These data suggest that the behavior of some teachers can be influenced by intervention and that intervention can alter students' perception and achievement. These data also suggest that teachers whose performance rankings of students are less tied to student IQ and student sex are more amenable to receiving and/or using information than are other teachers.

Two points should be made here. First, the alterable teachers' performance rankings correlated highly with student IQ, but not as highly as those of the unalterable teachers. Thus, there is correspondence between their ranking and the "objective" scores of students, but alterable teachers do not appear as dependent on IQ and sex cues as other teachers do. Second, these data do not tell us how alterable teachers form their expectations; they only tell us that these teachers are less dependent upon certain cues. Do alterable teachers place more importance on classroom behavior? Do such teachers use more information sources or integrate sources more efficiently than do other teachers? Are such teachers more intelligent or do they operate at a different level of cognitive complexity? We still know little about how teacher expectations are formed and how they are used in classroom decision making (Shulman & Elstein, 1975).

It must be remembered that Cooper's study is based on a small group of teachers and the findings may be restricted to subtle but unidentified factors operating in the research. It is still intriguing to speculate that the reason low achievers progressively fall farther behind their classmates is due to the fact that they make less effort, since they do not believe that a relationship exists between their effort and success.

Stipek (1977) studied the perceptions and achievement of students who were selected from an initial sample of 15 first-grade classrooms. She found that most students maintained a positive view of self as a learner as the year progressed. Her data also suggest that students' locus of control was not affected by school success or failure experiences. She argues that students' locus of control had more impact on academic performance than vice versa.

Hence some students, despite objective evidence indicating poor school performance, still expressed high levels of internal locus of control for perceived success at the end of the school year. Others have also noted the wide discrepancy between students' self-expectations and the objective feedback they receive from first-grade teachers (Entwisle & Hayduk, 1978).

Stipek feels that failure or success instances for a first grader may be defined less by actual performance than by the nature of the interactions with teachers. Since most first-grade teachers are warm and reinforcing, this may be sufficient "nourishment" for most of their pupils (even for those who are doing relatively poorly in school). Hence, to the extent that teachers influence highs and lows unevenly in the earliest grades, it may be more a direct (less teaching time) rather than an indirect influence (erosion of self-confidence). She also found that students' attitudes toward school became more positive during the year. To the extent that school experiences contribute to a decline in internality or interest in education, Stipek's data would suggest that such a decline occurs after first grade.

Stipek also failed to find differential teaching behavior toward boys and girls that some investigators have reported. Dweck et al. (1978) found that girls receive more noncontingent praise than boys, but Stipek's data did not support this conclusion. One possible reason for the difference between her results and those of Dweck et al. was grade level. Dweck et al. studied the upper elementary grades where the context of learning was perhaps more evaluative than Stipek found in first-grade classrooms.

One of Stipek's findings does suggest a teacher expectation effect. She noted that at the beginning of the school year teachers tended to rate students in a global way. Teachers saw good students as well behaved and possessing positive academic self-concepts. However, as the year progressed, teachers began to make sharper discriminations. She contended that the early, global nature of teacher perceptions might have harmful effects. She also noted that teachers may interpret poor classroom behavior as lack of ability rather than poor school adjustment. Later in the year the teacher may realize that a good academic student does engage in misbehavior, but it is less likely for the teacher to realize that a behavior problem student is also good academically.

Again we see that a comparison of individual studies often produces findings that are somewhat inconsistent. Cooper's data suggest that teaching acts may "cause" a shift in student perception and achievement. Stipek's data suggest that the "low" first graders show little evidence of internalizing lower achievement perceptions despite their relatively poor performance in school. However, given the wide differences in the ways in which teachers express differences and the methodological difficulties of testing young children, such differences are understandable. More research is called for, but the explanation for the difference may be that teachers in Cooper's sample were more critical of lows than teachers in Stipek's sample. Obviously, if teachers do not treat students differently there is little reason to expect that they will affect student perceptions or achievement.

There are nevertheless agreements in the two studies. For example, both Stipek and Cooper suggest that teachers' abilities to use a variety of student cues early in the year may be tied to the formation and expression of performance expectations for individual students (teachers who use more cues are less likely to develop and communicate inappropriately low expectations). Also, both investigators conclude that teacher expectancy effects are probably operative at one level or another and are deserving of continued study.

Another study illustrating that teacher behavior can be related to student learning was conducted by Good, Grouws, and others. They designed a mathematics program (Good et al., 1977) for use in fourth-grade classrooms. The program was built in part upon the investigators' previous naturalistic observation of relatively effective and ineffective teachers (Good & Grouws, 1975; 1977). After observing teachers for a long period of time, a behavioral profile was developed that characterized the differences between teachers who were getting good student achievement gains from those teachers who were not. The data were naturalistic, however, and many factors other than differences in teacher behavior might be responsible for the differences in student achievement.

To test the impact of instructional behavior on student achievement, an experimental study was conducted. Forty volunteer teachers were randomly assigned to treatment and control conditions, and the experimental teachers were trained to perform the behaviors that had been associated with successful mathematics learning.

All teachers (both treatment and control) were told that the program was based on an earlier observation of relatively effective and ineffective fourth-grade teachers and that the program was expected to work, but also that the project was the first test of those ideas. Control teachers were told that they would not get the details of the instructional program until mid-year, and they were also informed that then they would receive information about *their* classroom behavior (all teachers were being observed) as well as teaching tips from other teachers in the district who had used the program.

Given that control teachers knew that the research was designed to improve student achievement, that the school district was interested in the research, and that they were being observed, a strong Hawthorne control was probably created. With this motivational control, it could be argued that differences in performance between control and treatment groups were due to the program and not to motivational variables.

Interestingly, the results of the project show large differences in favor of the treatment classes and students (Good & Grouws, 1979). It should also be noted that certain teachers implemented the program more fully and got better results than did other teachers. Furthermore, certain students bene-fitted more from the treatment than did other students (Ebmeier & Good, 1979). Still, given the short time for the treatment and the magnitude of the positive results, the data are important, especially since these gains were made in urban, low-income neighborhood schools. Knowledge that achievement increments can occur in such schools is important information, given the low expectations that many educators hold for school achieve-ment in inner city schools.

The finding that is of primary relevance to the present discussion is that the project had positive effects on the control classrooms as well. That control students also exhibited marked improvement is no doubt due to the Hawthorne effect that was purposefully created. One possible interpretation of the improvement in the control classrooms is that the project information (*that teachers could make a difference*) enhanced teachers' feelings of personal efficacy and their willingness to think more about their mathemat-ics teaching.

The performance of the control group was notably less than that of the experimental group, and the program thus provides strong support for the contention that teaching behaviors can be related to student achievement. This same conclusion has also been reached recently by others who have successfully presented training information to teachers in the attempt to improve student learning (Anderson, Evertson, & Brophy, 1978; Crawford & Stallings, 1978).

There are also data to suggest that relatively easy treatments can bring about positive change. Miller, Brickman and Bolen (1975) have shown that teachers who repeatedly attributed to second graders either the ability or the motivation for doing well proved to be relatively effective in improving their mathematics achievement. These data indirectly suggest that teachers' attitudes can be related to student achievement. Unfortunately, the research just described does not measure the impact of changed teacher behavior on teacher or student expectations, but the studies do illustrate nicely a teacher-behavior-student achievement linkage.

Teacher expectation literature has illustrated that some teachers do exhibit differential behavior toward high and low expectation students. Moreover, teacher effectiveness research has shown that changes in teacher behavior can be related to improved student achievement. Unfortunately, the teacher expectation and teacher effectiveness thrusts have not been integrated systematically. Thus to date, evidence that can be used to test the model proposed by Brophy and Good (1970) is mainly relevant to Step 2. It now appears clear that some teachers do treat high and low students differently and sometimes in ways that appear to broaden the performance gap between these two groups of students. Whether differences in teacher behavior also influence students' motivational systems is more problematic given extant research data. The cause of differential teacher behavior is also an unresolved issue.

STUDENTS AS DETERMINANTS OF TEACHER BEHAVIOR

Differences in interaction between high and low achievers are frequently reported in the naturalistic literature. However, since one does not manipulate variables in naturalistic studies it is impossible to say that one variable causes another. If one observes that teachers wait longer for highs to respond than for lows, it is impossible to conclude that it is because teachers expect highs to answer. There are many rival reasons available for explaining why teachers might wait longer for highs. Perhaps the most basic alternative explanation is that *students cause* teacher behavior, and not vice versa (e.g., high students look relaxed).

The issue of teacher influence versus student influence is a relatively old one, but recently it has become a much discussed topic. Anderson and Brewer (1945) considered the matter some time ago. The question has also generated recent research and conceptual activity (for an extended discussion see West & Anderson, 1976). Openlander (1969) conducted a dissertation on the question. He observed four teachers who were instructing two sections of high and low ability students and found that teachers became more *indirect* in the low ability classes and more *direct* in high ability classrooms as the year progressed.

These data, at first glance, are consistent with the hypothesis that student characteristics cause teacher behavior. Still, it should be noted that these data are correlational and that it is possible that teachers behave more directly in classrooms with high ability students as a result of their beliefs (e.g., high students can benefit from abstract teacher explanations, but low students need concrete discussions).

It is clear that in a correlational study the same data can be used to support either a student influence hypothesis or a teacher influence hypothesis (i.e., teachers think high ability students learn best through lectures). My interpretation and hypothesis is that the teachers of more capable students have the belief that students can learn and thus they become more *serious* about teaching. When teachers become more serious about teaching, they spend more time actively trying to present concepts and are much more concerned with providing accurate and specific feedback to students.

I, too, have been involved in research that supports a student influence hypothesis (Emmer, Oakland, & Good, 1974). We found that some preservice teachers initially preferred an expository style, but shifted to a discovery style after presenting a micro teaching lesson. Whereas other teachers who preferred an expository style did not shift their preference after teaching a simulated lesson. These two groups of teachers differed significantly in terms of the amount of student participation they were able to obtain. Those teachers who switched their preference to a discovery style received more student-initiated discussion. Our results and those of Openlander can be interpreted to suggest that in certain ways students were systematically controlling the behavior of teachers. This research is also correlational research, and thus many interpretations are possible. In this instance, I find the student influence argument very persuasive. The basis for my belief is the fact that the sample utilized preservice teachers who were still searching for a teaching style and were hence very open (or vulnerable) to feedback.

Other studies have produced stronger results by manipulating pupil behavior in an attempt to cause predicted teacher outcomes. Jenkins and Deno (1969) found that when all students systematically acted in a responsive way teacher self-evaluations were higher than when students behaved in a passive, nonresponsive way. Klein (1971) studied the influence of positive and negative student behavior on guest lecturers in college classrooms. His findings indicated that negative student behaviors (e.g., lack of attention, disagreement) resulted in more negative teacher behaviors (criticism). Interestingly, though, positive student behavior did not elicit more positive teacher behavior. Perhaps the teachers were affected by the negative student behaviors because they were somewhat *atypical*, especially in a guest lecture situation. Although the evidence of a student effect per se in this research is compelling, one wonders how often teachers see systematic student reactions in the classroom. Typically, students present a variety of cues (some attentive, some bored, etc.) so that teachers may be able to infer several different affective states simultaneously.

This is not to argue that teachers are not affected by students in direct ways, because they are. For instance a teacher who carries a bundle of papers that look like a pop quiz may be deluged with so many student questions and comments that no time is left for the exam. All of us are aware of students who have successfully "conned" their instructor into giving them extra time and consideration because of alleged problems. My favorite example is an illustration shared with me by Professor Myron Dembo, at the University of Southern California, who has talked frequently with students about influence strategies that they use. He reports (personal communication) the successful manipulative activities of one student who frequently sought out instructors before exams and requested permission to take the exam *early*. Instructors typically preferred that she take the exam late, and often even gave her the same exam that was given to the class. Hence, she often received extra study time and a targeted exam. Obviously there are many ways in which students consciously attempt to manipulate teachers and in which students may inadvertently influence teachers (a look of disappointment, etc.).

One empirical attempt to deal with the teacher expectation versus the student achievement argument has been provided by Crano and Mellon (1978). They estimated the relative influences of teacher expectations and students' academic performance. A series of cross-lagged panel correlational analyses was conducted on a data set drawn from a 4-year longitudinal study of 4300 British elementary school children. Although cross-lagged analysis is correlational, the procedure allows one to make somewhat firmer conclusions about the direction of co-occurring variables than is generally the case in correlational research. To use such techniques one has to have a data set including variables that occur at different points in time. That is, one variable occurs before the other. Crano and Mellon's results indicated that teachers' expectations appeared to cause student achievement to a greater extent than the extent to which student achievement influenced teacher attitudes.

Specifically, the investigators examined the relationships between teachers' expectancies toward students and students' achievement at Grade 1. The same students were followed at Grades 2, 3, and 4 to see if teacher expectations (both performance and social expectations were measured) influenced subsequent achievement and the extent to which prior student achievement was influencing subsequent teacher expectations. It was found that teachers' expectations and evaluations of pupils' social development (assessed by questions such as, Do you like to have the student in class? Is the student obedient?) appeared to exert a greater influence on later academic performance than those expectations concerned more centrally with achievement potential. The study illustrates that expectations other than those pertaining to the academic performance of individual students are held by teachers and that such beliefs may be related to classroom outcomes.

Unfortunately, most research studies do not allow one to distinguish between teacher and student influence hypotheses. The way in which the research data have been collected makes it impossible to explain why teachers tend to wait longer for highs to respond. Is it because they believe that highs can respond, or do they wait longer because high students behave differently toward the teacher? An attempt to answer the wait time question would call for the measurement not only of the teacher expectations and wait time but also of student behavior during the wait time interval. To code both wait time duration and students' facial and postural cues simultaneously would probably necessitate the presence of two coders or video equipment. Hence, no data are available on this and similar questions.

It is likely the case that *both* student and teacher variables control wait time. Because teachers expect highs to answer, they wait longer *unless* the high student looks anxious. It is also likely that contextual variables also exert some control over wait time. For example, some teachers, because they expect less from lows, will wait less time for an answer *unless* they see a positive behavioral cue. During a reading group, however, they wait longer for a response, even without a positive behavioral cue (because the wait does not delay the whole class). To assess such effects, one must measure teacher and student behaviors under varying contextual conditions.

In general, the research done on teacher expectation effects has not explored interaction issues, and we have little data for speculating on complex but plausible hypotheses such as the one that follows: Whether or not teachers wait for a low student to respond depends upon teacher expectations for the individual student, on student behavior, and the context in which the interaction takes place. Whether or not the extra time improves student achievement is dependent upon student characteristics (e.g., extra time will not help students who are convinced that they cannot answer because they do not use the time to process information, but it will help lows who are still attempting to respond) and it is also dependent upon teacher behavior (extra wait time is helpful when the teacher helps the student to get the correct answer or to understand how to derive the answer in the future).

Teacher and student behavior are probably both responsible for the differential patterns of interactions that are sometimes found to occur in classrooms. Excellent conceptual statements and additional empirical references relevant to student influence issues can be found elsewhere (Winnie & Marx, 1977; Doyle, 1978). I concur with the general assertion that students exert influence upon teachers. However, because teachers possess more power (e.g., control of rewards), it would seem that most elementary school teachers, unless they decide to transfer power, are the major sources of classroom influence in the early grades. As noted previously, though, students doubtlessly mediate teachers' influence in a variety of ways.

Even if one concluded that student behavior controlled teacher behavior it would still seem apparent that the continued study of teacher expectations and behavior and ways to change them would be important. This is because in the short run it would seem that most intervention efforts would center on teacher behavior, not student behavior. For example, in the class McDermott observed, much of the "problem" could be solved by the teacher making changes in classroom structure or by making two changes in teaching behavior (a) do not allow students to interrupt reading group work; (b) generally call on all students to read in turn (even though the teacher may want to ask questions about the passage randomly). Still, the question, "Are student effects or teacher effects more important?" is inappropriate. To reiterate, rather than continuing a polemical discussion of whether teachers or students are more influential determinants of classroom behavior, future works might center more profitably on the conditions under which teacher and/or student characteristics are apt to be more fundamental.

IMPORTANCE AND FORM OF TEACHER EXPECTATIONS IN ELEMENTARY AND SECONDARY SCHOOLS

As noted previously, very little observational research relevant to the expectation issue has been done in secondary schools. What research has been done suggests that quantitative variables (frequency of interaction) become more important at the secondary level. In part, the reduced importance of qualitative variables may be due to the fact that teachers' use of affect (praise, criticism) diminishes rapidly as the grade level increases, at least those dimensions of affect that are commonly measured in classrooms.

In part, the apparent greater importance of contact per se at the secondary level may, as a vehicle of expectations, be due to the fact that achievement differences between high and low students are larger than they are in elementary school classrooms. Hence, many questions may be unanswerable by some of the lowest students, and some students have doubtlessly given up and have directly and indirectly "taught" teachers to leave them alone.

For a variety of reasons, it would seem that teacher expectations exert more influence on student achievement in elementary schools than in secondary schools. Young children are more impressionable and are more anxious to please adults than are older children. As Entwisle and Hayduk (1978) have pointed out, teachers have a great advantage over first graders. Children are exposed to many new activities in the first grade, and it is the teacher who controls the rewards for performance on these tasks. In short, teachers have the chance to define for young students the meaning of school work and their level of proficiency in performing it.[4]

Also, to the extent that a teacher fulfills an expectation, there is "less room" for a subsequent teacher to have a negative or positive impact. If a first-grade teacher is negatively overreactive to a particular pupil, then it is unlikely that the conditions that surround the beginning of Grade 2 for the student will be the same as those conditions associated with the first grade. The school record now has "solid" information documenting the child's academic difficulty and the child is likely to show classroom behavior consistent with his or her classification (not attempt to answer questions, etc.). Second-grade teachers who accept a low expectancy for the student would thus *sustain* the relationship between teacher expectation and achievement. Once a student begins to act as a slow student it is impossible to prove in future classes that unnecessarily low teacher expectations "cause" low achievement, although they could sustain unnecessarily low achievement (Cooper, 1979).

In secondary schools, teacher expectations may be important determinants of student behavior, but they are more likely to influence particular students rather than low achievers in general. For example, I know a student from a low-income family who had considerable talent for art, but who was denied access to art classes because he was in the wrong academic track. Fortunately for this individual, concerned teachers found a chance for the student to work with a commercial artist after school. Teachers may thus stimulate the behavior of individual students and exert some pressure on the achievement of lows in general. However, there are many other influences on the school behavior of lows at the secondary level. Some students find part-time jobs that leave little time for school preparation. Other students begin to sense the futility of unsuccessful job hunting and begin to conclude that school activity will not help them to obtain jobs immediately or in the future.

[4] Although secondary teachers probably do not generally teach students whether or not they are proficient at school tasks, they may help students to develop career expectations.

As Hurn (1978) notes, peer influence is exaggerated in some accounts, but the influence is real and does affect what can and cannot occur in classrooms. Although it is still probably true that some teachers are capable of directing peer influence toward educational goals (see Chapter 4), teachers exert progressively less influence on school achievement as students become older.

Educational decisions in secondary schools may still have important consequences, even though they might not modify students' achievement on a standardized test in a major way. For example, Williams (1976), on the basis of data from a study of 16,000 high school students, demonstrates that teacher expectations in secondary school are shaped mainly by previous school performance, not by student background characteristics. One would be surprised if this were not the case—given that students have been in school for 10 years. To reiterate, once a student begins to perform poorly, it becomes difficult to document a self-fulfilling prophecy in a given year.

Williams did report that teacher expectations influenced teacher grading. That is, students for whom teachers held low expectations received lower grades than their objective performance warranted, and high expectation students received higher grades than their performance merited. As Hurn (1978) has indicated, this is no trivial finding, since grades may influence future school placement and jobs.

Unfortunately, little research in general and very limited observational research has taken place in secondary schools. Until more is known about how teachers and students interact it will be hard to examine teacher influence issues in the secondary schools.

NEW RESEARCH

Research on teachers' expectations for the performance of individual students has provided some valuable information about unprofitable patterns of teacher–student interaction that occur in some classrooms. However, comparatively little is known about the cues that teachers use in forming expectations (Dusek, 1975) or the individual characteristics of teachers, students, and learning conditions that make expectations more or less likely to be fulfilled.

The amount of research collected in the past 10 years has been impressive, but much of it has been redundant, largely resulting from the speed with which the research was produced. Studies were generated in one large wave of activity; hence, researchers had little time to integrate the findings of others. Most researchers started with the intent to document the occurrence of differential behavior toward high and low students. There is now much experimental evidence to show that differential behavior does occur in some classrooms; it is time to answer other questions. It is impossible within the limits of this chapter to characterize all of the research that needs to be done on classroom expectations. However, I will take the opportunity to discuss three areas that seem to be rich topics for future study.

Other Expectations That Determine Teacher Behavior

This paper has focused on teacher expectations for the performance of individual students because most of the classroom expectation literature to date has centered on this question. However, it should be noted that many different types of expectations influence and interact with teachers' expectations for individual students. For example, teachers' general expectations about their teaching ability and the nature of school learning control their behavior to some extent. Similarly, decisions about how much emphasis to place on various subjects influences outcomes. Teachers who choose to spend but 15 minutes a day working with low readers will probably have more difficulty in achieving as much reading gain as teachers who decide to spend 40 minutes a day, even if teacher expectations are considerably higher in the 15-minute teaching situation.

An especially insightful description of the importance and influence of teacher goals on classroom behavior is provided by Carew and Lightfoot (1979). In their study of four first-grade teachers in two schools, the influence of teachers is carefully documented. Although two first-grade students may attend the same school, their school experience is sharply mediated by the particular teacher to whom they are assigned. Carew and Lightfoot found that pairs of teachers in different schools were more alike in some areas than teachers in the same school. Given the small sample size, it is not possible to tell how general such a finding is, but the data clearly illustrate that individual teachers can heavily influence the "face" of classroom life in some schools, independent of the broader school influences that may be operative in the school. Carew and Lightfoot found that teachers who placed more importance on social goals structured activities and interacted differently in the classroom than did teachers who placed more importance on cognitive goals. It would seem that being a low academic expectation student would not be the same experience in a socially oriented classroom as it would be in an achievement oriented classroom. Teachers' goals and general normative expectations about teaching will doubtlessly influence their classroom behavior, and this study is a good example of why it is impossible to find simple, consistent relationships between teachers' behavior and expectations for individual students. In future work more active attempts to understand the classroom work as teachers and students see it (in multidimensional form) are needed. Carew and Lightfoot's work is representative of this healthy trend.

The school context in which a teacher works may also influence the expression of that teacher's performance expectations for individual students. Surely it is easier for teachers to maintain optimism about their ability to teach and the ability of low students to learn when fellow teachers express similar beliefs. Indeed, Brookover et al. (1978) have produced data to illustrate that it is possible to find schools serving similar student populations where the achievement outcomes are considerably different. Achievement in some schools is better than in others, and one of the critical differences appears to be students' interest in achievement. In the low achievement schools, students are found to express negative attitudes that convey a sense of futility.[5]

Unfortunately, little is known about how teachers and students are influenced in such schools. However, Brookover and associates have described some of the ways that teachers express high expectations to their students. They have found that teachers in the higher achieving school identified fewer students as being incapable of learning, spent more time in instruction, and provided praise that was contingent upon performance. These data are consistent with the model that Jere Brophy and I presented sometime ago for explaining how expectation effects may be communicated to students (Brophy & Good, 1970). Brookover's data also suggest the possibility that some mechanisms at a school level may either serve to recruit teachers with higher expectations to a particular school and/or help teachers to maintain or to develop higher expectations once they arrive at the school.

What happens in classrooms and schools is also affected by expectations that are external to the physical boundaries of the school. Hall and Hall (1978), in a study funded by the National Institute of Education, are in part observing the effects that central administrations, boards of education, community groups, and government agencies have on expectations. Problems relating to expectational levels in any given area (e.g., curriculum, performance criterion, financial–budgetary statements) can emanate from

---

[5] Since this chapter was written, the author has become aware of an interesting work that provides good documentation of the school effect argument: that students do better in some secondary schools than do *comparable* students in other schools. (M. Rutter, B. Maughan, P. Mortimore, J. Ouston, & A. Smith, *Fifteen thousand hours: Secondary schools and their effects on children.* Cambridge, Massachusetts: Harvard University Press, 1979). Interestingly, the book provides support for the contention that higher but appropriate teacher expectations are one of the important characteristics of an "achieving" school. The interested reader may want to explore this intriguing book more fully.

any level, but tend to affect all other levels, and therefore necessitate negotiation, discussion, and interpretation in reaching solutions. For example, standardized tests issued by state departments of education are subject to any number of interpretations by administrations, school boards, and/or school personnel.

In the Hall and Hall (1978) study it was found that the media brought to public attention the results of a cross-section of schools and their standardized scores on a series of basic skills tests. Because there was a diversity of scores, local administration and school board members began receiving pressure from the community that reflected a concern on the part of the citizenry that their children were not performing up to expected levels as compared with other school systems. As a result, the administration has gone through a series of negotiations that have included reinterpretation of the meaning of these scores with community members, school board members, and teachers. The result of such negotiation has led the administration to implement programs within classrooms that instruct students in the needed skills included on the tests. Therefore, expectations for the children's performance resulted from a process of negotiation from the state department of education, the media, the central and school administration, school board, and finally the classroom teacher. Had the media not intervened in this case, the process may have occurred much differently. As an outcome, the public may have had quite different expectations for their children's performance on the test.

Social expectations would appear to make some outcomes more probable than others, at least indirectly. For example, it seems that young boys in this country do more poorly on verbal tasks in school than do young girls. However, these findings are reversed in other countries. Such findings suggest that societal expectations, which are expressed through differential parenting and classroom practices, the mass media, etc., appear to help boys and girls develop different skills and potentials. Interestingly, in some countries where academic and social expectations are more similar for boys and girls, early sex-related differences appear to be minimal (for a review of sex differences in achievement, see Bank, Biddle, & Good, in press).

It is important to note that classrooms, especially in elementary schools, are complex and busy settings, and that teachers have to monitor and to maintain an entire social setting while negotiating and interacting with individual students (Good & Brophy, 1980; Barr & Dreeben, 1977). Hence, teacher–child interactions are affected by variables other than beliefs about a particular student and the objective characteristics surrounding a given interaction. Surely teachers on occasion end an interaction with a student abruptly because they expect the student to fail. It is also true that some teachers end interactions quickly, not because they anticipate the failure of an individual pupil but because they anticipate a classroom disturbance and want to curb it before it starts. Cooper (1979) has contended that teacher behavior toward low students is influenced by expectations of retaining control of the classroom (e.g., some students are not encouraged because they may make a disruptive or excessively long response). Although teachers' concerns about control probably do influence teacher–student interaction, it is far from a complete explanation. To understand teacher expectations for individual pupils it is probably important to consider a number of other expectations that teachers possess (What is their definition of a good classroom?) as well as general needs of the teacher (Do they want to be liked by students or respected by other teachers?).

Student Characteristics

The extent to which students are susceptible to expectation effects probably relates to the students' beliefs about the classroom and the importance of school now (e.g., to their parents) and in the future. Although there are measures available for assessing individual student psychological difference variables (e.g., need achievement, locus of control), there is little information about students' personal reactions to the classroom.[6] What do students expect the teacher to do in a general sense? How do students feel when they cannot answer a teacher's questions? Why does the teacher ask questions in the classroom? Students who feel that teachers ask questions to provide students a chance to talk and/or allow the teacher to fill time may respond with different levels of attention and effort than the student who feels that he or she is being judged.

Braun (1976) has argued that children who possess a high self-concept may be less susceptible to teacher expectation effects. It is also possible that high and low self-concept students react differently to certain teacher behaviors. Perhaps different student expectations lead not only to differential effort but also to differential interpretation of teacher feedback about the response. That pen and paper measures of students' perceptions of effort-outcome relationships and student achievement do not have higher relationships with identifiable forms of teacher behavior may be in part due to the

---

[6] Fortunately, some researchers are beginning to turn their attention to students' classroom perceptions. For example, Rhona Weinstein, in the psychology department at the University of California, Berkeley, is in the midst of an intensive attempt to explore and understand students' views of classroom events. That students perceive teachers to differentiate certain teaching behavior toward male high and low achievers has been reported in a recent article, R. Weinstein & S. Middlestadt, Student perceptions of teacher interactions with male high and low achievers, *Journal of Educational Psychology*, 1979, 71(4), 421–431. The publication of this work came after this chapter had been written.

fact that certain patterns of interaction with the teacher mean different things to different students.

Similarly, different students may attach various meanings to other aspects of classroom life. Do some students view seatwork and homework assignments as "filler time" and tests and public recitation as real classroom tasks? If so, these students may respond differently to teacher seatwork messages than do students who feel that all teacher messages are important. Even students who are basically "pro-teacher" will likely react differently to similar teacher messages if they attach different values to different aspects of the classroom. Students, just as teachers, are likely to interpret classroom behavior selectively. Unfortunately, very little is known about student perceptions, although there have been some attempts to clarify students' perceptions of classroom events (Gannaway, 1976; Nash, 1976). Such information would seem to be very useful in attempting to understand school learning. Furthermore, information about the overlap of teacher and student expectations is also needed.

One study in progress illustrates an attempt at this type of integration. Evans and Byers (1978) are analyzing students' reading choices by asking students to select 5 to 10 books that they would like to read from a total of 30 descriptions. They want to determine why certain books are generally selected and how individual differences (e.g., grade level, sex, intelligence) influence selection decisions. The books represent a variety of themes and provide a basis for examining the stability of student choices over time. Also, the research team is interested in whether or not teachers use the same cues as students do to select books and why books are selected for classroom use. They also have an interest in examining influence effects (e.g., Do students' criteria come to be more like the teacher's as the year progresses?).

The extent to which teachers' judgments about students' reading interests match those of their students and the extent to which such knowledge enhances teachers' ability to influence students' reading habits are intriguing questions. This study is representative of the type of research that would help to clarify the extent to which teachers and students interpret the meaning of given behaviors similarly (e.g., Why and when do teachers criticize? Do students define criticism in the same way? If so, is the student definition similar to that of teachers?).

Earlier, the potential importance of attributions that teachers make in classrooms was noted. It would be important to see how students' interpretations of teachers' statements vary as a function of age and achievement level. Do first-grade students who are not a member of Joey's reading group infer a negative attribution from the teacher statement, "I'm asking Joey's group because they are fast?" Does the teacher have to be more explicit for young students to be influenced (e.g., "I'm asking Joey's group because they are so smart. Pay attention and someday you may get a chance to do this")?

One might ask, in light of the Evans and Byers research, if general statements of the teacher that are unrelated to attributions about students enhance, erode, or are irrelevant to students' perception of teacher credibility. Are teacher statements, "You'll like that book," basically accurate? If teachers are frequently *wrong* in predicting student interests, what impact does that have on student motivation? .

Observational research performed in the teacher expectation tradition has shown that differential and inappropriate behavior toward lows is a way of life in some classrooms. Attribution research has shown in laboratory settings that subjects' predictions of events do control motivational states. An integration of these research methods is needed. Fortunately, there is more attribution research being done in classrooms (e.g., Arkin & Maruyama, 1979). This bridge between laboratory and field setting data is important to explore since it has often been demonstrated that variables which are salient in the laboratory are not powerful in a social setting (Kounin, 1970).

The possibility that children's attributional reactions (particularly if teachers teach those reactions) are a determinant of school achievement should be of concern and of importance to educators. If Weiner (1976) is right—that high achievers accept responsibility for success and attribute failure to external causes (and low achievers do the opposite)—then it would seem important to help students alter this motivational stance.

However, when and how to intervene in the educational process is not clear. More observational research may help. Initial observational research is likely to illustrate that the problem is more complex than originally imagined. Stipek (1977) was intrigued by first graders' resistance to negative feedback. She noted that children who had done poorly in school and had received much feedback about their low performance (placement in the low reading group, frequent errors on papers) continued to claim (in interviews) that they were very smart and could easily learn. Some students would acknowledge that they had trouble with words in reading, but they still maintained that they were very smart (similar findings have been reported by Entwisle & Hayduk, 1978).

Stipek noted that there are at least two interpretations for this behavior. First, it is possible that first graders do not have a concept of "stable" traits such as ability. The second possibility is that they do not pay attention to objective or social comparisons available in the room and are responding to social reinforcement from the teacher (much of it gratuitous). Stipek thus suggests that teacher behavior may overshadow other cues available to children (e.g., class norms: how other students respond). She reports that teachers in her sample attempted to compensate for children's low performances by giving verbal reinforcement. When a poor performer gave a correct response teachers tended to respond with verbal reinforcement ("That's a very good answer"). When a good student made a correct response, the teacher frequently only gave "objective" feedback ("That's right"). She suggests that young children attend to the teacher's verbal praise and not to class norms. The unfortunate part of this may be that although teachers may be attempting to encourage low students for "good reasons," they may inadvertently fail to teach students to perceive the relationship between effort and outcome.

As noted earlier in this chapter, expectation literature has illustrated two types of inappropriate teaching styles for lows. Teachers who are either overly sympathetic or overly critical may exert a negative influence on student achievement, at least in the long run. Such findings suggest that the impact of a given teacher behavior is not always immediately obvious. However, more research on children's reactions to sequences of *behavior in their classrooms* may provide important cues. Stipek's data suggest that context conditions may influence the expression and/or interpretation of expectations. We now turn to a discussion of this possibility.

Context Effects

It would seem that many teacher behaviors could mean different things to students at different age levels, yet we have little data on this point. For example, *limited* use of noncontingent praise in the first grade might not be harmful (e.g., if used to strengthen interpersonal bonds and *if* the teacher works hard to help students develop academic skills and does not use praise as a consolation prize); however, for older students noncontingent praise might be detrimental under all circumstances. Teacher praise for an obviously poor response in a tenth-grade classroom would more likely be perceived negatively by students than in a second-grade classroom.

Research that examines student and teacher expectations under varying contextual conditions appears to be important. There are numerous contextual conditions (e.g., subject matter, architectural design of the school, classroom density) that might influence classroom behavior; however, two variables would seem to be especially interesting. Classroom size and variance in student achievement levels jointly appear to have potential for affecting the complexity of the classroom and the way in which students selectively attend and respond to classroom cues.

Educators have long discussed the possibility that the range of student ability in a class and class size may be important determinants of school achievement. However, the research on these two variables has produced conflicting results. The chief weakness of past research lies in the fact that variance in student ability and classroom size are seldom studied simultaneously; hence, there is very little information about the interactions of these two variables. Given the expense and difficulty involved in training teachers to engage in selected behavior, it would seem important to see if the manipulation of contextual variables (that are relatively easy to control) can produce classroom conditions that enhance classroom communication and student learning. Research on the contextual variables of size and ability variance also seems to be important considering the recent societal trends, such as decreasing school enrollment and legislative, judicial, and societal pressures to allow students of diverse backgrounds and abilities to share the same classroom.

Classroom size should have a direct impact on the way teachers and students interact. Teachers with large classes may find it difficult to wait for responses from hesitant students or to pursue correct responses after students have answered incorrectly. The pressure to maintain momentum in a large class may minimize teachers' efforts to monitor the learning of individual students. Similarly, the climate or pressures of a large class may suppress the willingness of lows to seek the teacher out for feedback.

The notion of ability grouping is very appealing. Logic would seem to dictate that teachers could do a better job if differences in student ability within a class were not great. It would seem that in the heterogeneous classroom teachers often go too slow for the high achiever and/or too fast for the low achiever. In contrast to the popular belief that ability grouping reduces "pacing problems," several reviews have suggested that ability grouping per se is unlikely to have a positive effect on student achievement. In fact, most studies suggest that when ability grouping does affect student achievement, the effect is usually negative: Students placed into the lower ability levels, relative to other students, suffer an educational decline.

In light of these findings, it may be that the change in mean class ability level (becoming either high or lower), which accompanies ability grouping, affects the teacher's expectation for class performance. The pacing of communications (frequency of repetition, detail of response to incorrect answers, questions accepted), the "depth" of communication (amount taught, complexity of student responses sought), and the level of abstractness of communications (whether concrete or abstract references are made) may all be less effective when class expectations are low.

The slow pace that heterogeneous classes create for fast learners may not be deleterious to their learning, since they perform as well as their tracked peers. However, the pace of the heterogeneous classroom may facilitate the learning of slow students by allowing them to be exposed to material they would otherwise miss. If this line of reasoning is correct, two conclusions seem warranted. First, since the process variables offered as mediating the effects of class size and those mediating the effects of ability variance are similar, there ought to be a set of relations between these two variables that optimizes learning.

In a complex classroom setting, teachers have to interpret a great deal of behavior and respond to it instantaneously. Hence, one can argue that process variations relating to high student-teacher ratios (e.g., restricted opportunity for teachers to monitor individual student performance; restricted opportunity for students to respond, to ask questions, and to get feedback) may make it difficult for some teachers to reassess their original hypotheses about students. *Large classes with diverse student populations may provide a milieu in which self-fulfilling prophecies are most likely to operate.* Reciprocally, large classes may make it difficult for the low achiever to respond to subtle cues or to actively alter a teacher's perception of his or her ability. It is thus contended here that the impact of size on interactions and achievement may be quite different for high and low expectation students. In particular, the forms of interactions created by large class size may adversely influence the education and achievement of low expectation students more than that of high expectation students. In large classes teachers may have to depend more on stereotypes to guide their responses, and low expectations may be difficult to alter.

The behavioral expression of teacher expectations may also vary as a function of classroom ability variation. Interactions in public settings must, to some extent, be geared to group needs. Long interactions with students in homogeneous low ability classrooms are likely to meet with more disruption and boredom than other student and classroom variance combinations. The pressure a teacher feels to behave differently with high and low expectation students may be strongest when they teach highs and lows separately. As stated earlier, having average and high ability students in classes with lows may dictate that the teacher maintain a communication style that exposes lows to more materials. To summarize, the changes in classroom interaction patterns accompanying size and variance changes may not be the same for high and low expectation students.

To reiterate, this discussion of size and variance is representative of a variety of context questions that can be raised. There are many context issues that could be explored profitably (open versus self-contained classrooms). For example, Chapter 4 in this book argues that potential benefits may follow when teachers adopt a more cooperative goal structure. One might ask how performance expectations are altered for students and teachers in cooperative and competitive situations.

Similarly one might ask about the meaning of interaction within the context of a given classroom. Does a given teacher behavior mean the same thing in different contexts in the same classroom? Does teacher praise or criticism following a student's response in a discussion involving the entire class mean the same thing to a student as criticism in a small reading group? Is the absolute criticism rate of the teacher more important or a more powerful way to express expectations? Does the influence of criticism vary with the context (what is the comparison group, general success rates in the activity, etc.) and individual characteristics of students? More research is needed to answer such questions. Again, the call is for research that more carefully defines the cognitive world of the classroom as teachers and students see it, and that simultaneously examines the influence of contextual variables upon such expectations and classroom behavior.

CONCLUSION

Implicitly, the call for new research here has been a request for activity that would place expectation research more centrally into the model proposed in Chapter 1. To understand why certain teacher behaviors influence some students and not others one must realize that the meaningfulness of the stimuli (teacher behavior) varies from student to student. In addition it is important to know more about what individual students expect from a teacher as well as the conditions under which an individual teacher becomes a significant other for a particular student.

We do not know the answers to such questions, except at a very general level. For example, it seems that teachers become less important to most students as they grow older. This appears to be the case in part because the needs of students become much more differentiated and the significant others who are relevant for providing feedback and goal directive motivation are no longer largely restricted to parents and teachers. Some students begin to rely more on themselves, peers, and other adults (e.g., coaches, employers) for such direction.

That teachers become less important, even as determinants of academic achievement, can be explained partly by the fact that behavior in familiar situations (i.e., classrooms) is progressively determined by students' past experiences and performances in similar situations. As students develop stable academic skills and motivations for academic work, it is less likely that an individual teacher can alter those behaviors and predispositions. If such reasoning is correct, the optimum time for teacher intervention would appear to be in kindergarten and in very early elementary school years.

Other useful intervention points may occur when students move away from familiar places and tasks to a new school. The opportunity to bring about motivational change in a junior high school may be considerably greater in seventh-grade classrooms than in eighth-grade classrooms. This is because in the seventh grade, students receive a new set of teachers, a new school record, a new school routine, and, in varying degrees, a new set of peer expectations. Also, because of developmental changes, new individual needs are also emerging at this grade level. Students may find that at least some teachers can recognize their emerging social needs. If teachers satisfy those needs, then their influence on cognitive student outcomes would also probably increase.

Teachers might be able to create these "unique" contextual conditions by assigning project work that is vastly different from previous assignments (and perhaps arousing the possibility in some students that they could complete the work successfully), especially if such assignments could also be related to the needs of a particular student. Teachers might also, as Johnson suggests in Chapter 4, create a "familiar" condition by altering the goal structure in classrooms.

The influence of a teacher is invariably related to what the teacher brings to the classroom (abilities, interests, expectations, goals) and those characteristics that students bring to the situation (need achievement, locus of control, interests, etc.). More insightful statements about the reciprocal effects of teacher and pupil expectations and behaviors will come about through a more careful documentation of the individual characteristics of those observed in future observational studies of classrooms. In short, the call for subsequent research is to make it more sensitive to the philosophy inherent in a person–situation interaction perspective.

Finally, it should be noted that research on teacher expectation effects has been successful in demonstrating that some low students receive teacher behavior that, at a minimum, sustains poor performance and that in some cases seems to worsen or lower the academic performance of lows. Those behaviors that have been associated with the communication of inappropriate expectations appear to be useful information for inclusion in teacher education programs, in order to sensitize teachers to the possible consequences of their behavior. However, it is now time for expectation research to move on to issues other than differential teaching behavior.[7] Especially

---

[7] Research on various relationships between teacher and student beliefs and behavior is being field tested in a program of research supported by the National Science Foundation under the direction of Harris M. Cooper and Thomas L. Good. Some of the preliminary data from this program of research were reported by H. M. Cooper, "Theoretical and Methodological Overview," and T. L. Good, "Studying and Modifying Classroom Behavior." In R. Baron (Chair), *Understanding Pygmalion: The Social Psychology of Self-Fulfilling Classroom Expectations.* Symposium presented at the meeting of the American Psychological Association, New York City, 1979. More integrative statements of this work will be available in book form, H. Cooper and T. Good, *Pygmalion grows up,* New York: Academic Press, in preparation.

important is how differential teacher behavior influences students' perception and motivation. There is also a need for more information about those teacher and student characteristics that make them more or less vulnerable to expectation effects. Finally, there needs to be a better understanding of the way in which student expectations and perceptions influence classroom achievement.

ACKNOWLEDGMENTS

The author would like to thank Sherry Kilgore for typing the manuscript, Gail Hinkel for a careful reading of the entire manuscript, and Jere Brophy, Jerry Burger, and Harris Cooper for their comments on certain aspects of this chapter.

REFERENCES

Anderson, H. & Brewer, H. Studies of teachers' classroom personalities, I: Dominative and integrative behavior of kindergarten teachers. *Applied Psychology Monographs*, 1945, 6.

Anderson, L., Evertson, C., & Brophy, J. Classroom organization at the beginning of school: Two case studies. Research and Development Center for Teacher Education, the University of Texas at Austin, Report No. 6003, 1978.

Arkin, R. & Maruyama, H. Attribution affect and college exam performance. *Journal of Educational Psychology*, 1979, 71, 85–93.

Barr, R. & Dreeben, R. Instruction in classrooms. In L. Shulman (Ed.), *Review of research in education*, No. 5. Itasca, Illinois: F. E. Peacock Publishers, 1977.

Bank, B., Biddle, B., & Good, T. Sex roles, reading instruction and pupil response. *Journal of Educational Psychology*, in press.

Braun, C. Teacher expectation: Socio-psychological dynamics. *Review of Educational Research*, 1976, 46, 185–213.

Brookover, W., Schweitzer, J., Schneider, J., Beady, C., Flood, P., & Wisebaker, J. Elementary school social climate and school achievement. *American Educational Research Journal*, 1978, 15, 301–318.

Brophy, J. & Evertson, C. *Learning from teaching: A developmental perspective*. Boston: Allyn & Bacon, 1976.

Brophy, J. & Good, T. Teachers' communication of differential expectations for children's classroom performance: Some behavioral data. *Journal of Educational Psychology*, 1970, 61, 365–374.

Brophy, J. & Good, T. *Teacher-student relationships: Causes and consequences*. New York: Holt, Rinehart & Winston, 1974.

Carew, J. & Lightfoot, S. Beyond bias: Perspectives on classrooms. *Harvard Educational Review* (1979).

Claiborn, W. Expectancy effects in the classroom: A failure to replicate. *Journal of Educational Psychology*, 1969, 60, 377–383.

Coleman, J., et al. Equality of educational opportunity. Washington, D.C.: Superintendent of Documents, U.S. Government Printing Office, 1966.

Cooper, H. Intervening in expectation communication: The "alterability" of teacher expectations. Technical Report No. 122. Center for Research in Social Behavior, University of Missouri, Columbia, Missouri, 1978.

Cooper, H. Pygmalion grows up: A model for teacher expectation communication and performance influence. *Review of Educational Research*, 1979, 49, 389–410.

Cooper, H. & Burger, J. Internality, stability and personal efficacy: A categorization of free response academic attribution. Technical Report No. 139, Center for Research in Social Behavior, University of Missouri, Columbia, Missouri, 1978.

Crandall, V. Reinforcement effects of adult reactions and nonreactions on children's achievement expectations. *Child Development*, 1963, 34, 335–354.

Crano, W. & Mellon, P. Causal influence of teachers' expectations on children's academic performance: A cross-lagged panel analysis. *Journal of Educational Psychology*, 1978, 70, 39–49.

Crawford, J. & Stallings, J. Experimental effects of in-service teacher training derived from process-product correlations in the primary grades. An unpublished paper, Center for Education Research at Stanford, Stanford University, Stanford, California, 1978.

Doyle, W. Student mediating responses in teaching effectiveness: An interim report. A paper read at the annual meeting of the American Educational Research Association, Toronto, March 1978.

Dusek, J. Do teachers bias children's learning? *Review of Educational Research*, 1975, 45, 661–684.

Dweck, C., Davidson, W., Nelson, S., & Enna, B. Sex differences in learned helplessness: II. The contingencies of evaluative feedback in the classroom; III. An experimental analysis. *Developmental Psychology*, 1978, 14, 268–276.

Ebmeier, H. & Good, T. An investigation of the interactive effects among student types, teacher types, and instruction types on the mathematics achievement of fourth grade students. *American Educational Research Journal*, 1979, 1, 1–17.

Emmer, E., Oakland, T., & Good, T. Do pupils affect teachers' styles of instruction? *Educational Leadership*, 1974, 31, 700–704.

Entwisle, D. & Hayduk, L. *Too great expectations*. Baltimore: The Johns Hopkins University Press, 1978.

Evans, T. & Byers, J., with Roehler, L. & Shulman, J. Teacher judgment of children's reading preferences. Research in progress. Cited in *Notes and News*. Institute for Research on Teaching, College of Education, Michigan State University, 1978, 6 (8).

Frieze, I. Causal attributions and information seeking to explain success and failure. *Journal of Research in Personality*, 1976, 10, 293–305.

Gannaway, H. Making sense of school. In M. Stubbs and S. Delamont (Eds.), *Explorations in classroom observation*. New York: Wiley, 1976.

Good, T. Teacher effectiveness in the elementary school: What we know about it now. *Journal of Teacher Education*, 1979, 30, 52–64.

Good, T. L. & Brophy, J. E. *Looking in classrooms*. New York: Harper & Row, 1973.

Good, T. L. & Brophy, J. E. *Educational psychology: A realistic approach*. 2d Ed. New York: Holt, Rinehart & Winston, 1980.

Good, T. L. & Brophy, J. E. *Looking in classrooms*. 2d Ed. New York: Harper & Row, 1978.

Good, T. & Grouws, D. The Missouri mathematics effectiveness project: An experimental study in fourth grade classrooms. *Journal of Educational Psychology*. 1979, 71, 355–362.

Good, T. & Grouws, D. Process-product relationships in fourth grade mathematics classrooms. Final Report of National Institute of Education Grant (NE-G-00-3-0123), University of Missouri, October 1975.

Good, T. & Grouws, D. Teaching effects: A process-product study in fourth grade mathematics classrooms. *Journal of Teacher Education*, 1977, 28, 49–54.

Good, T., Grouws, D., Beckerman, T., Ebmeier, H., Flatt, L., & Schneeberger, S. Teaching manual: Missouri mathematics effectiveness project. Technical Report No. 132, Center for Research in Social Behavior, University of Missouri, Columbia, Missouri, 1977.

Hall, P. & Hall, D. Personal communication. (Observations based upon research in progress.) 1978.

Hayden, T. & Mischel, W. Maintaining trait consistency in the resolution of behavioral inconsistency: The wolf in sheep's clothing. Unpublished Manuscript, Stanford University, 1973.

Hunter, D. Student on task behavior during reading group meeting. Unpublished Ph.D. dissertation, University of Missouri, Columbia, Missouri, 1978.

Hurn, C. *The limits and possibilities of schooling: An introduction to the sociology of education.* Boston: Allyn & Bacon, 1978.

Jackson, P. *Life in classrooms.* New York: Holt, Rinehart & Winston, 1968.

Jenkins, J. & Deno, S. Influence of knowledge and type of objectives on subject matter learning. *Journal of Educational Psychology,* 1971, *62,* 67–70.

Jones, R. *Self-fulfilling prophecies: Social, psychological, and physiological effects of expectancies.* Hillsdale, New Jersey: Lawrence Erlbaum Associates, 1977.

Klein, S. Student influence on teacher behavior. *American Educational Research Journal,* 1971, *8,* 403–421.

Kounin, J. *Discipline and group management in classrooms.* New York: Holt, Rinehart & Winston, 1970.

Martin, M. Equal opportunity in the classroom ESEA, Title III: Session A Report. Los Angeles: County Superintendent of Schools, Division of Compensatory and Intergroup Programs, 1973.

McDermott, R. Kids makes sense: An ethnographic account of the interactional management of success and failure in one first grade classroom. Unpublished Ph.D. dissertation, Stanford University, 1977.

McDonald, F. & Elias, P. The effects of teacher performance on pupil learning. Beginning Teacher Evaluation Study: Phase II, final report: Vol. I. Princeton, New Jersey: Educational Testing Service, 1976.

Miller, R., Brickman, P., & Bolen, D. Attribution versus persuasion as a means for modifying behavior. *The Journal of Personality and Social Psychology,* 1975, *31,* 430–441.

Nash, R. Pupils' expectations of their teachers. In M. Stubbs and S. Delamont (Eds.), *Explorations in classroom observation.* New York: Wiley, 1976.

Openlander, L. The relative influence of the group of pupils and of the teacher as determinants of classroom interaction. Paper presented at the annual meeting of the American Educational Research Association, 1969.

Rist, R. Student social class and teacher expectations: The self-fulfilling prophecy in ghetto education. *Harvard Educational Review,* 1970, *40,* 411–451.

Rosenthal, R. On the social psychology of the self-fulfilling prophecy: Further evidence for Pygmalion effects and their mediating mechanisms. New York: MSS Modular Publications, 1974.

Rosenthal, R. & Jacobson, L. *Pygmalion in the classroom: Teacher expectation and pupils' intellectual development.* New York: Holt, Rinehart & Winston, 1968.

Rutter, M., Maughan, B., Mortimore, P., Ouston, J., & Smith, A. *Fifteen thousand hours: Secondary schools and their effects on children.* Cambridge, Massachusetts: Harvard University Press, 1979.

Schrank, W. A further study of the labeling effect of ability grouping. *The Journal of Educational Research,* 1970, *63,* 358–360.

Shulman, L. & Elstein, A. Studies of problem solving, judgment, and decision making: Implications for educational research. In F. Kerlinger (Ed.), *Review of research in education III.* Itasca, Illinois: F. E. Peacock Publishers, 1975.

Snow, R. Unfinished Pygmalion. *Contemporary Psychology,* 1969, *14,* 197–199.

Spencer-Hall, D. A. Aligning actions in an elementary classroom. Unpublished Ph.D. dissertation, University of Missouri, Columbia, Missouri, 1976.

Stipek, D. Changes during first grade in children's social-motivational development. Unpublished Ph.D. dissertation, Yale University, New Haven, Connecticut, 1977.

Thomas, W. & Thomas, D. *The child in America.* New York: Knopf, 1928.

Tversky, A. & Kahneman, D. Belief in the law of small numbers. *Psychological Bulletin,* 1971, 76, 105–110.

Weiner, B. An attributional approach for educational psychology. In L. Shulman (Ed.), *Review of Research in Education IV.* Itasca, Illinois: F. E. Peacock Publishers, 1976.

Weinstein, R. Reading group membership in first grade: Teacher behaviors and pupil experience over time. *Journal of Educational Psychology,* 1976, 68, 103–116.

Weinstein, R. & Middlestadt, S. Student perceptions of teacher interactions with male high and low achievers. *Journal of Educational Psychology,* 1979, 71(4), 421–431.

West, C. & Anderson, T. The question of preponderant causation in teacher expectancy research. *Review of Educational Research,* 1976, 46, 185–213.

Williams, T. Teacher prophecies and the inheritance of inequality. *Sociology of Education,* 1976, 49, 223–235.

Winnie, P. & Marx, R. Reconceptualizing research on teaching. *Journal of Educational Psychology,* 1977, 69, 668–678.

chapter 4

Group Processes: Influences of Student–Student Interaction on School Outcomes

DAVID W. JOHNSON

INTRODUCTION: IMPORTANCE OF STUDENT–STUDENT RELATIONSHIPS

The classroom is first and foremost a scene of recurrent interpersonal interactions where a teacher and 30 or so students all interact with one another. Traditionally, educators and psychologists have viewed the interaction between the teacher and the student as the most important relationship for achieving the school's goals of subject matter mastery, socialization, and intellectual, social, and physical development. This view has been based on three assumptions. The first is that teaching and learning take place in a dyadic relationship between an adult and a child. Students' learning has been assumed to be primarily dependent on interaction with the teacher and, therefore, considerable research (as evidenced in Chapter 3) has focused on the teacher's (a) expectations of the student's ability to perform on academic tasks; (b) warmth, empathy, and democraticness in dealing with the student; (c) distribution of reinforcers to students for achievement and appropriate social behavior; and (d) feedback to the student concerning achievement and appropriate behavior. The second assumption has been that peer relationships in the classroom have little impact on the student and, therefore, should be ignored. And the third assumption has been that the infrequent and minor peer influences that do exist in the classroom are an unhealthy and bothersome influence on students' achievement, socialization, and development. Peer influences have been viewed as being in

123

THE SOCIAL PSYCHOLOGY
OF SCHOOL LEARNING

opposition to adult influences, aimed at discouraging academic achievement and encouraging off-task, disruptive behavior in the classroom.

Because of these three assumptions, student–student relationships have generally been suppressed in the classroom rather than constructively utilized. Most legitimate peer-group interaction in schools has been limited to extracurricular activities, which rarely deal with the basic issues of classroom life (McPartland, 1977). In many classrooms a system of instruction is used that emphasizes teacher lectures and students doing seatwork individually. Attempts by students to interact with each other are seen as off-task disruptiveness in such a system. Moreover, educators systematically fail to train students in the most basic social skills necessary for interacting effectively with peers, as they are not considered to be useful (Combs & Slaby, 1977). Without question, the dyadic, adult–child view of teaching and learning has lead to a deemphasis on student–student interaction and relationships in the classroom.

The assumption by psychologists that the most important relationships children form are with adults such as parents and teachers has so dominated that between the 1930s and the 1970s relatively few studies were conducted examining the impact of peer relationships on development and achievement. From both a psychoanalytic and Piagetian point of view, peer relationships were thought to be unimportant and, therefore, the study of children's early social behavior was directed toward child–parent interaction, especially child–mother relationships (Lewis & Rosenblum, 1975). Psychoanalytic theory emphasizes that children's early social experiences form the context for later social development and, therefore, that their social relationships are all greatly influenced by their interaction with their mothers and fathers. The infant–mother dyad is considered so important that other social relationships are considered to be derivatives and are neglected or not considered at all. Piagetian theory views cognitive–structural capacities of the young child as restricting the child's social behavior. Thus, for complex social behavior to occur, a person old enough to be capable of controlling and manipulating the dynamics of the relationship needs to be present (i.e., an adult). The view that children lack the cognitive faculties that are necessary for social interaction results in the restriction of the study of early child–peer relationships. The aspects of the psychoanalytic and the Piagetian theories that deemphasize the importance of peer relationships in development and socialization, however, are now being vigorously questioned.

The dyadic, adult–child view of teaching and learning is grossly oversimplified when the power of social dynamics among students that occur regularly in the classroom are taken into consideration (Schmuck, 1978). Whereas classroom teachers do interact frequently with individual students, virtually all of the teacher's classroom behavior occurs within the context of the student–peer group. A student responding to a teacher's directive, for example, does so while being aware of and influenced by the feelings, attitudes, and relationships shared with the student–peer group. A teacher's statements and actions are received by students in the context of their relationships with other students.

In the classroom the influences resulting from student–student relationships have more powerful effects on achievement, socialization, and development than any other factor. Yet the importance and power of peer interaction in the classroom are often ignored. In this chapter the impact of student–student relationships on achievement, appropriate behavior, and general socialization and development will be discussed. Secondly, the critical group dynamic variables teachers and educators can control that will ensure that constructive peer relationships are utilized for achievement, appropriate behavior, cognitive and social development, and general socialization will be covered.

CONSEQUENCES AND CORRELATES OF PEER RELATIONSHIPS

Experiences with peers are not superficial luxuries to be enjoyed by some students and not by others. Student–student relationships are an absolute necessity for healthy cognitive and social development and socialization. In fact, social interactions with peers may be the primary relationships in which development and socialization take place (Lewis & Rosenblum, 1975). There are many important ways in which student–student interaction contributes to the cognitive and social development and general socialization of children and adolescents, such as by:

1. Contributing to the socialization of values, attitudes, competencies, and ways of perceiving the world.
2. Being prognostic indicators of future psychological health.
3. Teaching the social competencies necessary to reduce social isolation.
4. Influencing the occurrence or nonoccurrence of potential problem behaviors in adolescence such as the use of illegal drugs.
5. Providing the context in which children learn to master aggressive impulses.
6. Contributing to the development of sex-role identity.
7. Contributing to the emergence of perspective-taking abilities.
8. Influencing educational aspirations and achievement.

Each of these consequences and correlates of peer relationships will be discussed in this chapter.

Socializing Influences

There is considerable evidence that peer relationships are of central importance in the socialization of the child, providing expectations, models, and reinforcements that shape a wide variety of social behaviors, attitudes, and perspectives (Hartup, 1976; Johnson & Johnson, 1978; Wahler, 1967). Schmuck (1971) states that peers constitute the immediate environment as well as the environment of greatest impact for students in school. On the basis of his review of the literature he concludes that compared to interactions with teachers, interactions with peers are more frequent, intense and varied. In their interactions with peers, children and adolescents directly learn attitudes, values, and information unobtainable from adults, such as the nature of sexual relations and how they are to be developed and managed with peers. In their interactions with each other children and adolescents imitate each other's behavior and identify with friends who have admired competencies. The way in which "ingroup" messages are phrased, the nature of clothes and hair styles, the music valued, what is defined as enjoyable and what is defined as distasteful, what competencies need to be practiced and developed, and so forth, are all based on identification with and imitation of peers. In their interaction with peers, children and adolescents try out, practice, and perfect social roles. Young children may play house, fire department, and a variety of other adult career roles; older children may experiment with various ways in which to be a friend; and adolescents may practice social roles aimed at obtaining acceptance into desired peer groups. Through practicing social roles in their relationships with peers, students have the opportunity for paced, slowly elaborating, enlargement of communicative, aggressive, defensive, and cooperative skills. The formation of relationships with peers, furthermore, not only promotes the values, attitudes, competencies, and perspectives needed to manage productively the challenges of adulthood but also creates coalitions that may last into adulthood to the benefit of children and their friends—partners.

The socialization importance of peers does not end during adolescence. Several studies have demonstrated that peers greatly influence the adoption and internalization of values and attitudes by college students (Chickering, 1969; Newcomb, et al., 1970, 1971; Vreeland & Bidwell, 1965; Wallace, 1966). Lacy (1978) found that frequency of interaction with peers was not a sufficient factor to affect the values of college students. For peers to be an important influence on the internalization of values and attitudes, the content of the interaction had to be relevant to the value dimension and students had to be generally satisfied with and responsive to their fellow students. Friends have an important impact on values throughout one's life.

While much of the evidence indicating that peer relationships are vital and important for socialization is correlational, it is consistent in indicating considerable peer influence on socialization and development.

Indicators of Future Psychological Health

The ability to build and maintain interdependent, cooperative relationships is often cited as a primary manifestation of psychological health (Adler et al., 1956; Fromm-Reichmann, 1950; Johnson & Matross, 1977; Jung & DeLaszlo, 1959; May, 1969; Murray, 1951; Sullivan, 1953). It is no surprise, therefore, that several studies have found a relationship between (a) poor peer relations in children and (b) destructive social conduct in adolescence and psychological pathology in adulthood. Kohn and Clausen (1955) found that a much higher percentage of adults diagnosed as psychotic were socially isolated as children than were a normal control sample. Roff (1961), in a study of servicemen who had formerly been patients in a child-guidance clinic, found that men receiving "bad conduct" discharges were more frequently rated by their childhood counselors as having poor peer adjustment than were men with successful service records. Roff (1963), in a study of adult males who were seen as children in child-guidance clinics, found that poor peer relationships were predictive of adult neurotic and psychotic disturbances of a variety of types, as well as disturbances in sexual behavior and adjustment.

Cowen and his associates (1973) found that poor peer adjustment in the third grade was an excellent predictor of emotional difficulties in early adulthood. They accumulated a variety of measures on the children, including IQ scores, school grades, achievement test results, school attendance records, teacher ratings, and peer ratings. Eleven years later, community mental health registers were examined to locate which members of the sample were consulting a mental health professional. Of all the measures secured in the third grade, the best predictor of adult mental health status was the peer rating. Roff, Sells, and Golden (1972) found a significant correlation between childhood peer acceptance and delinquency in adolescence. Among upper-lower-class and middle-class males, delinquency rates were higher among children who were not accepted by their peers than among those who were. Among lower-class males, both highly accepted and highly rejected children had higher delinquency rates than did those who were moderately accepted by peers, but individual case records suggested that the ultimate social adjustment of the peer-accepted children would be better than the rejected ones. Roff and his associates noted, furthermore, that no evidence exists to contradict the hypothesis that peer relations play a central role in psychological development. Finally, Johnson and Norem-Hebeisen (1977) found that adolescents oriented toward individualism and separation from peers displayed high levels of psychological pathology.

There is considerable correlational evidence, therefore, that poor peer relationships in elementary school predicts psychological disturbance in high school, and poor peer relationships in both elementary and high school predict adult psychological pathology.

Acquiring Social Competencies

There is some evidence that social isolation is related to a lack of social competencies. There is also evidence that constructive interaction with peers increases children's social skills. Children identified as social isolates in preschool situations tend to be deficient in leadership skills (Kohn & Rosman, 1972) and tend to not elicit reactions from other children (Stanley & Gottman, 1976). Koch (1935) identified seven distinctly unsocial children along with seven matched control children. For 30 minutes each day for 20 days, each "experimental child" was removed from the nursery along with one sociable child of the subject's own age and surrounded with play materials believed to stimulate cooperative play. The published reports are incomplete, but "changes in the direction of increased sociability were cumulative throughout the investigation [Page, 1936]." Furman, Rahe, and Hartup (in press) conducted a similar study in which they identified preschool children who were social isolates, paired them with a same-age or younger peer, and placed them in a playroom with toys aimed at stimulating cooperative play for ten play sessions. The socially withdrawn children were then observed in their regular classroom. The cooperative play significantly increased the frequency of social interaction of the withdrawn children, especially for those children who were paired with a younger peer. In addition, the withdrawn children positively reinforced their peers much more frequently, giving help and gifts, sharing, accepting guidance and suggestions, and engaging in cooperative play. The researchers concluded that the play sessions provided an opportunity for the isolates to have experiences that occurred infrequently in the regular classroom, such as being socially assertive by directing social activity.

Occurrence of Illegal Drug Use

Adolescents' peer groups and friends seem to have considerable influence on drug use patterns as well as on other problem or possible transition behaviors. There is considerable correlational evidence indicating that whether or not adolescents engage in the use of illegal drugs such as marihuana or engage in other problem or possible transition behaviors such as sexual intercourse and problem drinking is highly related to perceptions of one's friends as engaging in and being approving of the behaviors (Becker, 1953, 1955; Elseroad & Goodman, 1970; Goode, 1970; Jessor, 1975; Jessor, Jessor, & Finney, 1973; Johnson, 1973; Johnston, 1973; Josephson, 1974; Kandel, 1975; Lavenhar et al., 1972). The correlational nature of this evidence supports the position that providing adolescents with peers and friends who do engage in and disapprove of problem behaviors such as the use of illegal drugs may have considerable influence on adolescents' behavior.

Managing Agressive Impulses

Children learn to master aggressive impulses within the context of peer relations (Hartup, 1978). Peer interaction provides an opportunity to experiment aggressively with co-equals, and it is assumed that children who show generalized hostility and unusual modes of aggressive behavior, or children who are unusually timid in the presence of aggressive attack, may be lacking exposure to certain kinds of contacts with peers such as rough-and-tumble play. Rough-and-tumble play seems to promote the acquisition of a repertoire of effective aggressive behaviors and also establishes necessary regulatory mechanisms for modulating aggressive affect. Aggression occurs more frequently in child–child interaction than in adult–child interaction in many different cultures (Whiting & Whiting, 1975), and observational studies in the United States show clearly that feedback from peers escalates and deescalates rates of aggression among nursery school children (Patterson, Littman, & Bicker, 1967; Patterson & Cobb, 1971).

Socializing Sex-Role Identity

Hartup (1978) notes that although gender-typing first occurs in interactions between the child and its parents (Money & Ehrhardt, 1972), the peer culture extends and elaborates this process. Fagot and Patterson (1969) found that social rewards are exchanged within the peer culture according to the gender-appropriateness of the child's behavior. Furthermore, Kobasigawa (1968) found that peer models also contribute to the formation of appropriate sexual attitudes. Kinsey, Pomeroy, and Martin (1948) noted that sexual experimentation is pervasive in child–child interactions and must be seen as contributing positively rather than negatively to socialization. Roff (1966) has shown that adults who are arrested for committing crimes of sexual assault or who have disturbances in sexual adjustment have histories of peer rejection and social isolation. As Hartup (1976) has so aptly stated, if parents were to be given sole responsibility for the socialization of sexuality, humans would not survive as a species.

Acquiring Perspective-Taking Abilities

It is through interaction with peers that children develop the ability to view situations and problems from perspectives other than their own (Piaget, 1932). Perspective-taking is one of the most critical competencies for cognitive and social development as it has been found to be related to effective presentation of information, effective comprehension of information, the constructive resolution of conflicts, willingness to disclose information on a personal level, effective group problem-solving, cooperativeness, positive attitudes toward others within the same situation, autonomous moral judgment, intellectual and cognitive judgment, intellectual and cognitive development, and social adjustment (Johnson, 1975, 1980a). *Social perspective-taking* may be defined as the ability to understand how a situation appears to another person and how that person is reacting cognitively and emotionally to the situation. The opposite of perspective-taking is *egocentrism,* the embeddedness in one's own viewpoint to the extent that one is unaware of other points of view and of the limitations in one's perspective.

Piaget (1932) views all psychological development as a progressive loss of egocentrism and an increase in ability to take wider and more complex perspectives. In discussing Piaget's theorizing, Flavell (1963), for example, states: "In the course of this contact (and especially, his conflicts and arguments) with other children, the child increasingly finds himself forced to reexamine his own percepts and concepts in the light of others, and by so doing, gradually rids himself of cognitive egocentrism [p. 279]." There is correlational and experimental evidence that the development of perspective-taking ability and the reduction of egocentrism is dependent on interaction with peers. Gottmen, Gonso, and Rasmussen (1975) found that children who were able to take the perspective of others were more socially active and more competent in social exchanges with other children than were less able perspective-takers. Keasey (1973), in a study of fifth and sixth graders, found that those who belonged to many social organizations (and therefore interacted with peers more) had higher moral judgment scores (a major ingredient of which is perspective-taking) than did children who belonged to few clubs. Johnson and his colleagues (1976) found that individualistic learning experiences in which students were separated from each other and not allowed to interact promoted higher egocentrism and less perspective-taking ability than did learning in small cooperative groups.

Raising Educational Aspirations and Achievement

Peers have a great deal of influence on students' educational aspirations (Alexander & Campbell, 1964; Coleman, 1961; Coleman et al., 1966; Ramsøy, 1961; Turner, 1964; Wilson, 1959). Alexander and Campbell (1964), for example, found that a student is more likely to aspire to higher education and actually go to college if his best friend also plans to go to college. There is also evidence that students' achievement is related to the educational and economic levels of other students in the school (Coleman et al., 1966; Crain & Weisman, 1972). Freedman (1967) conducted an extensive review of the literature and concluded that student educational aspirations and actual achievement were more affected by fellow students than by any other school influence.

Two studies dealing with primary age students in elementary schools servicing children from low-income families found consistent negative correlations between subject matter achievement and high frequencies of students studying alone; consistent positive correlations were found between time spent with peers in moderate size groups (3–7 members) or large groups under the teacher's direction and subject matter achievement (Soar, 1973; Stallings & Kaskowitz, 1974). These studies imply that when students are young, and when they have poor study skills, interaction with peers can significantly increase achievement.

QUALITY OF STUDENT–STUDENT RELATIONSHIPS

Interpersonal interaction is the basis for learning, socialization, and development. While there has been considerable emphasis on teacher–student interaction, the educational value of student–student interaction has been largely ignored. There is evidence indicating that among other things student–student interaction will contribute to general socialization, future psychological health, acquisition of social competencies, avoidance of engaging in antisocial or problem behaviors, mastery and control of impulses such as aggression, development of a sex-role identity, emergence of perspective-taking ability, and development of high educational aspirations and achievement. *Simply placing students near each other and allowing interaction to take place does not mean, however, that these outcomes will appear.* The nature of the interaction is important. Some interaction leads to students rejecting each other and defensively avoiding being influenced by peers. When student–student interaction leads to relationships characterized by perceived support and acceptance, then the potential beneficial effects described in the previous section are likely to be found.

In order for peer relationships to be constructive influences, they must promote feelings of belonging, acceptance, support, and caring, rather than feelings of hostility and rejection. Perceptions of being accepted by peers affects the following aspects of classroom life:

1. Peer acceptance is positively correlated with willingness to engage in social interaction (Furman, 1977; Johnson & Ahlgren, 1976; Johnson, Johnson, & Anderson, 1978).
2. Peer acceptance is positively correlated with the extent to which students provide positive social rewards for peers (Hartup, Glazer, & Charlesworth, 1967).
3. Isolation in the classroom is associated with high anxiety, low self-esteem, poor interpersonal skills, emotional handicaps, and psychological pathology (Bower, 1960; Gronlund, 1959; Horowitz, 1962; Johnson & Norem-Hebeisen, 1977; Mensh & Glidewell, 1958; Schmuck, 1963, 1966; Smith, 1958; Van Egmond, 1960).
4. Rejection by peers is related to disruptive classroom behavior (Lorber, 1966), hostile behavior and negative affect (Lippitt & Gold, 1959), and negative attitudes toward other students and school (Schmuck, 1966).
5. Acceptance by peers is related to utilization of abilities in achievement situations (Schmuck, 1963, 1966; Van Egmond, 1960).

On the basis of this evidence it may be concluded that peer relationships will have constructive effects only when student–student interaction is characterized by support and acceptance. In order to promote constructive peer influences, therefore, teachers must first ensure that students interact with each other and, second, must ensure that the interaction takes place within a supportive and accepting context. In other words, teachers must control the group dynamics affecting student–student interaction.

When teachers promote student–student interaction in the classroom there are several dynamics of groups that should be taken into account. These include the way in which learning goals are structured, the way in which conflict among ideas are managed, the composition of the group, the norms instituted within the group, and the size of the group.

GROUP GOALS AND GOAL STRUCTURE

All groups have goals, and one of the most important aspects of group effectiveness is the group's ability to define its goals and achieve them successfully. The essence of a goal is that it is an ideal. It is a desired place toward which people are working, a state of affairs that people value. A *group goal* is a future state of affairs desired by enough members of the group to motivate efforts to achieve it. In order to teach successfully, teachers need to know what outcomes they hope to achieve. After their instructional goals are formulated appropriately, a decision must be made as to the type of goal interdependence to be structured among students as they learn.

There are three types of goal interdependence that teachers may structure during instruction (Deutsch, 1962; Johnson & Johnson, 1975): cooperative (positive goal interdependence), competitive (negative goal interdependence), and individualistic (no goal interdependence). A *cooperative* goal structure exists when students perceive that they can obtain their goal if and only if the other students with whom they are linked obtain their goals. A *competitive* goal structure exists when students perceive that they can obtain their goal if and only if the other students with whom they are linked fail to obtain their goals. An *individualistic* goal structure exists when students perceive that obtaining their goal is unrelated to the goal achievement of other students.

In the ideal classroom all three goal structures would be appropriately used. All students would learn how to work cooperatively with other students, compete for fun and enjoyment, and work autonomously on their own. Most of the time, however, students would work on instructional tasks within the goal structure that is the most productive for the type of task to be done and for the cognitive and affective outcomes desired. It is the teacher who decides which goal structure to implement within each instructional activity. The way in which teachers structure learning goals determines how students interact with each other and with the teacher. The interaction patterns, in turn, determine the cognitive and affective outcomes of instruction. There is no aspect of teaching more important than the appropriate use of goal structures.

Student–Student Interaction

Each goal structure will promote a different pattern of interaction among students. Aspects of student–student interaction important for learning include (Johnson & Johnson, 1975): accurate communication and exchange of information, facilitation of each other's efforts to achieve, constructive conflict management, peer pressures toward achievement, decreased fear of failure, divergent thinking, acceptance and support by peers, utilization of other's resources, trust, and emotional involvement in and commitment to learning. A summary of the research findings on the relationships among the three goal structures and these aspects of student–student interaction is presented in Table 4.1 (for specific references, see Johnson & Johnson, 1975, 1978). Cooperation provides opportunities for positive interaction among students, whereas competition promotes cautious and defensive student–student interaction (except under very limited conditions). When students are in an individualistic goal structure, they work by themselves to master the skill or knowledge assigned, without interacting with other students. When teachers wish to promote positive interaction among students, a cooperative goal structure should be used, and competitive and individualistic goal structures should be avoided.

Of special importance for students influencing each other in regard to achievement, appropriate social behavior, cognitive and social development, and general socialization is the degree to which each goal structure affects (a) students' perceptions that they are accepted, supported, and liked

Table 4.1
GOAL STRUCTURES AND INTERPERSONAL PROCESSES THAT AFFECT LEARNING

Cooperative	Competitive	Individualistic
High interaction	Low interaction	No interaction
Effective communication	No, misleading, or threatening communication	No interaction
Facilitation of other's achievement: helping, sharing, tutoring	Obstruction of other's achievement	No interaction
Peer influence toward achievement	Peer influence against achievement	No interaction
Problem-solving conflict management	Win–lose conflict management	No interaction
High divergent and risk-taking thinking	Low divergent and risk-taking thinking	No interaction
High trust	Low trust	No interaction
High acceptance and support by peers	Low acceptance and support by peers	No interaction
High emotional involvement in and commitment to learning by almost all students	High emotional involvement in and commitment to learning by the few students who have a chance to win	No interaction
High utilization of resources of other students	No utilization of resources of other students	No interaction
Division of labor possible	Division of labor impossible	No interaction
Decreased fear of failure	Increased fear of failure	No interaction

by their peers; (b) students' exchange of information; (c) students' motivation to learn; and (d) students' emotional involvement in learning.

Acceptance, Support, Liking

Cooperative learning experiences, compared with competitive and individualistic ones, have been found to result in stronger beliefs that one is liked, supported, and accepted by other students, and that other students care about how much one learns and want to help one learn (Cooper, Johnson, Johnson & Wilderson, 1980; Gunderson & Johnson, 1980; Johnson, Johnson, & Tauer, 1979; Johnson, Johnson, Johnson, & Anderson, 1976; Tjosvold, Marino, & Johnson, 1977). Furthermore, cooperative attitudes are related to the belief that one is liked by other students and wants to listen to, help, and do schoolwork with other students (Johnson & Ahlgren, 1976; Johnson, Johnson, & Anderson, 1978). Individualistic attitudes are related to *not* wanting to do schoolwork with other students, *not* wanting to help other students learn, *not* valuing being liked by other students, and *not* wanting to participate in social interaction (Johnson, Johnson, & Anderson, 1978; Johnson & Norem-Hebeisen, 1977). Furthermore, Deutsch (1962) and other researchers (Johnson, 1974a) found that trust is built through cooperative interaction and is destroyed through competitive interaction.

Exchange of Information

The seeking of information, and utilizing it in one's learning, is essential for academic achievement. Moreover, there is evidence that in problem-solving situations, students working within a cooperative goal structure will *seek* significantly more information from each other than will students working within a competitive goal structure (Crawford & Haaland, 1972). There is also evidence that students working within a cooperative goal structure will make optimal use of the information provided by other students, whereas students working within a competitive goal structure will fail to do so (Laughlin & McGlynn, 1967). Blake and Mouton (1961) provide evidence that competition biases a person's perceptions and the comprehension of viewpoints and positions of other individuals. A cooperative context, compared with a competitive one, promotes more accurate communication of information, more verbalization of ideas and information, more attentiveness to other's statements, and more acceptance of and willingness to be influenced by others' ideas and information. Furthermore, a cooperative context results in fewer difficulties in communicating with and understanding others, more confidence in one's own ideas and in the value that others attach to one's ideas, more frequent open and honest communication, and greater feelings of agreement between oneself and others (Johnson, 1974a; Johnson & R. Johnson, 1975).

Motivation

Motivation is most commonly viewed as a combination of the perceived likelihood of success and the perceived incentive for success. The greater the likelihood of success and the more important it is to succeed, the higher the motivation. Success that is intrinsically rewarding is usually seen as being more desirable for learning than is having students believe that only extrinsic rewards are worthwhile. There is a greater perceived likelihood of success and success is viewed as more important in a cooperative than in a competitive or individualistic learning situation (Johnson & R. Johnson, 1975).

The more cooperative students' attitudes, the more they see themselves as being intrinsically motivated: They persevere in pursuit of clearly defined learning goals; believe that it is their own efforts that determine their school success; want to be good students and get good grades; and believe that ideas, feelings, and learning new ideas are important and enjoyable (Johnson & Ahlgren, 1976; Johnson, Johnson, & Anderson, 1978). These studies also indicate that the more competitive students' attitudes are, the more they see themselves as being extrinsically motivated in elementary and junior high schools. Competitive attitudes are, however, somewhat related to intrinsic motivation, to being a good student, and to getting good marks in senior high school. Individualistic attitudes tend to be unrelated to all measured aspects of the motivation to learn. Being part of a cooperative learning group has been found to be related to a high subjective probability of academic success and continuing motivation for further learning by taking more advanced courses in the subject area studied (Gunderson & Johnson, 1980). There is also experimental evidence which indicates that cooperative learning experiences, compared with individualistic ones, will result in more intrinsic motivation, less extrinsic motivation, and less need for teachers to set clear goals for the students (Johnson, Johnson, & Anderson, 1976).

Emotional Involvement in Learning

Students are expected to become involved in instructional activities and to benefit from them as much as possible. There is evidence that the more cooperative students' attitudes are, the more they express their ideas and feelings in large and small classes and listen to the teacher, whereas competitive and individualistic attitudes are unrelated to indices of emotional involvement in instructional activities (Johnson & Ahlgren, 1976; Johnson, Johnson, & Anderson, 1978). There is evidence that cooperative learning experiences, compared with competitive and individualistic ones, result in a greater desire to express one's ideas to the class (Johnson, Johnson, Johnson, & Anderson, 1976; Wheeler & Ryan, 1973). Cooperative learning experiences, compared with competitive and individualistic ones, promote greater willingness to present one's answers and thus create more positive feelings toward one's answers and the instructional experience (Garibaldi, 1976; Gunderson & Johnson, 1980), as well as more positive attitudes toward the instructional tasks and subject areas (Garibaldi, 1976; Gunderson & Johnson, 1980; R. Johnson & Johnson, 1979; Johnson, Johnson, & Skon, 1979; Wheeler & Ryan, 1973).

Instructional Outcomes

There has been a great deal of research on the relationship among cooperative, competitive, and individualistic efforts and the cognitive and affective outcomes of instruction (Johnson & R. Johnson, 1975, 1978). According to hundreds of research studies that have been conducted, dramatically different learning outcomes will result from the use of the different goal structures. While space is too short in this chapter to review all of the research, the evidence concerning achievement, perspective-taking, self-esteem, psychological health, liking for other students, and positive attitudes toward school personnel such as teachers and principals will be discussed.

Achievement

Johnson, Maruyama, Johnson, Nelson, and Skon (1980) recently completed a meta-analysis of 108 studies comparing the relative effects of cooperative, competitive, and individualistic learning situations on achievement. The results strongly indicate that cooperative learning promotes higher achievement than do competitive and individualistic instruction. These results hold for all age levels, for all subject areas, and for tasks involving concept attainment, verbal problem-solving, categorizing, spatial problem-solving, retention and memory, motor performance, and guessing-judging-predicting. For rote-decoding and correcting tasks, cooperation does not seem to be superior. The average student in a cooperative situation performs at approximately the eightieth percentile of students in competitive and individualistic situations.

Perspective-Taking

An important instructional question is, "Which goal structure is most conducive to promoting the emergence of social perspective-taking abilities?" A series of studies have found that cooperativeness is positively related to the ability to take the emotional perspective of others, and that competitiveness is related to egocentrism (Johnson, 1980; Barnett, Matthews, & Howard, 1979). Cooperative learning experiences, furthermore, have been found to promote greater cognitive and emotional perspective-taking abilities than either competitive or individualistic learning experiences (Bridgeman, 1977; Johnson, Johnson, Johnson, & Anderson, 1976).

Self-Esteem

Schools are concerned with promoting student self-esteem for a variety of reasons, including school and postschool achievement and general psychological health and well-being. There is correlational evidence that cooperativeness is positively related to self-esteem in students throughout elementary, junior, and senior high school in rural, urban, and suburban settings; competitiveness is generally unrelated to self-esteem; and individualistic attitudes tend to be related to feelings of worthlessness and self-rejection (Gunderson & Johnson, 1980; Johnson & Ahlgren, 1976; Johnson, Johnson, & Anderson, 1978; Johnson & Norem-Hebeisen, 1977; Norem-Hebeisen & Johnson, 1980). There is experimental evidence indicating that cooperative learning experiences, compared with individualistic ones, result in higher self-esteem (Johnson, Johnson, & Scott, 1978); that cooperative learning experiences promote higher self-esteem than does learning in a traditional classroom (Blaney, et al., 1977; Geffner, 1978); and that failure in competitive situations promotes increased self-derogation (Ames, Ames, & Felker, 1977).

In a series of studies with suburban junior and senior high school students Norem-Hebeisen and Johnson (1980) examined the relationship among cooperative, competitive, and individualistic attitudes and ways of conceptualizing one's worth from the information that is available about oneself. Four primary ways of deriving self-esteem are: (a) basic self-acceptance (a belief in the intrinsic acceptability of oneself); (b) conditional self-acceptance (acceptance contingent on meeting external standards and expectations); (c) self-evaluation (one's estimate of how one compares with one's peers); and (d) real–ideal congruence (correspondence between what one thinks one is and what one thinks one should be). Attitudes toward cooperation are related to basic self-acceptance and positive self-evaluation compared to peers, whereas attitudes toward competition are related to conditional self-acceptance, and individualistic attitudes are related to basic self-rejection.

Psychological Health

The ability to build and maintain cooperative relationships is a primary manifestation of psychological health. Johnson and Norem-Hebeisen (1977) compared the attitudes of high school seniors toward cooperation, competition, and individualism with their responses on the Minnesota Multiphasic Personality Inventory (MMPI). They found that attitudes toward cooperation were significantly negatively correlated with 9 of the 10 scales indicating psychological pathology. Attitudes toward competition were significantly negatively correlated with 7 of the 10 psychological pathology scales. Attitudes toward individualism were significantly positively related to 9 of the 10 pathology scales. Both cooperation and competition involve relationships with other people, whereas individualistic activities involve isolation from other people. These findings indicate that an emphasis on cooperative involvement with other people and on appropriate competition during socialization may promote psychological health and well-being, whereas social isolation may promote psychological illness.

In addition, cooperative attitudes were significantly positively related to emotional maturity, well adjusted social relations, strong personal identity, the ability to resolve conflicts between self-perceptions and adverse information about oneself, amount of social participation, and basic trust and optimism. Attitudes toward competition were significantly related to emotional maturity, lack of a need for affection, the ability to resolve conflicts between self-perceptions and adverse information about oneself, social participation, and basic trust and optimism. Individualistic attitudes were significantly related to delinquency, emotional immaturity, social maladjustment, self-alienation, inability to resolve conflicts between self-perceptions and adverse information about oneself, self-rejection, lack of social participation, and basic distrust and pessimism.

Liking for Other Students

There is considerable evidence that cooperative experiences, compared with competitive and individualistic ones, result in more positive interpersonal relationships characterized by mutual liking, positive attitudes toward each other, mutual concern, friendliness, attentiveness, feelings of obligation to other students, and a desire to win the respect of other students (Johnson & R. Johnson, 1975, 1978). There is evidence that cooperative learning experiences, compared with individualistic ones, promote more positive attitudes toward heterogeneity among peers (Johnson, Johnson, & Scott, 1978), and that cooperativeness is related to liking peers who are smarter or less smart than oneself (Johnson & Ahlgren, 1976; Johnson, Johnson, & Anderson, 1978). In studies involving students from different ethnic groups, handicapped and nonhandicapped students, and male and female junior high school students, the evidence indicates that cooperative learning experiences, compared with competitive and individualistic ones, promotes more positive attitudes among heterogeneous students (Armstrong, Johnson, & Balow, 1980; Cook, 1978; Cooper, Johnson, Johnson, &

Wilderson, 1980; DeVries & Slavin, 1978; Johnson, Rynders, Johnson, Schmidt, & Haider, 1979; Rynders, Johnson, Johnson, & Schmidt, in press; Slavin, 1978).

Liking for School Personnel

The more favorable students' attitudes toward cooperation, the more they believe that teachers, teacher aides, counselors, and principals are important and positive; that teachers care about and want to increase students' learning; that teachers like and accept students as individuals; and that teachers and principals want to be friends with students (Gunderson & Johnson, 1980; Johnson & Ahlgren, 1976; Johnson, Johnson, & Anderson, 1978). Moreover, these findings hold in elementary, junior high, and senior high schools in rural, suburban, and urban school districts. In suburban junior and senior high schools, student competitiveness becomes positively related to perceptions of being liked and supported personally and academically by teachers. Individualistic attitudes are consistently unrelated to attitudes toward school personnel. There are also several field experimental studies that demonstrate that students experiencing cooperative instruction like the teacher better and perceive the teacher as being more supportive and accepting, academically and personally, than do students experiencing competitive and individualistic instruction (Gunderson & Johnson, 1980; Johnson, Johnson, Johnson, & Anderson, 1976; Johnson, Johnson, & Scott, 1978; Johnson, Johnson, & Tauer, 1979; Tjosvold, Marino & Johnson, 1977; Wheeler & Ryan, 1973).

Summary

Perhaps the most important aspect of group dynamics a teacher can control is the way in which learning goals are structured. The structure of the learning goals controls how students interact with each other which, in turn, greatly affects the cognitive and affective outcomes of instruction. When teachers wish to promote positive interaction among students (characterized by peer acceptance, support, and liking; student–student exchange of information; motivation to learn; and emotional involvement in learning), a cooperative goal structure should be used and competitive and individualistic goal structures should be avoided. The emphasis on positive goal interdependence among students not only will create the supportive, accepting, and caring relationships vital for socialization but will also promote achievement, perspective-taking ability, self-esteem, psychological health, liking for peers, and positive attitudes toward school personnel. Within any cooperative enterprise, however, controversies will inevitably arise. It is to the management of such conflicts that we now turn.

CONTROVERSY

In any learning situation, conflicts among ideas and opinions are inevitable. They will occur no matter what the teacher does. And, like all conflicts, controversies have the potential for producing highly constructive or highly destructive outcomes, depending on how they are managed. A *controversy* exists when one student's ideas, information, conclusions, theories, and opinions are incompatible with those of another, and the two then seek to reach an agreement. The conflict resides in the two students' attempts to reach a common position. When two students, for example, must come to an agreement on the answer to a math problem, and they disagree as to what the answer should be, a controversy exists.

If managed constructively, controversies can increase student motivation, creative insight, cognitive and social development, and learning. The process by which controversy sparks learning is outlined in Figure 4.1. It begins, as does all learning, with a student categorizing and organizing

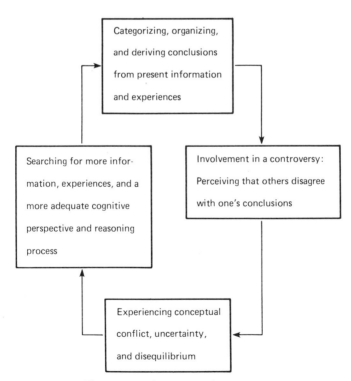

Figure 4.1. The process of controversy.

current information and experiences so that a conclusion is derived. When the student realizes that other students or the teacher are challenging the student's conclusion, a state of internal conceptual conflict, uncertainty, or disequilibrium is aroused. This uncertainty motivates an active search (called "epistemic curiosity" by Berlyne, 1971) for more information, new experiences, and a more adequate cognitive perspective and reasoning process in hopes of resolving the uncertainty. By adapting his or her cognitive perspective and reasoning through understanding the perspective and reasoning of others, a new or reorganized conclusion is derived. The outcomes of constructively managed controversy will be discussed and then the conditions determining whether controversy will be constructive or destructive will be reviewed.

Outcomes of Controversy

The process of controversy may lead to the following outcomes: epistemic curiosity, accuracy of cognitive perspective-taking, transition to a higher stage of cognitive reasoning, increased quality of problem-solving and decision making, greater creativity, and higher learning.

Epistemic Curiosity

Controversy among students creates conceptual conflict, which leads to epistemic curiosity. *Conceptual conflict* exists when two ideas do not seem to be compatible or when information being received does not seem to fit with what one already knows (Berlyne, 1957, 1966). Disagreement with another person can be a source of conceptual conflict that provokes attempts to explore the other person's ideas (Berlyne, 1966). The greater the disagreement among students, the more frequently the disagreement will occur. Moreover, the greater the number of people disagreeing with a student's position, the more competitive the context of the controversy; and the more affronted the student feels, the greater the conceptual conflict and uncertainty the student will experience (Asch, 1952; Burdick & Burnes, 1958; Festinger, 1964; Gerard & Greenbaum, 1962; Lowry & Johnson, 1980; Inagaki & Hatano, 1968, 1977; Tjosvold & Johnson, 1977, 1978; Tjosvold, Johnson, & Fabrey, 1978; Worchel & McCormick, 1963). Thus, there is evidence that controversy can create a conceptual conflict and epistemic curiosity.

Perspective-Taking

In resolving controversies, students need to be able to both comprehend the information being presented by their opposition and to understand the cognitive perspective their opposition is using to organize and interpret the information. A *cognitive perspective* consists of cognitive organization being used to give meaning to a person's knowledge and the structure of a person's reasoning. Tjosvold and Johnson (1977, 1978) and Tjosvold, Johnson, and Fabrey (1978) conducted three experiments in which they found that the presenoe of controversy promotes greater understanding of another person's cognitive perspective than does the absence of controversy. Students engaging in a controversy were better able subsequently to predict what line of reasoning their opponent would use in solving a future problem than were students who interacted without any controversy. Kurdek (in press) found that high cognitive perspective-taking skill was related to arguing with peers in students in the first through fourth grades.

Cognitive Reasoning

Cognitive development theorists (Flavell, 1963; Kohlberg, 1969; Piaget, 1948, 1950) have posited that it is repeated interpersonal controversies in which students are forced again and again to take cognizance of the perspective of others that promotes cognitive and moral development, the ability to think logically, and the reduction of egocentric reasoning. Such interpersonal conflicts are posited to create disequilibrium within students' cognitive structures, which motivate a search for a more adequate and mature process of reasoning. There are several studies that demonstrate that pairing a conserver with a nonconserver, and giving the pair conservation problems to solve, results in the conserver's answer prevailing on the great majority of conservation trials and in the nonconserver learning how to conserve (Botvin & Murray, 1975; Doise & Mugny, 1979; Doise, Mugny, & Perret-Clermont, 1976; Perret-Clermont, in press; Miller & Brownell, 1975; Mugny & Doise, 1978; Murray, 1972; Murray, Ames, & Botvin, 1977; Silverman & Geiringer, 1973; Smedslund, 1961; Silverman & Stone, 1972). There are a number of studies that demonstrate that when students are placed in a group with peers who use a higher stage of moral reasoning, and the group is required to make a decision as to how a moral dilemma should be resolved, advances in the students' level of moral reasoning result (Blatt, 1969; Blatt & Kohlberg, 1973; Crockenberg & Nicolayev, 1977; Keasey, 1973; Kuhn, Langer, Kohlberg, & Haan, 1977; LeFurgy & Woloshin, 1969; Maitland & Goldman, 1974; Rest, Turiel, & Kohlberg, 1969; Turiel, 1966). Taken together, these studies provide evidence that controversies among students can promote transitions to higher stages of cognitive and moral reasoning. Such findings are important as there is little doubt that higher levels of cognitive and moral reasoning cannot be directly taught (Inhelder & Sinclair, 1969; Sigel & Hooper, 1968; Sinclair, 1969; Smedslund, 1961a, 1961b; Turiel, 1973; Wallach & Sprott, 1964; Wallach, Wall, & Anderson, 1967; Wohlwill & Lowe, 1962).

Quality of Problem-Solving

The purpose of controversy within a group is to arrive at the highest quality problem solution or decision that is possible. There is evidence that the occurrence of a constroversy within a group does result in a higher quality problem solution and decision (Boulding, 1964; Glidewell, 1953; Hall & Williams, 1966, 1970; Hoffman & Maier, 1961; Hoffman, Harburg, & Maier, 1962; Maier & Hoffman, 1964; Maier & Solem, 1952). Furthermore, disagreements within a group have been found to provide a greater amount of information and variety of facts, and a change in the salience of known information which, in turn, results in shifts in judgment (Anderson & Graesser, 1976; Kaplan, 1977; Kaplan & Miller, 1977; Vinokur & Burnstein, 1974).

Creativity

Controversy is an important aspect of gaining creative insight by seeing a problem from a different perspective and reformulating it in a way that lets new orientations to a solution emerge. There is evidence that controversy increases the number of ideas, quality of ideas, feelings of stimulation and enjoyment, and originality of expression in creative problem-solving (Bahn, 1964; Bolen & Torrance, 1976; Dunnette, Campbell, & Jaastad, 1963; Falk & Johnson, 1977; Peters & Torrance, 1972; Torrance, 1970, 1971, 1973; Triandis, Bass, Ewen, & Mikesele, 1963). And there is also evidence that controversy results in more creative problem solutions, with more member satisfaction, compared to group efforts that do not include controversy (Glidewell, 1953; Hall & Williams, 1966, 1970; Hoffman, Harburg, & Maier, 1962; Maier & Hoffman, 1964; Rogers, 1970). These studies further demonstrated that controversy encourages group members to dig into a problem, raise issues, and settle them in ways that show the benefits of a wide range of ideas being used, as well as resulting in a high degree of emotional involvement in and commitment to solving the problems the group is working on.

Achievement

Finally, there is evidence that controversy increases the amount of mastery and retention of the subject matter being learned (Lowry & Johnson, 1980; Smith, Johnson & Johnson, 1980). Furthermore, students who experience conceptual conflict resulting from controversy are better able to generalize the principles they learn to a wider variety of situations than are students who do not experience such conceptual conflict (Inagaki & Hatano, 1968, 1977).

Student–Student Interaction

Although controversy can operate in a beneficial way, it will not do so under all conditions. As with all conflict, the potential for either constructive or destructive outcomes is present in a controversy. Whether positive or negative consequences result depends on the conditions under which controversy occurs and the way in which it is managed. These conditions and procedures include: the goal structure within which the controversy occurs, the heterogeneity among students, the amount of relevant information distributed among students, the ability of students to disagree with each other without creating defensiveness, and the perspective-taking skills of the students.

Duetsch (1973) emphasizes that the context in which conflicts occur has important effects on whether the conflict turns out to be constructive or destructure. There are two possible contexts for controversy: cooperative and competitive. Furthermore, there are several ways in which a cooperative context facilitates constructive controversy whereas a competitive context promotes destructive controversy:

1. In order for controversy to be constructive, information must be accurately communicated. As was discussed previously, communication of information is far more complete, accurate, encouraged, and utilized within a cooperative rather than a competitive context.
2. Constructive controversy requires a supportive climate in which students feel safe enough to challenge each other's ideas. This evidence has already been reviewed, and it indicates that cooperation provides a far more supportive climate than does competition.
3. In order for controversy to be constructive, it must be valued. Cooperative learning experiences, compared with individualistic ones, promotes a belief that controversy is constructive (Johnson, Johnson, & Scott, 1978).
4. Constructive controversy requires dealing with feelings as well as with ideas and information. There is evidence that cooperativeness is positively related and competitiveness negatively related to the ability to understand what other people are feeling and why they are feeling that way (see previous discussion).
5. How controversies are defined has great impact on how constructively they are managed. Within a cooperative context, conflicts tend to be defined as problems to be jointly solved, whereas within a competitive context conflicts tend to be defined as "win–lose" situations (Deutsch, 1973; Rubin & Brown, 1975).
6. Constructive controversy requires that students recognize similarities

between positions as well as differences. Students participating in a controversy within a cooperative context identify more of the similarities between their positions than do students participating in a controversy within a competitive context (Judd, 1978).

A second major factor influencing whether controversy results in constructive or destructive outcomes is the heterogeneity among the students involved. While the research concerning this issue is reviewed within the section on group composition, it may be stated here that the differences among students in terms of personality, sex, attitudes, background, social class, cognitive reasoning strategies, cognitive perspectives, information, and skills, lead to diverse organization and processing of present information and experiences, which in turn begins the cycle of controversy. There is evidence that more controversy occurs in heterogeneous than in homogeneous groups (Fiedler, Meuwese, & Oonk, 1961; Torrance, 1961).

If controversy is to lead to learning, the group members must possess information that is relevant to the solution of the problem on which they are working. The more information available, the easier it should be to solve their problem. There are a number of studies that demonstrate that groups that have more information about a problem usually perform better than do groups with less information (Goldman, 1965; Laughlin & Branch, 1972; Laughlin & Johnson, 1966; Laughlin, Branch, & Johnson, 1969; Laughlin, Keer, Davis, Haiff, & Marciniak, 1975; Tuckman, 1967). Having relevant information available, however, does not mean that it will be utilized. For example, when the task is such that the correct answer is immediately recognizable when it is proposed, it tends to be immediately accepted (Laughlin & Bitz, 1975), but when the task is such that the correct answer is not immediately recognizable, it may take one group member to propose it and another member to support the answer before the group adopts it (Laughlin, Keer, Davis, Haiff, & Marciniak, 1975). This later study, furthermore, found that even when the expertise of the group members was uniformly very low, the group would still successfully solve the problem about 20% of the time.

In order for controversies to be managed constructively, students need to be able to disagree with each other's ideas while confirming each other's personal competence. There is evidence that disagreeing with other people while imputing that they are incompetent tends to increase their commitment to their own ideas and their rejection of the other's ideas (Brown, 1968, Tjosvold, 1974). Tjosvold, Johnson, and Fabrey (1980) and Tjosvold, Johnson, and Lerner (in press) conducted a pair of studies in which disagreeing while confirming the other's competence was compared with disagreeing while imputing the other was incompetent. They found that confirmation of the opponent's competence resulted in being better liked, the opponent being less critical of one's ideas, more open-minded to and more interested in learning more of one's ideas, and the opponent being more willing to incorporate one's information and reasoning into the opponent's own analysis of the problem.

Perhaps the most important set of skills for exchanging information and opinions within a controversy is perspective-taking. More information, both personal and impersonal, is disclosed when one is interacting with a person engaging in perspective-taking behaviors (Colson, 1968; Noonan-Wagner, 1975; Sermat & Smyth, 1973; Taylor, Altman, & Sorrentino, 1969). Perspective-taking ability increases people's ability to phrase messages so that they are easily understood by others and to comprehend accurately other people's messages (Feffer & Suchotliff, 1966; Flavell, 1968; Hogan & Henley, 1970). Engaging in perspective-taking behaviors in conflicts results in increased understanding and retention of the opponent's information and perspective (Johnson, 1971). During controversies, perspective-taking behaviors (compared with egocentrically emphasizing one's own information and perspective) results in more creative and higher quality solutions (Falk & Johnson, 1977) and in greater gains in accuracy of problem-solving (Johnson, 1977). Finally, perspective-taking behaviors promote more positive perspections of the information exchange process, fellow problem-solvers, and the problem-solving experience (Falk & Johnson, 1977; Johnson, 1971, 1977; Noonan-Wagner, 1975).

GROUP COMPOSITION

There has been a considerable emphasis on homogeneous grouping within education. Ability grouping or tracking separates students defined as being high, medium, and low in academic ability into separate classrooms within such basic areas as reading. Yet there is no consistent evidence supporting such practices and, in fact, there is evidence indicating that such practices produce negative consequences for both achievement and development.

It is reasonable to believe that a group's behavior will be affected by the distribution and patterning of such member characteristics as abilities, knowledge, resources, attitudes, interests, personality dispositions, age, sex, and social status. Within educational endeavors, the issue of homogeneity or heterogeneity of students must be considered in terms of the influence of group composition on achievement, cognitive and social development, and socialization. Group composition must be evaluated in reference to the demands confronting the group, rather than in a vacuum. In addressing the issue of how group composition affects academic achievement, cognitive and social development, and socialization, current research on group problem-solving, ability grouping, and cross-age interaction will be reviewed.

Achievement and Problem-Solving

There is contradictory evidence concerning the effectiveness of homogeneous and heterogeneous groups in problem-solving. Several studies have found heterogeneous groups to be superior to homogeneous groups in terms of the quality of the solution, creativity of the group solution, and member satisfaction with the solution (Amaria, Brian, & Leith, 1969; Ghiselli & Lodahl, 1958; Goldman, 1965; Hoffman, 1959; Hoffman & Maier, 1961; Hoffman, Harburg, & Maier, 1962; Pelz, 1956; Triandis, Hall, & Ewen, 1965; Ziller, 1955; Ziller & Exline, 1958). Whereas, other studies have found that either homogeneous groups arrive at better solutions than do heterogeneous groups or that there is no difference between heterogeneous and homogeneous groups in terms of the quality of group solutions (Altman & McGinnies, 1960; Fiedler, Meuwese, & Oonk, 1961; Haythorn, et al., 1956; Shaw, 1960; Falk & Johnson, 1977). The failure of heterogeneous groups to always outperform homogeneous groups raises possibilities that when relevant expertise is lacking in the group, heterogeneity may not affect the quality of problem solving, or when group members do not have the skills to exchange information effectively, heterogeneity may not be utilized productively. In general, literature indicates that when there are varied functions to perform in the group, when group members have the social skills needed to exchange and utilize information, and when expertise relevant to the group's task is present in the group, heterogeneity is an asset.

Ability Grouping

It is a common practice in many schools to separate students through ability grouping or tracking so that the rapid learners are placed in one class, the average learners in another, and the slow learners in a third. The rationale for ability grouping is that narrowing the ability range in the classroom facilitates the provision of more appropriate learning tasks, makes more teacher time available to students of a given ability level, and stimulates teachers to gear their teaching to the level of the group (Goldberg, Passow, & Justman, 1966). While the practice has been widespread for at least 80 years, and heavily researched for 50 years, there is no solid evidence that any student benefits from such segregation. Ability grouping remains a very dubious practice. Some of its more serious problems include (Johnson, 1979):

1. The reliability and validity of the measures to differentiate slow, average, and rapid learners are low. IQ tests are not precise enough to make such judgments concerning students, especially if the students are not white middle-class children. Lower-class students, impulsive students, students whose basic language is not English, and many other types of students are consistently misclassified on the basis of IQ tests. Furthermore, there is more to being gifted intellectually than IQ. Creativity and leadership, for example, are also important qualities. Psychologists have not yet derived a definition of intelligence that is adequate enough to construct a valid and reliable measure of it. For many reasons, the tools needed to differentiate among slow, average, and rapid learners are not available at present.

2. Because of the lack of validity and reliability of the measures used to assign students to ability levels, many students are originally sent to the wrong level. The second problem with using ability grouping is that once misclassified, it is difficult for a student to be reassigned. Once labeled, always labeled! Jackson (1964) found that while 40% of all students should be transferred from one ability level to another, only between 1 to 5% were actually transferred. The rigidity of level membership once students are assigned invalidates the practice of ability grouping in schools.

3. There is considerable evidence that ability grouping is segregated on the basis of social class and ethnic membership (Eash, 1961; Yates, 1966; Goldberg, Passow, & Justman, 1966; Husen & Svensson, 1960; Johnson, 1970; Douglas, 1964). White students who come from middle- or upper-class families and who are clean, well-clothed, and well-behaved have a greater chance of being placed in the high ability track than their measured ability would seem to justify.

4. There is no consistent evidence that ability grouping will increase the achievement of students at any ability level. The rapid learners do not benefit with higher achievement and in some cases the average and slow learners' achievement is damaged by the absence of more intellectually oriented peers to interact with (Borg, 1964; Eash, 1961; Goldberg, Passow, & Justman, 1966; Millman & Johnson, 1964; Svensson, 1962).

5. There is no consistent evidence that ability grouping either raises or lowers students' self-esteem. Some studies find that the stigma attached to being placed in the low ability track reduces self-esteem, while other studies find that high achievers' self-esteem is somewhat reduced by homogeneous grouping. Yet other studies contradict such findings or find that ability grouping in and of itself has no effect on self-esteem.

6. There is evidence that teachers expect less of students placed in low ability tracks and generally underestimate the capabilities of each student (Goldberg, Passow, & Justman, 1966; Tillman & Hull, 1964; Wilson, 1963).

7. Ability grouping, by reducing the heterogeneity among students in the classroom, prevents students from obtaining needed socializing experiences and from gaining valuable insights from others. The basic social competencies needed for healthy psychological development may be better provided for in heterogeneous classrooms.

Because of these and other problems, ability grouping does not seem to be justifiable as a procedure to improve instruction or to facilitate intellectual or social development. There are other more effective means of ensuring every student is fully challenged and learns maximally. The instructional strategies teachers use have far more powerful effects on student achievement and socialization than does the separation of students into ability levels.

Same Age versus Mixed Age

Age homogeneity, which was not introduced into American schools until the mid-nineteenth century, is now firmly entrenched (Kett, 1974). Most school classrooms are age-graded so that students spend most of the school day in the presence of peers who are within 12 months of being the same age. This is an unusual situation in the sense that in most cultures children interact with multiage peers rather than with peers of the same chronological age (Hartup, 1978). Barker and Wright (1955) in a study done in the United States found that approximately 65% of children's interactions with other children outside the school environment involved individuals who differed in age by *more* than 12 months.

Hartup (1978) argues that mixed-age groups are well-suited to children's needs. He states:

Social adaptation requires skills in both seeking help (dependency) and giving it (nurturance); being passive and being sociable; being able to attack others (aggression) and being able to contain one's hostility; being intimate and being self-reliant. Since there is a greater likelihood that some of these behaviors will occur in interaction with younger children than with older children (e.g., nurturance), some in interaction with agemates rather than non-agemates (e.g., aggression), and some in interaction with older children rather than younger children (e.g., dependency), mixed-age social contacts would seem to serve children in ways that same-age contacts cannot [p. 147].

There is some evidence that mixed-age classes might be preferable to same-age classes in elementary schools. Ferguson (1965) found that both second and fifth graders worked harder at simple tasks when social rewards were supplied by a non-agemate than by an agemate. On a social problem-solving task third graders worked with greater speed, success, and task persistence when they were the only third grader in a triad than when they were in the majority (Graziano, French, Brownell, & Hartup, 1976).

There is some evidence that social learning occurs more effectively in interaction with older children. Allen and Feldman (1976) found that in tutoring situations, children prefer to be taught by children older than themselves. In addition, Thelen and Kirkland (1976) found that reciprocal imitation is more characteristic of children's interactions with older children than with younger children, and Peifer (1971) found that older children are more effective models than younger children. Finally, Lougee (1977) found that older children are especially good models in situations calling for difficult perceptual judgments or complicated skills rather than declarations of personal preferences or tastes.

There is evidence that the effects of previous isolation from peers may be best repaired in interaction with younger than with same-age peers. Furman, Rache, and Hartup (1977) located 24 socially withdrawn children in five childcare centers by means of observations conducted over 2-week periods. The identified children were social isolates but were not autistic or emotionally disturbed. For 8 children, an intervention was devised consisting of 15 daily play sessions involving a second child who was 18 months younger than the subject. For 8 children, daily play sessions with a peer who was within 4 months of their age were arranged. The remaining 8 children received no treatment at all. Significant improvement in sociability occurred in both experimental groups as contrasted to the no-treatment group (which did not change), but greater increases in sociability occurred among the children exposed to younger peers than among those exposed to same-age peers.

Summary

The question facing teachers concerning group composition is whether students should be placed in homogeneous or heterogeneous groups. Traditionally, students have been tracked on the basis of ability into separate classrooms or have been placed into homogeneous groups with regard to ability, skills, or learning deficits within the classroom. While the research findings are not consistent, the overall weight of the evidence indicates that higher achievement by rapid, average, and slow learners will result when they are placed in heterogeneous learning groups. This is especially true when students learn within cooperative groups (Johnson & Johnson, 1978; Johnson, Skon, & Johnson, 1978; Skon, Johnson, & Johnson, 1980; Wodarski et al., 1973). The weight of the evidence, furthermore, is against the use of ability grouping and tracking, and there are a variety of experiences important for socialization and cognitive and social development in classrooms where students of various ages are given the opportunity to interact and learn together.

CLASSROOM AND GROUP NORMS

Students should not run in the hallways. Students should not use foul language in the classroom. Students should not strike classmates or peers. Students should pay attention when the teacher speaks. Students should do their homework. Students should not arrive for class late. All of these expectations are norms. *Norms* refer to the common beliefs regarding appropriate behavior (Johnson, 1970). They dictate how members of the school, classroom, or group are expected to behave. Some norms apply to all people within the classroom whereas others apply only to the teacher or to the students. Because norms refer to the expected behavior sanctioned (reinforced or punished) by members of the classroom or group, they have a specific "ought to" or "must" quality; group members must not disrupt the group's work, group members ought to participate in discussions, and so on. The norms of any group vary in their importance. Those that are less important for the objectives and values of the classroom or group usually allow for a greater range of behavior and bring less severe pressures for people to conform than do norms that are highly relevant for group functioning.

For a classroom or group norm to influence students' behavior, they must recognize that it exists, be aware that other group members accept and follow the norm, and accept and follow it themselves. At first students may conform to a classroom or group norm because groups typically reward conforming behavior and punish nonconforming behavior. Later students may internalize the norm and conform to it automatically, even when no other group members are present.

Norms influence interpersonal relationships by helping people to know what is expected of them and what they should expect from others. Classroom and group life is orderly and predictable partly because of norms. Furthermore, norms have powerful influences on the behavior of students and teachers. They also influence how people view their physical and social worlds (Festinger, 1950; Sherif, 1936), and what attitudes and values people adopt (Newcomb, 1952). Group norms can support and liberate members so that each one can react as one personally feels (Asch, 1952, Milgram, 1965). Finally, they greatly influence how students and teachers will behave in the classroom and during instructional activities.

It is evident that the norms develop in student peer groups may help or hinder the educational process. Coleman (1961) found in a survey of 10 midwestern high schools that the student norms valued athletic achievement over academic success. In the schools where these norms were most powerful, the students who endorsed academic values were not the most intelligent but were the ones most willing to work hard at an activity that was relatively unrewarded by their peers. Orth (1963) in a study of the Harvard Graduate School of Business found that the greatest number of overachievers were in a student subgroup that endorsed academic values, whereas the greatest number of underachievers were in a student subgroup that was nonacademically oriented. Hargreaves (1967) found that while some student informal peer groups valued academic achievement and looked down upon "mucking around in class," other student informal peer groups valued obstructing teachers so that less material was covered in class and looked down upon students who cooperated with teachers' efforts to instruct. In one informal peer group truancy was encouraged, physical violence was used against students who cooperated with teachers, and destruction of school property was valued. Other studies in both educational (Hughes, Becker, & Geer, 1962) and industrial (Roethlisberger & Dickson, 1939) settings suggest that informal peer group norms can influence members to achieve at a lower level than is desired by the organization. It is not uncommon for informal peer group norms among students to explicitly express disapproval towards those who achieve too high or who overexert themselves for grades (don't be a "curve-breaker"). Yet when teachers can successfully initiate classroom norms valuing high achievement and cooperation with the instructional program, a positive classroom climate can result.

Traditionally, schools in the United States have chosen not to utilize group norms systematically as a way to increase student achievement and control disruptive student behavior. Consequently, peer group norms have often hindered academic efforts. Yet the systematic use of peer group norms have been successfully used to resocialize delinquents (Pilnick, et al., 1966; Empey & Rabow, 1961; McCorkle, Elias, & Bixby, 1958), drug addicts (Yablonsky, 1962), and alcoholics. Consciously changing peer group norms has also been shown to eliminate discipline problems (Lippitt, 1964). One of the major advantages of structuring learning goals cooperatively (as compared with competitively and individualistically) is that the peer group norms will encourage achievement and involvement in instructional activities (Bronfenbrenner, 1962; Deutsch, 1949; DeVries & Edwards, 1974; DeVries, Edwards, & Wells, 1974; DeVries, Muse, & Wells, 1971; Hulten, 1974; Spilerman, 1971; Haines & McKeachie, 1967), as well as more on-task, studying behavior and less off-task, apathetic, nonstudying, and disruptive behaviors on the part of students (Wodarski et al., 1973; DeVries, Edwards, & Wells, 1974a).

GROUP SIZE

The number of students within a class or learning group has several important implications for academic achievement, cognitive and social development, and general socialization. Although optimum group size depends on the group's task, composition of members, time available, level of social skills of students, and many other factors, some of the more important aspects of group size are as follows:

1. As the size of the group increases, the total resources of the group increases, but not the usable resources (Deutsch, 1969; Thomas & Fink, 1963). The range of abilities, expertise, and skills that are available to the group increases with the increasing group size, as well as the sheer number of "hands" that are available for acquiring and processing information. The usable resource per member, however, will often increase at a slower rate than will the total resources and often will, beyond a certain point, not increase at all. Adding a new member to a group of three will have more impact, for example, than adding a new member to a group of thirty.

2. As the size of the group increases, the heterogeneity among members will also increase. The probability that any given characteristic will appear increases as the size of the group increases, but the probability that all members have a given characteristic decreases as the size of the group increases.

3. As the size of the group increases, the opportunity for individual participation and reward decreases. The larger the group, the less opportunity each student has to participate in a discussion, the greater the feelings of threat and the greater the inhibition of impulses to participate, and the more a few members will dominate (Bales, Strodtbeck, Mills, & Roseborough, 1951; Gibb, 1951; Stephan & Mishler, 1952). Barker and Gump (1964) found that as school size increases, individual participation in high school life decreases.

4. As the size of the group increases, the more the member's energy will have to be directed towards coordinating and assembling the contributions of the individual members (Deutsch, 1969).

5. As the size of the group increases, the less liked, supported, and valued individual members will be, and the greater the absenteeism, formality, conflict, and dissatisfaction with the group (Baumgartel & Sobol, 1959; Cleland, 1955; Katz, 1949; O'Dell, 1968; Slater, 1958). Olson (1971) found that as class size became larger, interpersonal regard among students decreased.

6. As the size of the group increases, the clarity of member's perceptions of each other's degree of mastery of the material being learned will decrease.

Steiner (1972) argues that the type of task interacts with group size, so that in additive tasks (i.e., the outcome is the result of some combination of individual efforts) and disjunctive tasks (i.e., the outcome depends on at least one group member successfully performing the task) achievement will increase as the size of the group increases. But on conjunctive tasks (i.e., the outcome depends on everyone in the group accomplishing the task) performance may go down as group size increases. There are several studies that suggest that class size makes no difference in student achievement, but Sitkei (1968) stresses that there are twice as many studies that favor smaller classes over larger classes than vice versa. In a recent review of the research, Glass and Smith (1978) conducted a meta-analysis of the research on class size and achievement and, when the well-controlled studies were separated from the poorly controlled studies, a clear relationship between class size and achievement was demonstrated. They found that achievement increases dramatically as class size decreases from above 20 to 2. Since it does not seem realistic to recommend that class size in American schools be reduced to under 5, 10, or even 15 students, Glass and Smith's findings may imply that more instruction should take place in small learning groups rather than with an entire class as a whole.

Taken in its entirety, the evidence concerning group size indicates that the optimal size of learning groups within the classroom might be from 4 to 6 members. Such a group is large enough that enough diversity and resources are present to facilitate achievement, and is small enough that everyone's reosurces are utilized, everyone will participate and receive rewards for their contributions. This size group also minimizes the energy needed to coordinate members' contributions, acceptance and support is highlighted, and the achievement level of each student is clearly perceived by other group members. When students are very young, however, or when there is a marked lack of the social skills necessary for working productively with other students, pairs and triads may be more productive than larger groups.

GROUP PROCESSES AND THE COGNITIVE SOCIAL-PSYCHOLOGICAL VIEW OF LEARNING

In the first chapter a cognitive social-psychological view of learning is presented that emphasizes as a primary determinant of behavior the information concerning appropriate behavior gained from interaction with others. There are two ways in which messages concerning appropriate behavior are sent by significant others; directly through expectations and indirectly through structural influences such as the goal structure of the situation and the situational norms. There can be little doubt that developmentally, peers become increasingly important influences on students' behavior and attitudes as students grow older and become more and more independent of adults. Despite the prevailing concentration on adult–child relationships in education, it is the messages from peers that in most cases students choose to attend to, believe, and incorporate into their decisions.

The group processes of the classroom determine the indirect influences on students' perceptions of what is appropriate behavior. By definition group norms communicate such expectations. Of equal importance is the goal structure of the situation. Watson and Johnson (1972) highlight the importance of situational structure in the Structure-Process-Attitude theory of attitude change. Each goal structure implies certain patterns of behavior that are expressed in the definition of the student role. The role of the student includes facilitating each other's learning in the cooperative situation, frustrating each other's learning in the competitive situation, and ignoring each other's learning in the individualistic situation. Such role expectations determine how students interact with classmates. The interaction patterns determine what information is received from peers and the value attached to the information, as well as achievement and other instructional outcomes. Especially important to learning is the feedback from peers in a cooperative situation that achievement-oriented behavior is desired and appropriate, as compared to the peer feedback that off-task, nonachievement-oriented behavior is appropriate in the competitive situation. Goal structures establish role expectations as to how students should behave, and in the process of carrying out the role, the information they receive and the value they attach to the information are affected. Cooperative interaction, furthermore, strengthens the positiveness of relationships among students, thus increasing the importance of peer feedback concerning appropriate behavior. In essence, the goal structure influences students' perceptions of appropriate behavior and affects the probability that students place on the likelihood of being able to fulfill such needs as affiliation and belonging. Thus, the evidence reviewed in this chapter indicates that the nature of student–student interaction and group dynamics affects the quality and quantity of perceived messages from others regarding appropriate or expected behavior.

SUMMARY AND CONCLUSIONS

Teaching and learning do not typically take place within a dyadic relationship between an adult and a child. Students' learning takes place within a network of relationships with peers, and it is these relationships that form the context within which all learning takes place. Student–student relationships are an important and vital aspect of classroom learning and students' development and socialization. There is considerable evidence that peer relationships within the classroom contribute to general socialization, development of social competencies and general psychological health, management of agressive impulses, socialization of sex roles, internalization of values, acquisition of perspective-taking abilities, and achievement. Constructive peer relationships, however, do not take place automatically. They must be characterized by acceptance, liking, and support.

In order to ensure that accepting and supportive student–student relationships are developed, teachers may control the group dynamics affecting the interaction among students. There are several aspects of group dynamics that are important for such a purpose:

1. *The structure of learning goals.* It is important that students be primarily placed in cooperative learning groups and that competitive and individualistic learning are used sparingly.
2. *The way in which controversies are managed.* It is important that controversies be structured by the teacher in ways that ensure their constructive resolution.
3. *The heterogeneity among students.* It is important that students have the opportunity to interact with diverse peers with different perspectives, attitudes, backgrounds, abilities, and opinions, and of different ages.
4. *The classroom norms.* It is important that the norms of the classroom support achievement and appropriate behavior by students.
5. *The size of the learning groups.* It is important that the learning groups be large enough so that needed resources and diversity are present, but small enough so that everyone's resources are fully utilized, participation is high, acceptance and support of all members is possible, coordination is easy, and individual accountability for learning is feasible.

REFERENCES

Adler, A. H., Ansbacher, H. L., & Ansbacher, R. R. (Eds.). *The individual psychology of Alfred Adler.* New York: Basic Books, 1956.

Alexander, C., & Campbell, E. Peer influences on adolescent aspirations and attainments. *American Sociological Review,* 1964, *29,* 568–575.

Allen, V., & Feldman, R. Studies on the role of tutor. In V. L. Allen (Ed.), *Children as tutors.* New York: Academic Press, 1976.

Altman, I., & McGinnies, E. Interpersonal perception and communication in discussion groups of varied attitudinal composition. *Journal of Abnormal and Social Psychology,* 1960, *60,* 390–395.

Amaria, R., Brian, L., & Leith, G. Individual versus cooperative learning. *Educational Research,* 1969, *11,* 95–103.

Ames, C., Ames, R., & Felker, D. Informational and dispositional determinants of children's achievement attributions. *Journal of Educational Psychology,* 1977, *68,* 63–69.

Anderson, N., & Graesser, C. An information integration analysis of attitude change in group discussion. *Journal of Personality and Social Psychology,* 1976, *34,* 210–222.

Armstrong, B., Johnson, D. W., & Balow, B. Cooperative goal structure as a means of integrating learning-disabled with normal-progress elementary pupils. *Contemporary Educational Psychology,* in press, 1980.

Asch, S. E. *Social psychology.* Englewood Cliffs, New Jersey: Prentice-Hall, 1952.

Bahn, C. *The interaction of creativity and social facilitation in creative problem solving.* Doctoral dissertation, Columbia University, 1964. University Microfilms, No. 65–7499.

Bales, R., Strodtbeck, F., Mills, T., & Roseborough, M. Channels of communication in small groups. *American Sociological Review,* 1951, *16,* 461–468.

Barker, R., & Gump, P. *Big school, small school: High school size and student behavior.* Stanford, California: Stanford University Press, 1964.

Barker, R., & Wright, H. *Midwest and its children.* New York: Harper and Row, 1955.

Barnett, M., Matthews, K., & Howard, J. Relationship between competitiveness and empathy in 6- and 7-year-olds. *Developmental Psychology,* 1979, *15,* 221–222.

Baumgartel, H., & Sobol, R. Background and organizational factors in absenteeism. *Personnel Psychology,* 1959, *12,* 431–443.

Becker, H. Becoming a marijuana user. *American Journal of Sociology,* 1953, *59,* 235–242.

Becker, H. Marijuana use and the social context. *Social Problems,* 1955, *3,* 35–44.

Berlyne, D. Uncertainty and conflict: A point of contact between information-theory and behavior-theory concepts. *Psychological Review, 64,* 1957, 329–339.

Berlyne, D. Notes on intrinsic motivation and intrinsic reward in relation to instruction. In J. Bruner (Ed.), *Learning about learning* (Cooperative Research Monograph No. 15). Washington, D.C.: U.S. Department of Health, Education, and Welfare, Office of Education, 1966.

Berlyne, D. *Aesthetics and psychobiology.* New York: Appleton-Century-Crofts, 1971.

Blake, R. R., & Mouton, J. S. Comprehension of own and outgroup positions under intergroup competition. *Journal of Conflict Resolution,* 1961, *5,* 304–310.

Blaney, N., Stephen, C., Rosenfield, D., Aronson, E., & Sikes, J. Inter-dependence in the classroom: A field study. *Journal of Educational Psychology,* 1977, 69, 139–146.

Blatt, M. *The Effects of classroom discussion upon children's level of moral judgment.* Unpublished doctoral dissertation, University of Chicago, 1969.

Blatt, M., & Kohlberg, l The effects of classroom moral discussion upon children's level of moral judgment. In L. Kohlberg (Ed.), *Collected papers on moral development and moral education.* Harvard University: Moral Education and Research Foundation, 1973.

Bolen, L., & Torrance, E. *An experimental study of the influence of locus of control, dyadic interaction, and sex on creative thinking.* Paper presented at the meeting of the American Educational Research Association, San Francisco, April, 1976.

Borg, W. R. *An evaluation of ability grouping.* Cooperative Research Project, No. 577. Salt Lake City: Utah State University, 1964.

Botvin, G., & Murray, F. The efficacy of peer modeling and social conflict in the acquisition of conservation. *Child Development,* 1975, *45,* 796–799.

Boulding, E. Further Reflections on conflict management. In R. Kahn and E. Boulding (Eds.), *Power and conflict in organizations.* New York: Basic Books, 1964, 146–150.

Bower, S. *Early identification of emotionally handicapped children in school.* Springfield, Illinois: Thomas, 1960.

Bridgeman, D. *Cooperative, interdependent learning and its enhancement of role-taking in fifth grade students.* Paper presented at the meeting of the American Psychological Association, San Francisco, August, 1977.

Bronfenbrenner, U., Soviet methods of character education: Some implications for research. *Religious Education,* 1962, *57*(4, Res. Suppl.), 545–561.

Brown, B. Effects of the need to maintain face on interpersonal bargaining. *Journal of Experimental Social Psychology,* 1968, *4,* 107–122.

Burdick, H. A., & Burnes, A. J. A test of "strain toward symmetry" theories. *Journal of Abnormal and Social Psychology,* 1958, *57,* 367–369.

Chickering, A. *Education and Identity.* San Francisco: Jossey-Bass, 1969.

Cleland, S. *Influence of plant size on industrial relations.* Princeton, New Jersey: Princeton University Press, 1955.

Coleman, J. S. *The adolescent society.* New York: Macmillan, 1961.

Coleman, J. S., Campbell, E. Q., Hobson, C. J., McPartland, J., Mood, A. M., Weinfeld, F. D., & York, R. L. *Equality of educational opportunity.* Washington, D.C.: U.S. Office of Health, Education, & Welfare, 1966.

Colson, W. N. *Self-disclosure as a function of social approval.* Unpublished master's thesis, Howard University, 1968.

Combs, M., & Slaby, D. Social skills training with children. In B. Lahey & A. Kazdin (Eds.), *Advances in Clinical Child Psychology.* Vol. 1. New York: Plenum Press, 1977.

Cook, S. Interpersonal and attitudinal outcomes in cooperating interracial groups. *Journal of Research and Development in Education,* 1978, *12,* 97–113.

Cooper, L., Johnson, D. W., Johnson, R., & Wilderson, F. The effects of cooperation, competition, and individualization on cross-ethnic, cross-sex, and cross-ability friendships. *Journal of Social Psychology,* 1980.

Cowen, E., Pederson, A. Babijian, H., Izzo, L., & Trost, M. Long-term follow-up of early detected vulnerable children. *Journal of Consulting and Clinical Psychology,* 1973, *41*(3), 438–446.

Crain, R., & Weisman, C. *Discrimination, personality, and achievement: A survey of Northern Blacks.* New York: Seminar Press, 1972.

Crawford, J., & Haaland, G. Predecisional information seeking and subsequent conformity in the social influence process. *Journal of Personality and Social Psychology,* 1972, *23,* 112–119.

Crockenberg, S., & Nicolayev, J. *Stage transition in moral reasoning as related to conflict experienced in naturalistic settings.* Paper presented at the meeting of the Society for Research in Child Development, New Orleans, March, 1977.

Deutsch, M. An experimental study of the effects of cooperation and competition upon group process. *Human Relations,* 1949, *2,* 199–232.

Deutsch, M. Cooperation and trust: Some theoretical notes. In M. R. Jones (Ed.), *Nebraska symposium on motivation.* Lincoln, Nebraska: University of Nebraska Press, 1962, 275–320.

Deutsch, M. Conflicts: Productive and Destructive. *Journal of Social Issues,* 1969, *25,* 7–43.

Deutsch, M. *The resolution of conflict.* New Haven, Connecticut: Yale University Press, 1973.

DeVries, D. L., & Edwards, K. J. *Cooperation in the classroom: Towards a theory of alternative reward-task classroom structures.* Paper presented at the meeting of the American Educational Research Association, Chicago, Illinois, April, 1974.

DeVries, D. L., Edwards, K. J., & Wells, E. H. Teams-games-tournament in the social studies classroom: Effects on academic achievement, student attitudes, cognitive beliefs, and classroom climate. Report No. 173, Center for Social Organization of Schools. Baltimore: Johns Hopkins University, 1974.

DeVries, D. L., Muse, D., & Wells, E. H. The effects on students of working in cooperative groups: An exploratory study. Report No. 120, Center for Social Organization of Schools. Baltimore: Johns Hopkins University, 1971.

DeVries, D., & Slavin, R. Teams-games-tournaments: Review of ten classroom experiments. *Journal of Research and Development in Education,* 1978, *12,* 28–38.

Doise, W., & Mugny, G. Individual and collective conflicts of centrations in cognitive development. *European Journal of Social Psychology,* 1979, *9,* 105–108.

Doise, W., Mugny, G., & Perret-Clermont, A. Social interaction and cognitive development: Further evidence. *European Journal of Social Psychology,* 1976, *6,* 245–247.

Douglas, J. W. B. *The home and the school.* London: MacGibbon & Kee, 1964.

Dunnette, M. D., Campbell, J., & Jaastad, K. The effect of group participation on brainstorming effectiveness of two industrial samples. *Journal of Applied Psychology,* 1963, *47,* 30–37.

Eash, M. J. Grouping: What have we learned? *Educational Leadership,* 1961, *18,* 429–434.

Elseroad, H., & Goodman, S. *A survey of secondary school students' perceptions and attitudes towards use of drugs by teenagers: Parts I, II, III.* Rockville, Maryland: Montgomery County Public Schools, 1970.

Empey, L. T., & Rabow, J. The Provo experiment in delinquency rehabilitation. *American Sociological Review,* 1961, *26,* 679–695.

Fagot, B., & Patterson. G. An *in vivo* analysis of the reinforcing contingencies for sex-role behaviors in the preschool child. *Developmental Psyohology,* 1969, *1*(5), 563–568.

Falk, D., & Johnson, D. W. The effects of perspective-taking and egocentrism on problem solving in heterogeneous and homogeneous groups. *Journal of Social Psychology,* 1977, *102,* 63–72.

Feffer, M., & Suchotliff, L. Decentering implications of social interaction. *Journal of Personality and Social Psychology,* 1966, *4,* 415–422.

Ferguson, N. *Peers as social agents.* Unpublished master's thesis. University of Minnesota, 1965.

Festinger, L. Informal social communication. *Psychological Review,* 1950, *57,* 271–282.

Festinger, L., & Maccoby, N. On resistance to persuasive communications. *Journal of Abnormal and Social Psychology,* 1964, *68,* 359–366.

Fiedler, F. E., Meuwese, W., and Oonk, S. An exploratory study of group creativity in laboratory tasks. *Acta Psychology,* 1961, *18,* 100–119.

Flavell, J. *The developmental psychology of Jean Piaget.* Princeton, New Jersey: Van Nostrand, 1963.

Flavell, J. *The development of role-taking and communication skills in children.* New York: Wiley, 1968.

Freedman, M. B. *The student and campus climates of learning.* Washington, D.C.: U.S. Department of Health, Education, and Welfare, 1967.

Fromm-Reichmann, F. *Principles of intensive psychotherapy.* Chicago: University of Chicago Press, 1950.

Furman, W. *Friendship selections and individual peer interactions: A new approach to sociometric research.* Paper presented at biennial meetings of the Society for Research in Child Development, New Orleans, 1977.

Furman, W., Rache, D., & Hartup, W. Social rehabilitation of low interactive preschool children by peer intervention. *Child Development,* 1979, *50,* 915–922.

Garibaldi, A. *Cooperation, competition, and locus of control in Afro-American students.* Unpublished doctoral dissertation, University of Minnesota, 1976.

Geffner, R. *The effects of interdependent learning on self-esteem, interethnic relations, and inra-ethnic attitudes of elementary school children: A field experiment.* Unpublished doctoral dissertation, University of California at Santa Cruz, 1978.

Gerard, H., & Greenbaum, C. Attitudes toward an agent of uncertainty reduction. *Journal of Personality,* 1962, *30,* 485–495.

Ghiselli, E., & Lodahl, T. Patterns of managerial traits and group effectiveness. *Journal of Abnormal and Social Psychology,* 1958, *57,* 61–66.

Gibb, J. The effects of group size and of threat reduction upon certainty in a problem-solving situation. *American Psychologist,* 1951, *6,* 324.

Glass, G. & Smith, M. Meta-analysis of research on the relationship of class-size and achievement. San Francisco: Far West Laboratory for Educational Research and Development, Final Report, 1978.

Glidewell, J. C. *Group emotionality and productivity.* Unpublished doctoral dissertation, University of Chicago, 1953.

Goldman, M. A comparison of individual and group performance for varying combinations of initial ability. *Journal of Personality and Social Psychology,* 1965, *1,* 210–216.

Goldberg, M. L., Passow, A. H., & Justman, J. *The effects of ability grouping.* New York: Teachers College Press, 1966.

Goode, E. *The marijuana smokers.* New York: Basic Books, 1970.

Gottman, J., Gonso, J., & Rasmussen, B. Social interaction, social competence, and friendship in children. *Child Development,* 1975, *45*(3), 709–718.

Graziano, W., French, D., Brownell, C., & Hartup, W. Peer interaction in same- and mixed-age triads in relation to chronological age and incentive condition. *Child Development,* 1976, *47*(3), 707–714.

Gronlund, N. *Sociometry in the classroom.* New York: Harper, 1959.

Gunderson, B., & Johnson, D. W. Promoting positive attitudes toward learning a foreign language by using cooperative learning groups. *Foreign Language Annuals,* 1980, *13,* 39–46.

Haines, D. B., & McKeachie, W. J. Cooperative versus Competitive Discussion Methods in Teaching Introductory Psychology. *Journal of Educational Psychology,* 1967, *58:* 386–390.

Hall, J., & Williams, M. S. A comparison of decision-making performances in established and ad hoc groups. *Journal of Personality and Social Psychology,* 1966, *3,* 214–222.

Hall, J., & Williams, M. S. Group dynamics training and improved decision making. *Journal of Applied Behavioral Science,* 1970, *6,* 39–68.

Hargreaves, D. *Social relations in a secondary school.* New York: Humanities Press, 1967.

Hartup, W. Peer interaction and the behavioral development of the individual child. In E. Schopler & R. Reichler (Eds.), *Psychopathology and child development.* New York: Plenum, 1976.

Hartup, W. Children and their friends. In M. McGurk (Ed.), *Childhood social development.* London: Methuen, 1978.

Hartup, W., Glazer, J., & Charlesworth, R. Peer reinforcement and sociometric st1tus. *Child Development,* 1967, *38,* 1017–1024.

Haythorn, W. A., Couch, D. H., Haefner, D., Langham, P., & Carter, L. The behavior of authoritarian and equalitarian personalities in groups. *Human Relations,* 1956, *9,* 57–74.

Hoffman, L. R. Homogeneity of member personality and its effect on group problem-solving. *Journal of Abnormal and Social Psychology,* 1959, *58,* 27–32.

Hoffman, L. R., Harburg, E., & Maier, N. R. F. Differences and disagreement as factors in creative problem solving. *Journal of Abnormal and Social Psychology,* 1962, *64,* 206–214.

Hoffman, L. R., & Maier, N. R. F. Sex differences, sex composition, and group problem solving. *Journal of Abnormal and Social Psychology,* 1961, *63,* 453–456.

Hogan, R., & Henley, N. *A test of the empathy-effective communication hypothesis.* Report No. 84, Center for Social Organization of Schools. Baltimore: Johns Hopkins University, 1970.

Horowitz, F. The relationship of anxiety, self-concept, and sociometric status among 4th, 5th, and 6th grade children. *Journal of Abnormal and Social Psychology,* 1962, *65,* 212–214.

Hughes, E., Becker, H., & Geer, B. Student culture and academic effort. In N. Sanford (Ed.), *The American college.* New York: Wiley, 1962.

Hulten, B. H. *Games and teams: An effective combination in the classroom.* Paper presented at the American Educational Research Association Convention, Chicago, April 1974.

Husen, T., & Svensson, N. Pedagogic milieu and development of intellectual skills. *School Review,* 1960, *68,* 36–51.

Inagaki, K., & Hatano, G. Motivational influences on epistemic observation (in Japanese with English summary). *Japanese Journal of Educational Psychology,* 1968, *16,* 221–228.

Inagaki, K., & Hatano, G. Amplification of cognitive motivation and its effects on epistemic observation. *American Educational Research Journal,* 1977, *14,* 485–491.

Inhelder, B., & Sinclair, H. Learning cognitive structures. In P. H. Mussen, J. Langer, & M. Covington (Eds.), *Trends and issues in developmental psychology.* New York: Holt, Rinehart & Winston, 1969, 2–21.

Jackson, B. *Streaming: An education system in miniature.* London: Routledge & Kegan Paul, 1964.

Jessor, R. Predicting time of onset of marijuana use: A developmental study of high school youth. In D. Lettier (Ed.), *Predicting adolescent drug abuse.* Washington, D.C.: National Institute on Drug Abuse, 1975.

Jessor, R., Jessor, F., & Finney, J. A social psychology of marijuana use: Longitudinal studies of high school and college youth. *Journal of Personality and Social Psychology*, 1973, *26*, 1–15.

Johnson, D. W. *The social psychology of education.* New York: Holt, Rinehart & Winston, 1970.

Johnson, D. W. Role-reversal: A summary and review of the research. *International Journal of Group Tensions*, 1071, *1*, 318–334.

Johnson, D. W. Communication and the inducement of cooperative behavior in conflicts: A critical review. *Speech Monographs*, 1974, *41*, 64–78.

Johnson, D. W. Distribution and exchange of information in problem-solving dyads. *Communication Research*, 1977, *4*, 283–298.

Johnson, D. W. *Educational psychology.* Englewood Cliffs, New Jersey: Prentice-Hall, 1979.

Johnson, D. W. Constructive peer relationships, social development, and cooperative learning experiences: Implications for the prevention of drug abuse. *Journal of Drug Education*, 1980, *10*, 7–24.

Johnson, D. W., & Ahlgren, A. Relationship between student attitudes about cooperation and competition and attitudes toward schooling. *Journal of Educational Psychology*, 1976, *68*, 92–102.

Johnson, D. W., & Johnson, R. *Learning together and alone: Cooperation, competition, and individualization.* Englewood Cliffs, New Jersey: Prentice-Hall, 1975.

Johnson, D. W., & Johnson, R. (Eds.). Social interdependence within instruction. *Journal of Research and Development in Education*, 1978, *12*(1).

Johnson, D. W., Johnson, R., & Anderson, D. Relationship between student cooperative, competitive, and individualistic attitudes and attitudes toward schooling. *Journal of Psychology*, 1978, *100*, 183–199.

Johnson, D. W., Johnson, R., Johnson, J., & Anderson, D. The effects of cooperative vs. individualized instruction on student prosocial behavior, attitudes toward learning, and achievement. *Journal of Educational Psychology*, 1976, *68*, 446–452.

Johnson, D. W., Johnson, R., & Scott, L. The effects of cooperative and individualized instruction on student attitudes and achievement. *Journal of Social Psychology*, 1978, *104*, 207–216.

Johnson, D. W., Johnson, R., & Skon, L. Student achievement on different types of tasks under cooperative, competitive, and individualistic conditions. *Contemporary Educational Psychology*, 1979, *4*, 99–106.

Johnson, D. W., & Matross, R. The interpersonal influence of the psychotherapist. In A. Gurman & A. Razin (Eds.), *The effective therapist: A handbook.* Elmsford, New York: Pergamon Press, 1977.

Johnson, D. W., & Norem-Hebeisen, A. Attitudes toward interdependence among persons and psychological health. *Psychological Reports*, 1977, *40*, 843–850.

Johnson, D. W., Maruyama, G., Johnson, R., Nelson, D., & Skon, L. The effects of cooperative, competitive, and individualistic goal structures on achievement: A meta-analysis. University of Minnesota, *Psychological Bulletin*, 1980.

Johnson, D. W., Skon, L., & Johnson, R. Effects of cooperative, competitive, and individualistic conditions on students' problem-solving performance. *American Educational Research Journal*, 1980, *17*, 83–94.

Johnson, R., & Johnson, D. W. Type of task and student achievement and attitudes in interpersonal cooperation, competition, and individualization. *Journal of Social Psychology*, 1979, *108*, 37–48.

Johnson, R., Johnson, D. W., & Tauer, M. Effects of cooperative, competitive, and individualistic goal structures on students' achievement and attitudes. *Journal of Psychology*, 1979, *102*, 191–198.

Johnson, R., Rynders, J., Johnson, D. W., Schmidt, B., & Haider, S. Producing positive interaction between handicapped and nonhandicapped teenagers through cooperative goal structuring: Implications for mainstreaming. *American Educational Research Journal*, 1979, *16*, 161–168.

Josephson, E. Trends in adolescent marijuana use. In E. Josephson & E. Carroll (Eds.), *Drug use: Epidemiological and sociological approaches*. New York: Halstead-Wiley, 1974.

Judd, C. Cognitive effects of attitude conflict resolution. *Conflict Resolution*, 1978, *22*, 483–498.

Jung, C., & DeLaszlo, V. (Eds.). *The basic writings of C. G. Jung*. New York: Random House, 1959.

Kandel, D. Some comments on the relationship of selected criteria variables to adolescent illicit drug use. In D. Lettier (Ed.), *Predicting adolescent drug abuse*. Washington, D.C.: National Institute on Drug Abuse, 1975.

Kaplan, M. Discussion polarization effects in a modern jury decision paradigm: Informational influences. *Sociometry*, 1977, *40*, 262–271.

Kaplan, M., & Miller, C. Judgments and group discussion: Effect of presentation and memory factors on polarization. *Sociometry*, 1977, *40*, 337–343.

Katz, D. Morale and motivation in industry. In W. Dennis (Eds.), *Current trends in industrial psychology*. Pittsburgh: University of Pittsburgh Press, 1949, 145–171.

Keasey, C. Social participation as a factor in moral development of preadolescents. *Developmental Psychology*, 1971, *5*(2), 216–220.

Keasey, C. Experimentally induced changes in moral opinions and reasoning. *Journal of Personality and Social Psychology*, 1973, *26*, 30–38.

Kett, J. History of age grouping in America. In J. Coleman *et al.* (Eds.), *Youth: Transition to adulthood*. Chicago: University of Chicago Press, 1974, 9–29.

Kinsey, A., Pomeroy, W., & Martin, C. *Sexual behavior in the human male*. Philadelphia: W. B. Saunders, 1948.

Kobasigawa, A. Inhibitory and disinhibitory effects of models on sex-inappropriate behavior in children. *Psychologia*, 1968, *11* (1–2), 86–96.

Koch, H. The modification of unsocialness in preschool children. *Psychological Bulletin*, 1935, *32*, 700–701.

Kohlberg, L. Stage and sequence: The cognitive-developmental approach to socialization. In D. A. Goslin (Ed.), *Handbook of socialization theory and research*. Chicago: Rand McNally, 1969, 347–480.

Kohn, M., & Clausen, J. Social isolation and schizophrenia. *American Sociological Review*, 1955, *20*(3), 265–273.

Kohn, M., & Rosman, B. A social competence scale and symptom checklist for the preschool child: Factor dimensions, their cross-instrument generality, and longitudinal persistence. *Developmental Psychology*, 1972, *6*, 445–452.

Kuhn, D., Langer, J., Kohlberg, L., & Haan, N. S. The development of formal operations in logical and moral judgment. *Genetic Psychological Monographs*, 1977, *55*, 97–188.

Lacy, W. Interpersonal relationships as mediators of structural effects: College student socialization in a traditional and experimental university environment. *Sociology of Education*, 1978, *51*, 201–211.

Laughlin, P. Ability and group problem solving. *Journal of Research and Development in Education*, 1978, *12*, 114–120.

Laughlin, P., & Bitz, D. Individual versus dyadic performance on a disjunctive task as a function of initial ability level. *Journal of Personality and Social Psychology*, 1975, *31*, 487–496.

Laughlin, P., & Johnson, H. Group and individual performance on a complementary task as a function of initial ability level. *Journal of Experimental Social Psychology*, 1966, *2*, 407–414.

Laughlin, P., Keer, N., Davis, J., Haiff, H., Marciniak, K. Group size, member ability, and social decision schemes on an intellective task. *Journal of Personality and Social Psychology*, 1975, *31*, 522–535.

Laughlin, P., & Branch, L. Individual versus tetradic performance on a complementary task as a function of initial ability level. *Organizational Behavior and Human Performance*, 1972, *8*, 201–216.

Laughlin, P., Branch, L., & Johnson, H. Individual versus triadic performance on a unidimensional complementary task as a function of initial ability level. *Journal of Personality and Social Psychology,* 1969, *12,* 144–150.

Laughlin, P., & McGlynn, R. Cooperative versus competitive concept attainment as a function of sex and stimulus display. *Journal of Personality and Social Psychology,* 1967, *7,* 398–402.

Lavenhar, M., Wolfson, E., Shesset, A., Einstein, S., & Louria, D. A survey of drug abuse in six suburban New Jersey high schools: II Characteristics of drug users and nonusers. In S. Einstein and S. Allen (Eds.), *Student drug survey.* Farmingdale, New York: Baywood, 1972.

LeFurgy, W., & Woloshin, G. Immediate and long-term effects of experimentally induced social influence in the modification of adolescents' moral judgments. *Journal of Personality and Social Psychology,* 1969, *12,* 104–110.

Lewis, M., & Rosenblum, L. (Eds.). *Friendship and peer relations.* New York: Wiley, 1975.

Lipitt, R. The effects of authoritarian and external controls on the development of mental health. In A. H. Ojemann (Ed.), *Recent research on creative approaches to environmental stress.* Iowa City, Iowa: University of Iowa Press, 1964.

Lippitt, R., & Gold, M. Classroom social structure as a mental health problem. *Journal of Social Issues,* 1959, *15,* 40–58.

Lorber, N. Inadequate social acceptance and disruptive classroom behavior. *Journal of Educational Research,* 1966, *59,* 360–362.

Lougee, M. *Children's imitation of younger and older peers.* Unpublished doctoral dissertation, University of Minnesota, 1977.

Lowry, N., & Johnson, D. W. The effects of controversy on students' motivation and learning. University of Minnesota, submitted for publication, 1980.

May, R. *Love and will.* New York: Norton, 1969.

Maier, N. R. F., & Hoffman, L. R. Financial incentives and group decision in motivating change. *Journal of Social Psychology,* 1964, *64,* 369–378.

Maier, N., & Solem, A. The contributions of a discussion leader to the quality of group thinking: The effective use of minority opinions. *Human Relations,* 1952, *5,* 277–288.

Maitland, D., & Goldman, J. Moral judgment as a function of peer group interaction. *Journal of Personality and Social Psychology,* 1974, *30,* 699–704.

McCorkle, L. W., Elias, A., & Bixby, F. L. *The highfields story. A unique experiment in the treatment of juvenile delinquency.* New York: Holt, 1958.

McPartland, J. *School authority systems and student motivation.* Paper presented at the Annual Meeting of the American Educational Research Association, New York, April, 1977.

Mensh, I., & Glidewell, J. Children's perceptions of relationships among their family and friends. *Journal of Experimental Education,* 1958, *27,* 23–39.

Milgram, S. Liberating effects of group pressure. *Journal of Personality and Social Psychology,* 1965, *1,* 127–234.

Miller, S. A., & Brownell, C. A. Peers, persuasion, and Piaget: dyadic interaction between conservers and nonconservers. *Child Development,* 1975, *46,* 992–997.

Millman, J., & Johnson, M. Jr. Relation of section variance to achievement gains in English and mathematics in grades 7 and 8. *American Educational Research Journal,* 1964, *1,* 47–51.

Money, J., & Ehrhardt, A. *Man and woman, boy and girl.* Baltimore: Johns Hopkins University Press, 1972.

Mugny, G., & Doise, W. Socio-cognitive conflict and structure of individual and collective permances. *European Journal of Social Psychology,* 1978, *8,* 181–192.

Murray, H. A. Thematic Apperception Test in various. *Military clinical psychology.* Washington, D.C.: U.S. Government Printing Office, 1951, 59–71.

Murray, F. Acquisition of conservation through social interaction. *Developmental Psychology,* 1972, *6,* 1–6.

Murray, F., Ames, G., & Botvin, G. Acquisition of conservation through cognitive dissonance. *Journal of Educational Psychology,* 1977, *69,* 519–527.

Newcomb, T. M. Attitude development as a function of reference groups: The Bennington study. In G. E. Swanson, T. M. Newcomb, & E. L. Hartley (Eds.), *Readings in social psychology* (rev. ed.). New York: Holt, Rinehart & Winston, 1952.

Newcomb, T., Brown, D., Kulik, J., Reimer, D., & Revell, W. The University of Michigan's residential college. In P. Dressel (Ed.), *The new colleges: Toward an appraisal.* The American College Testing Program and the Amerioan Association for Higher Education, Monograph No. 7. Iowa City, Iowa: The American College Testing Program, 1971, 99–142.

Newcomb, T., Brown, D., Kulik, J., Revell, W., & Reimer. Self-selection and change. In J. Gaff (Ed.), *The cluster college.* San Francisco: Jossey-Bass, 1970, 137–160.

Noonan-Wagner, M. P. Intimacy of self-disclosure and response processes as factors affecting the development of interpersonal relationships. Unpublished doctoral dissertation, University of Minnesota, 1975.

Norem-Hebeisen, A., & Johnson, D. W. The relationship between cooperative, competitive, and individualistic attitudes and differentiated aspects of self-esteem. University of Minnesota, mimeographed report, submitted for publication, 1980.

O'Dell, J. Group size and emotional interaction. *Journal of Personality and Social Psychology,* 1968, *8,* 75–78.

Olson, M. Ways to achieve quality in school classrooms: Some definitive answers. *Phi Delta Kappan,* 1971, *53,* 63–65; 448–450.

Orth, C. *Social structure and learning climate: The first year at the Harvard Business School.* Boston: Harvard Business School, 1963.

Page, M. The modification of ascendant behavior in preschool children. University of Iowa Studies in Child Welfare, Vol. 12, No. 3, 1936.

Patterson, G., & Cobb, J. A dyadic analysis of "aggressive" behaviors. In J. Hill (Ed.), *Minnesota symposia on child development.* Vol. 5. Minneapolis: University of Minnesota Press, 1971.

Patterson, G., Littman, R., & Bricker, W. Assertive behavior in children: A step toward a theory of aggression. *Monographs of the society for research in child development,* 1967, *32,*(113).

Peifer, M. The effects of varying age-grade status of models on the imitative behavior of six-year-old boys. Unpublished doctoral dissertation, University of Delaware, 1971.

Pelz, D. C. Some social factors related to performance in a research organization. *Administrative Science Quarterly,* 1956, *1,* 310–325.

Perret-Clermont, A. *Social interaction and cognitive development in children.* London: Academic Press, in press.

Peters, R., & Torrance, E. Dyadic interaction of preschool children and performance on a construction task. *Psychological Reports,* 1972, *30,* 747–750.

Piaget, J. *The moral judgment of the child.* Glencoe, Illinois: The Free Press, 1932, 1948.

Piaget, J. *The psychology of intelliger* . New York: Harcourt, 1950.

Pilnick, S., Elias, A., & Clapp, N. W. The Essexfields concept: A new approach to the social treatment of juvenile delinquents. *Journal of Applied Behavioral Science,* 1966, *2,* 109–130.

Ramsøy, N. R. *American high schools at mid-century.* New York: Bureau of Applied Social Research, Columbia University, 1961.

Rest, J., Turiel, E., & Kohlberg, L. Relations between level of moral judgment and preference and comprehension of the moral judgment of others. *Journal of Personality,* 1969, *37,* 225–252.

Roethlisberger, F. J., & Dickson, W. J. *Management and the worker.* Cambridge, Massachusetts: Harvard University Press, 1939.

Roff, M. Childhood social interaction and young adult bad conduct. *Journal of Abnormal and Social Psychology,* 1961, *63*(2), 333–337.

Roff, M. Childhood social interaction and young adult psychosis. *Journal of Clinical Psychology,* 1963, *19,* 152–157.

Roff, M., Sells, S., & Golden, M. *Social adjustment and personality development in children.* Minneapolis: University of Minnesota Press, 1972.

Rogers, V. R. *Teaching in the British primary schools.* London: Macmillan, 1970.

Rubin, J., & Brown, B. *The social psychology of bargaining and negotiation.* New York: Academic Press, 1975.

Rynders, J., Johnson, R., Johnson, D. W., & Schmidt, B. Effects of cooperative goal structuring in producing positive interaction between Down's Syndrome and nonhandicapped teenagers: Implications for mainstreaming. *American Journal of Mental Deficiencies,* in press.

Schmuck, R. Some relationships of peer liking patterns in the classroom to pupil attitudes and achievement. *School Review,* 1963, *71,* 337–359.

Schmuck, R. Some aspects of classroom social climate. *Psychology in the School,* 1966, *3,* 59–65.

Schmuck, R. Influence of the peer group. In G. Lesser (Ed.), *Psychology and educational practice.* Glenview, Illinois: Scott, Foresman, 1971, 502–529.

Schmuck, R. Applications of social psychology to classroom life. In D. Bar-Tal & L. Saxe (Eds.), *Social psychology of education.* Washington, D.C.: Hemisphere, 1978, 231–256.

Sermat, V., & Smyth, M. Content analysis of verbal communication in the development of a relationship: Conditions influencing self-disclosure. *Journal of Personality and Social Psychology,* 1973, *26,* 332–346.

Shaw, M. E. A note concerning homogeneity of membership and group problem-solving. *Journal of Abnormal and Social Psychology,* 1960, *60,* 448–450.

Sherif, M. *The psychology of social norms.* New York: Octagon, 1936.

Sigel, I. E., & Hooper, F. H. (Eds.). *Logical thinking in children: Research based on Piaget's theory.* New York: Holt, Rinehart & Winston, 1968.

Silverman, I. W., & Geiringer, E. Dyadic interaction and conservation induction: A test of Piaget's equilibration model. *Child Development,* 1973, *44,* 815–820.

Silverman, I. W., & Stone, J. M. Modifying cognitive functioning through participation in a problem-solving group. *Journal of Educational Psychology,* 1972, *63,* 603–608.

Sinclair, H. Developmental psycho-linguistics. In D. Elkind & J. H. Flavell (Eds.), *Studies in cognitive development: Essays in honor of Jean Piaget.* New York: Oxford University Press, 1969, 315–336.

Sitkei, E. The effects of class size: A review of the research. Washington, D C: U.S. Department of Health, Education, and Welfare, 1968. (ERIC CED 043124, EA 003 074)

Skon, L., Johnson, D. W., & Johnson, R. Cooperative peer interaction versus individual competition and individualistic efforts: Effects on the acquisition of cognitive reasoning strategies. University of Minnesota, submitted for publication, 1980.

Slater, P. Contrasting correlates of group size. *Sociometry,* 1958, *21,* 129–139.

Slavin, R. Students teams and achievement divisions. *Journal of Research and Development in Education,* 1978, *12,*

Smedslund, J. The acquisition of conservation of substance and weight in children: II. External Reinforcement of conservation and weight and of the operations of addition and subtraction. *Scandinavian Journal of Psychology,* 1961, *2,* 71–84a.

Smedslund, J. The acquisition of conservation of substance and weight in children: III. Extinction of conservation of weight acquired 'normally' and by means of empirical controls on a balance. *Scandinavian Journal of Psychology,* 1961, *2,* 85–87b.

Smedslund, J. The acquisition of conservation of substance and weight in children: V. Practice in conflict situations without external reinforcement. *Scandinavian Journal of Psychology,* 1961, *2,* 156–160c.

Smith, L. The concurrent validity of six personality and adjustment tests for children. *Psychological Monographs,* 1958, *77*(457).

Soar, R. Follow-through classroom process measurement and pupil growth. Final report. Gainesville, Florida: College of Education, University of Florida, 1973.

Spilerman, S. Raising academic motivation in lower class adolescents: A convergence of two research traditions. *Sociology of Education,* 1971, *44,* 103–118.

Smith, K., Johnson, D. W., & Johnson, R. The effects of controversy on the motivation and achievement of students. University of Minnesota, submitted for publication, 1980.

Stallings, J., & Kaskowitz, D. *Follow-through classroom observation evaluation.* Menlo Park, California Stanford Research Institute, 1974.

Stanley, C., & Gottman, J. Popularity, social structure, and social interaction in children. Manuscript submitted for publication, 1976.

Steiner, I. *Group process and productivity.* New York: Academic Press, 1972.

Stephan, F., & Mishler, E. The distribution of participation in small groups: An exponential approximation. *American Sociological Review,* 1952, *17,* 598–608.

Sullivan, H. S. *The interpersonal theory of psychiatry.* New York: Norton, 1953.

Svensson, N. *Ability grouping and scholastic achievement.* Stockholm: Almqvist & Wiksell, 1962.

Taylor, D. A., Altman, I. & Sorrentino, R. Interpersonal exchange as a function of rewards and costs and situational factors: Expectancy confirmation-disconfirmation. *Journal of Experimental Social Psychology,* 1969, *5,* 324–339.

Thelen, M., & Kirkland, K. On status and being imitated: Effects on reciprocal imitation and attraction. *Journal of Personality and Social Psychology,* 1976, *33*(6), 691–697.

Thomas, E. J., & Fink, C. Effects of group size. *Psychological Bulletin,* 1963, *60,* 371–384.

Tillman, R., & Hull, J. H. Is ability grouping taking schools in the wrong direction? *Nations' Schools,* 1964, *73,* 70–71; 128–129.

Tjosvold, D. Threat as a low-power person's strategy in bargaining: Social face and tangible outcomes. *International Journal of Group Tensions,* 1974, *4,* 494–510.

Tjosvold, D., & Johnson, D. W. The effects of controversy on cognitive perspective-taking. *Journal of Educational Psychology,* 1977, *69,* 679–685.

Tjosvold, D., & Johnson, D. W. Controversy within a cooperative or competitive context and cognitive perspective-taking. *Contemporary Educational Psychology,* 1978, *3,* 376–386.

Tjosvold, D., Johnson, D. W., & Lerner, J. The effects of affirmation of one's competence, personal acceptance, and disconfirmation of one's competence on incorporation of opposing information in problem-solving situations. *Journal of Social Psychology,* in press.

Tjosvold, D., Johnson, D. W., & Fabrey, L. The effects of controversy and defensiveness on cognitive perspective-taking. Pennsylvania State University, submitted for publication, 1980.

Tjosvold, D., Marino, P., & Johnson, D. W. Cooperation and competition and student acceptance of inquiry and didactic teaching. *Journal of Research in Science Teaching,* 1977, *14,* 281–288.

Torrance, E. P. Can grouping control social stress in creative activity? *Elementary School Journal,* 1961, *62,* 139–145.

Torrance, E. Influence of dyadic interaction on creative functioning. *Psychological Reports,* 1970, *26,* 391–394.

Torrance, E. Stimulation, enjoyment, and originality in dyadic creativity. *Journal of Educational Psychology,* 1971, *62,* 45–48.

Torrance, E. *Dyadic interaction in creative thinking and problem solving.* Paper read at the meeting of the American Educational Research Association, New Orleans, February 1973.

Triandis, H., Bass, A., Ewen, R., & Mikesele, E. Teaching creativity as a function of the creativity of the members. *Journal of Applied Psychology,* 1963, *47,* 104–110.

Triandis, H. C., Hall, E. R., & Ewen, R. B. Member heterogeneity and dyadic creativity. *Human Relations,* 1965, *18,* 33–55.

Tuckman, B. Group composition and group performance on structure and unstructured tasks. *Journal of Experimental Social Psychology,* 1967, *3,* 25–40.

Turiel, E. An experimental test of the sequentiality of developmental stages in the child's moral judgment. *Journal of Personality and Social Psychology*, 1966, *3*, 611–618.

Turiel, E. Stage transition in moral development. In R. Travers (Ed.), *Second handbook of research on teaching*. Chicago: Rand McNally, 1973, 732–758.

Turner, R. H. *The social context of ambition*. San Francisco: Chandler, 1964.

Van Egmond, E. *Social interrelationship skills and effective utilization of intelligence in the classroom*. Unpublished doctoral dissertation, University of Minnesota, 1960.

Vinokur, A., & Burnstein, E. Effects of partially shared persuasive arguments on group-induced shifts. *Journal of Personality and Social Psychology*, 1974, *29*, 305–315.

Vreeland, R., & Bidwell, C. Organizational effects in students' attitudes: A study of the Harvard houses. *Sociology of Education*, 1965, *38*, 233–250.

Wahler, R. Child–child interactions in five field settings: Some experimental analysis. *Journal of Experimental Child Psychology*, 1967, *5*(2), 278–293.

Wallace, W. *Student culture: Social structure and continuity in a liberal arts college*. Chicago: Aldine, 1966.

Wallach, L., & Sprott, R. L. Inducing number conservation in children. *Child Development*, 1964, *35*, 1057–1071.

Wallach, L., Wall, A. J., & Anderson, L. Number conservation: The roles of reversibility, addition-subtraction, and misleading perceptual cues. *Child Development*, 1967, *38*, 425–442.

Watson, G., & Johnson, D. W. *Social psychology: issues and insights*. Philadelphia: Lippincott, 1972.

Wheeler, R., & Ryan, F. Effects of cooperative and competitive classroom environments on the attitudes and achievement of elementary school students engaged in social studies inquiry activities. *Journal of Educational Psychology*, 1973, *65*, 402–407.

Whiting, B., & Whiting, J. *Children of six cultures: A psychocultural analysis*. Cambridge, Massachusetts: Harvard University Press, 1975.

Wilson, A. B. Residential segregation of social classes and aspirations of high school boys. *American Sociological Review*, 1959, *14*, 836–845.

Wilson, A. B. Social stratification and academic achievement. In A. H. Passow (Ed.), *Education in depressed areas*. New York, Teachers College Press, Columbia University, 1963, 217–235.

Wodarski, J. S., Hamblin, R. L., Buckholdt, D. R., & Ferritor, D. E. Individual consequences versus different shared consequences contingent on the performance of low-achieving group members. *Journal of Applied Social Psychology*, 1973, *3*, 276–290.

Wohlwill, J. F., & Lowe, R. C. Experimental analysis of the development of the conservation of number. *Child Development*, 1962, *33*, 153–167.

Worchel, P., & McCormick, B. Self-concept and dissonance reduction. *Journal of Personality*, 1963, *31*, 589–599.

Yablonsky, L. The anticriminal society: Synanon. *Federal Probation*, 1962, *26*, 50–57.

Yates, A. (Ed.). *Grouping in education*. New York: Wiley, 1966.

Ziller, R. Scales of judgment.. a determinant of the accuracy of group decisions. *Human Relations*, 1955, *8*, 153–164.

Ziller, R. C., & Exline, R. V. Some consequences of age heterogeneity in decision-making groups. *Sociometry*, 1958, *21*, 198–211.

chapter 5

The School Organization

RICHARD A. SCHMUCK

Systematic study of the interaction between individuals and institutions is at the heart of social psychology. However, the extension of this kind of study to the social psychology of education has been slow to develop. Educational social psychologists have been preoccupied with the micro processes of classroom interaction, teacher–student relationships, and student attitudes. In this chapter, I go beyond that micro focus to ways of conceiving and assessing how interactions between student and school relate to academic learning.

The school is a social institution composed of a multitude of parts. It is an integral aspect of the community, a complex organization, and a loosely knit collection of small groups. It is also an arena in which faculty members work together or apart, in which committees are formed or dissolved, and in which crucial problems are solved or ignored. The school is a complex organization composed of both formal and informal relationships among faculty members and between faculty and students. Whereas it is integrally bound to the norms of its community and other important societal conditions, its students and teachers create their own living curriculum as they interact in classrooms. In short, the school constitutes a diverse and complex social system with a multiple of interdependent parts. As a living open system, the school and its classrooms continually adapt to changes from within—to the teachers, committees, and students—and respond to forces from without—to budgets, parents, and boards.

Although the school has an objective reality that is shared by all participants, like all complex social phenomena it is experienced differently

169

THE SOCIAL PSYCHOLOGY
OF SCHOOL LEARNING

from various perceptual vantage points. From the social-psychological view, the school is constituted of multiple existential realities. Like the elephant that, when touched by three blind men in different places, seemed like a very different beast to each, the school takes on a different sense when it is experienced by its various participants.

The problem that this chapter addresses is how the multiple realities of the school organization influence student learning, both by setting a stage on which only certain behaviors may be expressed and through a complex filtering of the social structures and norms that have an impact on the individual student's perceptual field and behavioral repertoire. Before presenting concepts and data let us offer illustrations of how the school is perceived by some of its participants as well as by some scholars and policy makers who have been concerned about public education.

MULTIPLE REALITIES OF THE SCHOOL

I prepare this chapter as a social psychologist in the Lewinian tradition who is committed to consultation and action research for school improvement. I prefer to interact with school participants as a co-creator in the systematic study of their own organizational life because to do so is both good practice and good science. My point of departure in this chapter, therefore, is to consider an assortment of quotations from school participants themselves on the special meanings that their school has for them.

Let us begin with the words of an alienated tenth grader who undoubtedly will be dropping out of school next year:

> This school is just a place I have to go until I'm 16. I won't graduate because the teachers can't teach. I hate the vice principal who has kicked me out of school several times. Little I care when he kicks me out. No, I don't have any friends at this dump. All of my friends are out of school, mostly working or just hanging around.

And a math teacher who teaches in the same high school attended by the tenth grader said:

> This school has changed a lot. There used to be close relationship between parents and teachers. The teachers worked together and the principal was a close friend. But now the community has changed. It's dangerous—lots of muggings and assaults—my husband takes me to

*school and picks me up. I stay in my classroom all day. I seldom see
other teachers or the principal.*

Again in the same school I listened to an administrator who took an
innovative job a few years ago designated by the title, instructional assistant
principal:

*The paperwork is out of sight! I don't have time at all to meet with
teachers about the instructional program. Imagine a matrix with 10 rows
and 10 columns—that makes for 100 cells. Now fill each cell with a
form to complete. Whether its federal, state, county, or the district
makes no difference to me. I'm overwhelmed by it.*

Let us turn to sample quotes from another very different school. For
example, here are the thoughts of an eleventh grader who is part of the
school's football team:

*Our school is the greatest. We have the best football team in the
conference and the best looking cheerleaders. Lots of kids attend the
games; the school spirit is super. The principal speaks at the pep rallies
and the teachers attend the games. It's easy to get out of classes for
practices and trips.*

But, here is another very different point of view from another eleventh
grader at the same school:

*There is a bunch around the school who do everything right. The
teachers like them and they'll go to college. But not our gang! You don't
act too smart or too dumb with us. You don't talk about school at all.
You stay away from the teachers and the vice-principal. You don't see
the counselor. You get C's, just enough to get by.*

Turning to a fourth-grade teacher in a new multi-unit school, we get a
glimpse of the constructive energy that can be mustered by an enthusiastic
staff member:

*I'm really excited about our school. In my last job I worked alone,
didn't talk much with others about the students or the program, and got
pretty bored just following the daily routine. But now we have a new
principal and some new teachers who want to do more teaming and
working together. We're organizing ourselves into teams that meet
several times a week. I really like the people I'm working with. The*

students are doing well and I've been rejuvenated. Teaching can be fun.

In contrast, the head of the English department in an innovative high school presents a far different reality:

> *I'm trying to get teachers to participate more in running meetings, but many just want to be left alone to teach. I get frustrated in not knowing what to do. It seems as if most teachers don't want to discuss how to improve the department. They say that's what I'm getting paid for. But still when I do decide many don't agree, saying that they weren't involved. What am I to do?*

And let us consider the perspective of an assistant superintendent who views the schools from the district office:

> *Some schools have it and some don't. It's mostly the principal, I think. You can visit some schools and you know right away that they have it together. Others are the dregs. In the good schools the principal knows how to stimulate staff involvement and the parents are usually organized and supportive. If we could only get good principals, our schools would be a lot better.*

Another array of multiple realities about the school organization come from scholars who have studied it. Here are three quotes from prominent researchers, indicating the variety that exists among scholarly treatments.
Charles Bidwell (1965), a sociologist of education, notes how school organizations offer teachers considerable freedom in how they will teach:

> Teachers . . . resist authority in the instructional area and press for professional discretion, defining the administrator as a colleague. . . . Teachers seem likely to ignore or redefine rules of procedure, especially as they impinge on matters of professional techniques. Insofar as instruction is concerned, . . . school-system rules bear more heavily on content than method, for example, system-wide curricula or courses of study [p. 1014].

Later in this chapter we will reiterate these notions about the instructional autonomy of teachers when the "loosely coupled" nature of school structures is discussed. Now, consider a quotation from Robert Dreeben (1968), who views life in the school as communicating the "hidden curriculum" of particular cultural values:

> The social experience available to pupils in schools, by virtue of the nature and sequence of their structural arrangements, provide opportunities for children to learn norms charac-

teristic of several facets of adult life, occupation being but one. The social properties of schools are such that pupils, by coping with the sequence of classroom tasks and situations, are more likely to learn the norms of independence, achievement, universalism, and specificity than if they had remained full-time members of the household [p. 65].[1]

Finally, the scholarly view of school organizations comes from the Bank Street Study (Minuchin et al., 1969), in which several organizational norms of schools were shown to affect students differentially:

Given these findings . . . educators, psychologists, parents, cannot rest with the idea that the school is in charge of intellectual education . . . and that the rest (of personality development) is not its province. . . . Our data confirm that schools cannot choose to limit the scope of their impact by fiat—by declaring certain areas off limits and out of bounds. . . . We saw some of the clearest effects of the contrasting educational systems in areas related to self-development. Whether they noticed it or wanted it, the traditional schools were affecting the attitudes, styles, and values of their pupils in important areas of development, just as modern schools were, but the nature of impact was different [p. 400].[2]

From still another horizon, policy makers have discovered the school organization as a target for improvement. Members of school boards, county departments, state offices, the federal bureaucracy, and foundations have heeded the following remarks from the Rand study (1975):

The strategies that significantly promoted teacher change in the classroom include staff training in methods of collaborative problem solving with their colleagues, frequent, regular task-oriented staff meetings, and local materials development. In addition, a project's perceived success was reduced when the teachers did not participate together in making day-to-day decisions about how to implement the project. A top-down strategy for school change typically was not successful. The teachers could sabotage such efforts because of the highly differentiated nature of the structure of schools [p. 18].

Similarly, the following statements, paraphrased from a report of the National Institute of Education (1977), indicate that the importance of organizational life in schools has also been noted by funders of school improvement:

On the basis of research, what can be said about the necessary conditions for educational improvement?

1. Provide funds only when the school people who are going to implement the program design it and think it will help them address a problem they think is important.

---

[1] From Robert Dreeben, On What Is Learned in School. © 1968, Addison-Wesley Publishing Co., Reading, Mass., p. 65. Reprinted with permission.

[2] From The Psychological Impact of School Experience, by Patricia Minuchin et al., p. 400, © 1969 by Basic Books, Inc., Publishers, New York.

2. Concentrate on individual schools for improvement. Stimulate communication and exchange of ideas among principals, other administrators, teachers, students, and parents.
3. Help school staffs develop skills and organizational structures that will enable them to help one another to make decisions collaboratively, engage in continuous planning, and implement instructional programs that meet the objectives the school sets for itself.

Given the different perspectives and multiple realities, what are the implications of the school organization? What can be derived from an informal content analysis of these various quotes? It is obvious that the same school organization can be perceived in very contrasting ways. In the first school discussed, each participant in his or her own unique manner showed the varieties of alienation to which the school experiences can give rise; marking time, anxiety and fear, feelings of overload, and the like. The two eleventh graders of a second school expressed very different emotions about the same school, one was turned on by the school's spirit whereas the second felt turned off by it. The last student, the head of the English department, Dreeben, and Minuchin et al., all saw ways the school can constrict opportunity and freedom. The assistant superintendent viewed the school as a collection of individuals, granting the principal a very special potency. This view of principal power contrasts with Bidwell's perception of the autonomous teacher.

Clearly, the organizational life of a school can communicate powerful and different messages to the participants, the scholars and the policy makers. The school as an institution embodies a cultural identity with a vibrant life of its own. It presents a mini-culture of values, cognitive maps, and feelings with a unity that sets it off from exterior demands and from the idiosyncracies of personalities.

The school offers the context or stage on which the instructional program is implemented, yet it offers much more. It shapes values, attitudes, and even personality structures. It influences hopes and aspirations; it can cause alienation and self rejection. Attempted alterations in the instructional program that might be planned by an individual or subgroup will have to be integrated into the school's norms and structures. Whereas there is a variety of norms and structures that are possible, the ones that characterize any particular school organization tend to become tenacious and to require planned, long-range efforts to change.

The individual alone, except perhaps for the principal in some schools, cannot alter the complex norms, structures, and procedures of the school organization; that is apparent to all who get to know even a small part of the school, but the administrators, scholars, and policy makers understand it best. Change in the school organization requires the concerted efforts of administrators, teachers, and students working together. Moreover, whereas the cooperative efforts of several parties within may lead to change, outside support from key members of the district office and the community are also critical. Where instructional changes are sought, there must be a reciprocal condition of mutual adaptation between the innovation as a social process and the school's norms and structures. When student learning is the focus, we should look, too, for mutual adaptation between the individual and the institution.

THEORIES OF THE SCHOOL ORGANIZATION

American schools became bureaucratized during the middle of the nineteenth century. According to Katz (1971), it was during the 1870s that increasing numbers of students finally made democratic localism and community control of schools unfeasible, and when the lay-run one-room schoolhouse gave way to the professionally managed bureaucracy. With reduced lay involvement in directly administering the schools, the professional educators began to establish a managerial structure, partly to cope with the logistics of mass education, and partly, according to Katz, to establish their own hegemony and protect their self-interests.

In his history of the Boston school district, for example, Katz argued that the Boston schools began to display many of the essential attributes of a Weberian bureaucracy during the 1880s. In line with the Weberian model, Katz enumerated the essential features of the developing Boston school bureaucracy as (a) increased centralization of control, in the form of a district office that would attempt to standardize programs across schools; (b) differentiation of function by creating new job titles and roles; (c) standardized qualifications for office; (d) objectivity and rationality in performance; (e) precision and consistency in decision making, along with a clear chain of command; and (f) the general exercise of discretion.

Thus, during the latter part of the nineteenth century, the primary-group atmosphere of schools changed to the more rationalized and impersonal norms and procedures of large-scale industries. Schools, along with the rest of the Victorian society, had entered the industrial revolution, and like the small-craft families of the first half of the nineteenth century, gave way to mass production. Norms in support of particularism and ascription changed to norms of universalism and achievement. Competition became much more prominent. The affective, familial support of whole persons working together gave way to the rational attention on large members of youngsters in the role of student. Indeed, the school superintendents of that period believed that division of labor, standardized treatment of all, and the centralization of control were part of an ameliorative process of social development and societal progress.

Perhaps the most prominent characteristic of schools that emerged was a highly individuated division of labor. Teachers became specialized either in an academic subject or in working with a particular age of student. Grade level took over as a prominent feature of school structure, and teachers became known as grade-level specialists. Indeed, the strength of this organizational division of labor continues to survive even in the face of today's efforts to return to the community-controlled "one-room schoolhouse" in the form of alternative schools.

According to an analysis by Firestone (1977), despite radical alterations in organizational structure and norms, the character of teacher autonomy (the individuated division of labor) in alternative schools is remarkably similar to that in public ones. Consequently, administrative changes such as decentralization and community control appear unlikely to lead to lay-inspired instructional reform (that is, a return to the first half of the nineteenth century) because those changes may give community residents control over administrators but *not* over teachers. In fact, as was expressed previously in the quote from Bidwell, the frequent failure of innovations for instructional change may well stem from the substantial autonomy of teachers.

The School as Traditional Bureaucracy

The superintendents that came into authority during the last half of the nineteenth century believed that bureaucratization, in the sense described by Max Weber, represented a rational solution to the complexities of modern problems. Specialization of teachers, clear division of labor, and the chain of accountability would help the school to overcome the intellectual limits of individuals. They viewed the bureaucracy as an adaptive device to the psychology of the human being. It is instructive to explore a few twentieth-century theorists' views about the unanticipated responses of organizational members to rational bureaucracy, and to relate such responses to some of the managerial problems of schools.

The Merton Analysis

Merton's (1949) concern was with behavioral rigidity as an unplanned consequence of a chain of accountability. He argued that the demand for control issued by the top managers encourages the reliability of staff behavior. Through their authority, the managers hope to establish both accountability and predictability of worker performance. Standard operating procedures are instituted, and control consists of checking to ensure the procedures are being followed.

Three consequences may follow (a) a reduction in personalized relationships as staff members interact with one another in terms of roles and positions; (b) an increase in the internalization of rules of the organization; and (c) an increased use of categorization to make decisions, thus reducing a search for alternatives. All three social-psychological consequences may lead to an increase in the behavioral rigidity of staff. At the same time, an "esprit de corps" may very well develop, particularly as the organizational goals and procedures are viewed increasingly as the "way we do things here." That sense of the common fate of an ingroup can increase the tendency of staff members to defend one another against outside pressures, and that defense may strengthen even further the tendency toward rigid behavior.

Behavioral rigidity can eventuate in three consequences (a) satisfying management's demands for staff reliability and standardization; (b) legitimizing the defensibility of staff actions; and (c) increasing the difficulty in meeting the demands of the organization's clients. The last two consequences can become interlocked in an unproductive circular process, that is, difficulty with clients increases the defensiveness of staff members, which leads in turn to more difficulties with clients.

Parallels to the modern school organization seem clear. As the district administrators exert demands for control, stressing standardized and reliable action, they also are unwittingly encouraging behavioral rigidity, thus reducing the innovativeness that would be risked by a staff member. The typical reaction of staff members becomes, "Don't rock the boat—Do it as they want it done—Do it according to the book." Filling out forms, having lesson plans prepared according to a set format, writing narrow behavioral objectives, and the like can lead to a rigid and ritualistic adherence to administrative demands and can also serve as a crutch to a staff member's defense against criticism from parents or students. "Well, that's the way we do it; we professionals know better because of our training and experience!" Difficulties with students or parents can be written off as reactions from trouble makers or from citizens who are unsophisticated about the complexities of education. And when parents do criticize a staff member or two, the conceptions of common fate and mutual professional interest may bring administrators and teachers together in defense against the attacks of the unprofessionals.

The Selznick Analysis

In comparison to Merton's emphasis on rigidity, Selznick (1949) stressed the delegation of authority as a key variable of bureaucracies. In particular, he was concerned with the unplanned results that arise when delegation is employed for hierarchical control. Delegation results eventually in departmentalization and a "bifurcation of interests" among the departments. Frequently, the maintenance of departments dictates concern for achieving departmental goals first, and organizational purposes second. Another aspect of delegation is an increase in the specialized capabilities that are expected of departmental members. As their specialities are increased, it becomes costly to move personnel from one department to another, and psychological attachments to departments deepen even further. Contributions to overall organizational goals may be sufficient, but the departments can become so entrenched that they will not change even in the face of demands on the organization for change.

The parallels of the school with Selznick's theory seem even more familiar than those with Merton's. Indeed, delegation of responsibility constitutes a strong norm in public education. The board delegates district responsibilities to the superintendent; the superintendent delegates site responsibilities to the principals; and the principals delegate classroom authority to the teachers. In the end, all are granted considerable autonomy to function as they wish. Moreover, staff members such as counselors, psychologists, curriculum specialists, and nurses are given the authority to carry out their specialized functions almost free of managerial control. And, as in Selznick's analysis, the emergence of departments in districts abounds, each with its own purposes and specialities. There are academic departments, grade level groups, administrative cabinets, counseling staffs, teaching teams, and the like. Each establishes its own goals, competencies, and skills, and it is usually difficult for a member of one department to function effectively in another. Organizational change becomes difficult as the separate departments solidify. District office administrators bemoan the lack of flexibility in school staffs; principals complain about the rigidity of an academic department; department heads become angered over the lack of flexibility of a cluster of classroom teachers; and frustrations over the intractibility of others carry on.

The Gouldner Analysis

Gouldner (1954) argued that a bureaucracy maintains stability by using universalistic rules about how jobs should be executed and procedures should be carried out. Since the rules are general and impersonal, a norm of "equality under the law" arises, which decreases the extent to which power differences within the organization are noticed. This could work well, since cooperation would be enhanced in an equalitarian climate; however, the impersonal rules provide cues, at the same time, for staff members beyond those originally intended by the authorities. Specifically, by clearly defining acceptable behavior, management increases the visibility of what is minimally acceptable performance, and it attempts to pressure members to upgrade their work which in turn heightens the visibility of power differences, flying in the face of the equalitarian norms. Increased closeness of supervision exacerbates interpersonal tensions between workers and supervisors, culminating in the introduction of new rules about what is appropriate behavior in the bureaucracy—and the cycle repeats itself.

Schools suffer from the bureaucratic dysfunctions noted by Gouldner, particularly urban schools where pressures for change continue to be strong. There exists among all educators a strong norm of equality. Indeed, the elementary staff frequently is referred to as "one big, happy family," and in secondary schools, administrators strive to treat all teachers alike, regardless of department and tenure. However, the norm of equality and professional collaboration is violated every time the district administrators evaluate the performance of teachers as falling short. Since principals are held responsible for weak performances in their schools and are urged to tighten up on their supervision, it is difficult for them to relate with teachers on an equalitarian basis. In some instances a new supervisory role is introduced into the school to upgrade teacher performance and to take the principal "off the hook." Tensions inevitably arise, just the same, between the supervisor and the teachers; and new group agreements must be reached to reduce the tension. Sometimes a district-wide committee is formed or a school-based steering group is established to seek ways of upgrading all teachers' performances. Eventually, staff members learn how to live within the new norms and procedures, and to perform adequately. But again, performance that is minimally adequate will be subsequently viewed as falling short of an ideal, and the vicious cycle is reinstituted.

The School as Nonprofit Bureau

Michaelsen (1977) offered another theory for understanding aspects of how the school works, different from the model of the Weberian bureaucracy, by borrowing concepts from economists' treatments of behavior in profit-making, market-oriented organizations. Economic theory posits that the entrepreneur primarily aims to maximize profit. The social machinery, which insures that the entrepreneur will serve the public interest, at least in the long run, is the dependency of the entrepreneur on sales. Without sales there can be no budget and the entrepreneur cannot continue on in business. Moreover, there inevitably emerges competing entrepreneurs for most markets and the presence of competition, à la Adam Smith, forces every entrepreneur to act efficiently in the production and distribution of desired goods and services or the business cannot survive.

According to Michaelsen, this classical economic view of profit-seeking enterprises can serve as a useful conceptualization for aspects of the school as an organization. He refers to the school as a bureau and offers illustrations in how it differs from the profit-seeking firm. The bureau's environment differs in two primary ways from the classical firm. First, its budget is not derived from sales but from politics. Consequently, the bureau's staff must satisfy the appropriate politicians, not customers or clients, to procure a budget. It is important to note that the clients' withholding purchases does not directly provide them with power. The second difference is that bureaus typically face little if any competition from alternative sources for the same services, save for the 10% of students enrolled in private schools. Thus, the coordination and direction of the bureau's activities are *not* influenced by interactions of buyers and sellers.

The school is thus a nonprofit bureau, concerned with politics more than sales and client responses. And since there are no profits but only political hegemony, it can be assumed that school staffs will seek to enlarge the scope of their activities, to gain prestige and credibility, to avoid conflict and tension, to control their daily activities, and finally to survive. Achieving those objectives represents symbolic profit to the politically minded staff of the school. Being granted tenure becomes the holy grail of the individual staff member.

Seen in this way, administrators and teachers are viewed as striving to maximize politically related activities over which they might have some control. For the administrators, budgets rather than profits would be maximized. Larger budgets could help administrators to survive, to increase their prestige, and generally to gain control over their environments. For teachers, classroom space, materials, freedom of movement, autonomy, equality, and tenure would be emphasized. Those resources that are mostly psychological could help the teachers to survive, to increase their prestige, and to gain self-respect as professionals.

The School as Cultural Reflection

This perspective emphasizes how the school organization embodies and indirectly teaches societal norms and values. This "curriculum of cultural transmission" is only partly planned or formalized; it most often gets acted out in the daily structures and routines of the school. The intellectual roots of this point of view can be found in Durkheim (trans. by S. D. Fox, 1956), revisited in the more recent extensions of Durkheim by Parsons (1951), and applied to contemporary schools by both Eisenstadt (1956) and Dreeben (1968).

Eisenstadt states that industrially oriented societies possess jobs demanding norms much different from the norms of nuclear families or kinship units. Thus, in being socialized for work, individuals must undergo psychological changes of considerable magnitude to make the transition from family to occupation. Using Parsons's "pattern variables" to describe fundamental forms of social interaction, Eisenstadt points out that the typical social interactions that take place in schools help youngsters bridge the cultural gaps between dependence and independence, particularism and universalism, ascription and achievement; and diffuse-affectivity and specific-rationality.

Those bipolar pairs describe the kinds of social exchange and interaction that take place in different societal settings. In the family, for example, one initially acts dependently, comes to feel a special individuality because of others' reactions, comes to feel included by ascription of birth and family name, and learns to expect affect-laden, whole-person relationships with others. The family is the proper stage for primary relationships. In contrast, industrial organizations demand different social relationships. The successful employee learns to work independently or at least interdependently, expects that all employees will be given the same treatment, believes that one achieves by dint of hard work and personal effort, and that one should view organizational life as task-focused and as designed for rational and logical relationships among the employees.

Following the Parsons and Eisenstadt sociological perspectives is Dreeben, who spells out how the school organization provides opportunities for children to learn norms that are characteristic of adults in industrial society. The norms of concern to Dreeben are independence, achievement, universalism, and specificity. I have already summarized the heart of Dreeben's argument in the quote presented in the section on multiple realities of the school.

It should be noted in relation to Dreeben's argument that American culture is changing from an industrial emphasis to one of social service, and that we might, therefore, expect demands for new norms and for new socialization experiences in schools. Some recent research also bears this out. In a small-scale study contrasting a few alternative schools with a few traditional schools, Swidler (1976) showed that while the academic outcomes of the contrasting sets of schools did *not* differ, the "hidden curriculum" taught in the form of norms and values did differ. Swidler showed that in place of the values of independence and achievement, the alternative schools were teaching group skills, interdependence, and collaboration. Students of the alternative schools were *not* learning how to take tests, how to cope with the anxiety of personal evaluation, and about the importance of risking failure. Instead, they were being encouraged to develop emotional openness, self-direction, and intellectual autonomy. In contrast to the norms of universalism, achievement, and task specificity, the alternative schools were organized to stress particularism through individualization and diffuse intimacy between teachers and students and within the peer group. The picture painted by Swidler is not unlike the one given in the Bank Street Study quoted previously in the section on multiple realities of the school.

The School as Loosely Coupled

Weick (1976) has proposed quite a different perspective from the others just described on the school organization, arguing that instead of putting emphasis on the school as bureaucracy, nonprofit bureau, or cultural reflection (all of which strongly imply that the organizational components of schools are connected through dense, tight linkages), the organizational components of schools are actually *loosely coupled.* By loose coupling, Weick conveys the image that while interdependent events may be responsive, each event also preserves its identity and its physical or logical separateness. For example, high school classes are loosely coupled; students do move from one to another and therefore formal interdependence exists, but the identity and separateness of each class is strong. In a similar vein the counselor's office as a behavior setting is loosely coupled to classrooms and to the principal's office. Attachments across these components, while present, are infrequent, weak, or delayed in their mutual effects.

In theories about bureaucracies, the most commonly discussed organizational mechanisms for coupling are the technical and the authority subsystems. For schools, the former concerns instruction in classrooms, while the latter concerns the chain of accountability from the superintendent through the principal to teachers and then on to the students. In both subsystems, the components are rather loosely coupled. We would expect, therefore, that routines implemented in one classroom would influence routines of other classes only in minor ways, and that educational planning carried out by administrators would have only minimal impact on teachers. Much of what takes place in such loosely coupled organizational structures would be up to how the particular individuals carry out their roles. Thus, administrators would be expected to have very different impacts on different teachers, different teachers will execute their instructional plans quite differently, etc.

There are some potential functions and dysfunctions for the school that are implied by their theory. For example, loose coupling allows some organizational components to remain insulated from environmental threats, offering functional protection for innovative practices, while carrying the dysfunction of perpetuating out-of-date practices. Loose coupling preserves independent sensing components to help the organization diagnose complex environments, yet at the same time makes it more difficult to mobilize the components to respond to the diagnoses because of low integration and cohesiveness. Loosely coupled components can respond more adaptively to different clients, but wherever standardization is desirable—such as when students transfer from one school to another—the looseness becomes a disadvantage. And, if there is a weakness in one component of a loosely coupled system, then the weakness may be sealed off, not affecting other components. However, these isolated weak components are difficult to change by virtue of their being sealed off. Thus, it is likely that schools perpetuate many inadequate practices that are inaccessible to change efforts.

Meyer and Rowan (1976) have argued that, on balance, loose coupling is more functional for the political survival of school organizations than tight coupling. They point out that the school establishes its legitimacy in the society by proffering its fundamental role in educating youth for the betterment of all and for social progress. Enforced inspection, coordination, or evaluation of the school (all forms of tight coupling) would have the potential of demonstrating inconsistencies among procedures, student needs, and societal goals. Consequently, the school deals with its uncertainties, challenges, and inconsistencies through the maintenance of loosely coupled components.

Contributions of Theory

Just as the participants' multiple realities of life in schools had validity for every individual, but only partly described the school organization, so does each of the theories discussed make only a partial contribution to an understanding of how the school as an organization functions. The contributions of the theories reside in the cognitive maps they offer to alert us to particular social-psychological events in our search for the relationships between student learning and the school organization.

There are, for example, important aspects of school life that resemble the pictures drawn by the theorists of bureaucracy. Specialization and a differentiated task structure are prominent organizational features of schools, and some of the results of attempting to control them are similar to those described by Merton, Selznick, and Gouldner. In many urban schools, for example, increased social distance has arisen among the professionals and the students and their parents. The professionals, irritated by the pressures of having to account for the academic achievement of students, have banded together to defend against criticisms and pressures. In some districts, teachers have formed into unions or autonomous professional associations to cope politically with the attacks. As a consequence, many schools now more closely resemble a union–management structure than they did a generation ago, with the community's representatives—the superintendent and the board—in combat with teacher leaders.

We have also seen what Selznick refers to as the "bifurcation-of-interests" phenomenon occurring between components of the school district. As one department establishes its own identity, program, budget, and cohesiveness, it frequently fails to contribute to the changing academic goals of the district. For example, the different interests of counselors and teachers may clash with each other, undermining the establishment of consistent rules and procedures for the students. As students' problems increase, the counselors and the teachers become even more rigidly committed to doing what they respectively believe they do best.

As another example, the phenomenon of "just getting by" is not an uncommon complaint in school districts, and the theories help us to understand it. Since the norms in support of equality and autonomy both are strong among professional educators, it is easy to understand that teachers and administrators want to treat one another as colleagues. At the same time, it is difficult to reconcile collegiality with supervision, and the former frequently wins out over the latter. Collegiality typically allows for considerable autonomy among teachers and what may commence as a tacit acceptance of doing enough to meet standards can gradually degenerate into doing just enough to get by and its attendant mediocre performance. When close supervision is tried, the resulting tensions can lead to new agreements about how to behave in the school, but after the supervision is removed the power of collegiality reasserts itself and the possibility of mediocre performances are once again increased.

While the theories of bureaucracy can facilitate our understanding of the dysfunctions of school life for student learning, they were developed primarily to describe the problems of industrial or other noneducational organizations. The other three theories, on the other hand, dealt directly with schools. Viewing the school as a nonprofit bureau helps us to remember the importance of the politics between the school and the larger society and within the school itself. The maintenance of power and control on the part of the educational professionals will often compete with the energy and attention they have available for student learning.

Viewing the school as a reflection of the culture helps us to remember the hidden curriculum that is manifest in how the organization operates. Thus, regardless of the power of the planned and formal academic curriculum, the processes of social interaction that occur within the school and the classroom will also communicate norms and values to students. For example, the amount of encouragement that a teacher gives to student participation can communicate democratic values even though the subject matter of the class has nothing to do with politics.

Viewing the school as loosely coupled helps us to remember that, however powerful organizational effects are, they are unlikely to be monolithic and all encompassing. Within most school organizations there will be a great deal of variability and variety. Teachers, in particular, can stay insulated from administrative pressures and from the community's attempts to influence the school.

In the actual lives of the participants as well as in the conceptions of the scholars, we find a multiplicity of pictures of the school as an organization. Clearly, schools do differ one from the other, and clearly they do house considerable variability within themselves. They are not Hobbesian leviathans, controlling every behavior of the participants, nor are they figments of the sociologist's imagination with no collective meaning beyond the individuals that make them up. They do, I believe, make a difference for student learning. How school organizations may influence the academic learning of students is what we turn to in the rest of the chapter.

STUDIES OF THE SCHOOL ORGANIZATION

There is now evidence that one or another aspect of the school organization can influence, directly or indirectly, such crucial aspects of students' behavior as the length of time devoted to academic tasks, involvement in school activities, anxiety about learning, expectations of success, motive satisfaction, and self-esteem. To keep clear the sources of the social influence process and the kinds of available evidence, I shall first discuss the social variables under three headings: (a) contextual factors; (b) formal structural variables; and (c) informal climate conditions. In the next major section of this chapter, I indicate the ways in which the three sorts of social influences impinge upon the perceptual field of the student, creating the kinds of multiple realities that were illustrated earlier. An overview depicting the complexity of how the three classes of social variables causally relate to one another and finally to student learning is shown in Figure 5.1.

Contextual Factors

The variables most frequently studied that relate to the extra organizational context are school size, the sociological character of the neighbor-

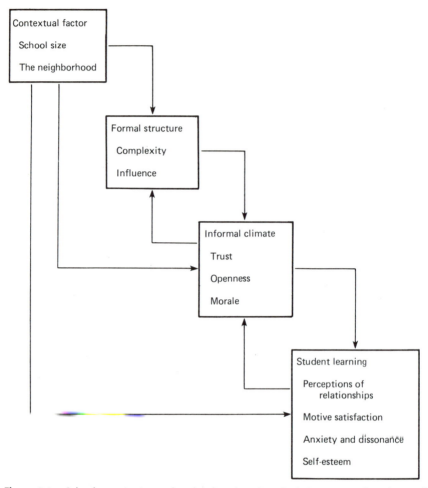

Figure 5.1. School organization and student learning: Causal relations among four classes of key variables.

hood, and the peer relationships that students enter into both outside and inside the school.

Size of School

Many sociological studies support the conclusion that large size groups or organizations are dysfunctional. Indeed, the cautions about bureaucracy offered by Merton, Selznick, and Gouldner seemingly describe best what might go on in large schools and large districts rather than small ones. For examples of some recent empirical support, Kasarda (1975) and Stavig and

Barnett (1977) have shown morale, satisfaction, absenteeism, communication, and cohesiveness all to have been negatively influenced by increasing organizational size.

The number of students and staff members within a single school, I believe, can be critical in influencing many aspects of the school's organization. There are some obvious effects such as the typical student–teacher ratio within learning groups, or the number or diversity of classes available to the student body. There are also some less obvious effects such as those having to do with characteristic patterns of interaction between teachers and students and among the students.

Barker and Gump (1964), Baird (1969), and Moracco (1978) have presented impressive empirical evidence on the relationships between school size and the behavior of students in relation to one another. The three studies showed that whereas small and large high schools had about the same number of "behavioral settings"—places and activities in which students interact with one another—larger proportion of students in small schools participated in a greater variety of the activities offered by the school than did the students of large schools. Furthermore, a greater proportion of small-school students held positions of importance and responsibility, whereas in the larger high schools, fewer students proportionately held such positions. Students of small schools reported more personal kinds of satisfactions; for example, developing new competencies, being challenged, participating in activities they considered important, and becoming clear about their values. In contrast, students from large schools reported more impersonal satisfactions that were less goal-directed, more vicarious enjoyments, more learning about persons and affairs, and receiving more external rewards such as points for participation.

Despite the fact that students in small schools are more involved in relationships with peers, the research also shows that there is a greater probability that large-school students' attitudes and values are more strongly influenced by their peer group. Youngsters in large schools become just as intimate with some peers as their small-school counterparts, but their friendships more often take place outside the school's formal program. Moreover, students in a large school are faced with many alternatives of the kinds of persons they will choose for friends. Not as many alternatives are present within the relatively homogeneous group of small-school students. Large-school students may choose people different from themselves, and the peer structure of small cliques and dating couples are important factors in the students' developing personalities. As a student chooses friends outside of classroom experiences, the importance of school-related activities decreases and the influence of out-of-school peer relationships increases.

In analogous studies of colleges, Pace (1967) and Astin (1968) reported that size was negatively related to students' perceptions of their campus's friendliness, cohesiveness, and supportiveness. In the larger colleges, there was less concern for the individual student, lack of psychological involvement in classes, little familiarity with instructors, greater competitiveness, and lower cohesiveness. Exceptions were found, but generally smaller institutions were the more psychologically supportive environments.

This research runs counter to the belief that large schools are better than small schools because they can concentrate resources, develop more impressive activities, and stimulate more learning. Large high schools can indeed engage in many different activities and provide a diversity of curricula that would allow a heterogeneous student body to follow courses of study best suited for each individual. The diversity and potential for satisfying the needs of an array of individuals would seem at first to go with big schools. However, research on school size suggests that the distribution of the actual use that is made of existing facilities is more important than the variety of facilities presumably available. On the average, students in small schools make better use of their facilities, at least in terms of individual and group participation in educationally valuable activities, than do the students of large schools. The data offer clear evidence that some of the very important ingredients to support academic learning—involvement, participation, and commitment—are not encouraged by large and impersonal schools.

The Neighborhood

Whereas size influences the sorts of behavioral settings and social interactions that are possible, the sociology of a neighborhood imposes many norms and values on the school. It starts by shaping the basic resources that are present in the school. Sexton (1961), for example, illustrated how the organizational resources of a school district are allocated in relation to the immediate socioeconomic environment of the school. She found that money spent for schools in a large urban district, as well as the quality of education offered, varied in relation to the incomes of families in the school's neighborhood. Sexton found inequalities in (a) adequacy of school buildings and facilities; (b) school and class crowding; (c) competence of teaching staff; (d) methods of testing student performance; (e) methods of selecting and segregating students; (f) thoroughness of the secondary curriculum; (g) vocational and educational counseling of students; (h) opportunities for completion of secondary school and admission to college; (i) use of school buildings by adults; (j) enrollment in preschool programs; (k) health, recreation, and food services facilities; and (l) total costs of educating students. All were correlated with the poorer academic performance of lower-income students. Her findings also held obvious implications for race relations. Indeed, she pointed out that in another city, appropriations for school expenses in white schools were almost 25% greater per student, teachers' salaries were 18% higher, and nonteaching expenses were 50% higher than in black schools (1963 *Handbook*).

Differences in resource allocation across schools set the stage for variations in what happens in classrooms. Herriott and St. John (1966) showed, for example, that both teachers and principals of schools in low socioeconomic neighborhoods were less experienced and less satisfied in their jobs than those in high status areas. In the highest status areas, only 17% of principals wanted more prestige, compared to 43% in the lowest. Furthermore, 42% of teachers in the lowest compared with only 18% in the highest status schools wanted to transfer to a school in a better neighborhood. The teachers of schools in the lowest status neighborhood were younger, less experienced, newer to the school, and receiving less pay. Poor physical conditions, overcrowding, outdated curriculum supplies, and inexperienced, harsh, and punitive teachers made up the school's reality for lower-class students. Furthermore, measures of the quality of both teaching performance and classroom group processes were lowest in schools of poorest socioeconomic status. Moreover, as a large survey on security in schools has shown, (National Institute of Education, 1977), it is the urban lower-class neighborhoods that have schools in which crime and violence is high and in which both the students and faculty feel anxious about their security.

The psychological fall-out from these objective deficiencies are perhaps even more devastating to the teachers and students. Finn (1972), for example, found that teachers in lower-class urban schools had much lower expectations for students and paid more attention to IQ scores and achievement tests in evaluating student work than did the teachers in middle-class schools. He pointed to the socioeconomic character of schools to account for his findings. Teachers in middle-class suburban schools had lower class loads, more teaching resources, and more support from psychologists, counselors, and curriculum personnel than their urban counterparts. The teachers in the lower-class urban schools did not have resources, nor did they have to make adequate diagnoses of the students' problems. Consequently, out of frustration, urban teachers used "objective indicators" of mental test scores to determine the worth of a student's performance.

Other research indicates that classroom conditions, teachers' expectations, and circumstances of the family and neighborhood combine to reduce the likelihood that lower-class students will do well in school. Still, a few studies have questioned this apparently inevitable relationship between a student's socioeconomic background and academic achievement. McDill et al. (1969) studied 20 high schools and found that parental involvement and community support for academic achievement were important variables in affecting student achievement. In 1966 Gross conducted a similar study of low socioeconomic elementary schools and also found parental interest (measured by teacher's perceptions) differentiated low and high academic productivity in schools with relatively homogeneous sociological groupings. Although the literature seems clear that a neighborhood's socioeconomic character has a significant influence on the school's functioning, especially with regard to academic achievement, the results are *not* so conclusive that educators can justify failures to improve the quality of instructional programs by "writing off" schools in low socioeconomic neighborhoods.

The sociology of the school's neighborhood also makes a difference in student behavior through the influence of peers. Wilson (1959), for example, provided evidence showing how the norms of peers influence adolescent aspirations about higher education. He measured student aspirations in schools with three types of predominant populations as follows: (School A) upper-middle-class white collar; (School B) lower-middle-class white collar; and (School C) industrial working class. Wilson found that in School A, 80% wanted to go to college; in School B, 57% wanted to go to college; and in School C, 38% wanted to attend college. Wilson found that each of these schools embodied a different pattern of norms about college attendance. His data showed that 93% of the sons of professionals in School A wanted to go to college whereas only 64% of the upper-middle-class boys in School B wanted to go to college. In contrast, only 33% of the sons of manual workers in School C wanted to go to college, whereas 59% of working class boys in School A wanted a college education. The influences of peer norms were shown to alter the participating students' aspirations about college.

Boyle (1966), Michael (1961), and Sewell and Armer (1966) obtained similar findings indicating the relation between the predominant social class of students and their aspirations to attend college. Derision, ridicule, and rejection faced the boys who had different college aspirations and career orientations than their peers. Therefore, peer influence may be even more important than the formal educational programs in determining a student's plans about college.

Indeed peer norms can have a powerful influence on students of all social classes and personality styles. McDill *et al.* (1969) measured the relative effects of the neighborhood and norms of the peer group on the behavior of students. The analysis revealed that the effect of the socioeconomic context of a school's neighborhood disappeared when important personality and ability variables were held constant. In contrast, even when the school's socioeconomic context and the personal attributes were simultaneously held constant, various normative dimensions (e.g., competitiveness, negative attitudes about college, etc.) of the peer group continued to have significant effects on students' performances.

In another study of peer norms, Winter, Alpert, and McClelland (1963) assessed value changes of bright, rural boys who were exposed to an intensive summer education at an elite private boarding school in New England. The results indicated that the students changed their values toward what the researchers called the *classic personal style*. They became more cynical and sophisticated, had more self-control over impulses, and showed increased antihumanitarianism. These values were not only promoted by school peers but were apparently effective in influencing the thinking of those boys who were exposed to them for only 6 weeks.

In some schools, staff members are continuously battling the student peer group, especially when its norms are antagonistic to the achievement values of the school. Educators frequently find fault with parents, neighborhood groups, or the larger community for socializing youngsters who have little conception of the "value of education." Recently, it has been commonplace to see police within the hallways of schools to keep order. In some of these instances, social relationships within the school itself serve to perpetuate and accentuate the antischool norms of the peer group.

Formal Structure

Two structural aspects of formal school organization that are influenced by both size and neighborhood, and that interact with the informal climate of the participants in a circular manner, are *complexity* and *influence*. Both serve to differentiate one school from another and both can indirectly impact upon student learning through the influence they have on the school climate.

Complexity

We already have shown that in both large industries and large schools there are high amounts of absenteeism, dissatisfaction and low amounts of worker morale and energy. In both, too, a feasible remedy for organizational bigness has been the introduction of small, interdependent work groups or teaching teams in which staff members carry out the lion's share of their daily work. However, increased organizational complexity can present a mixed blessing to the participants in the organization. Whereas the dysfunctions of bigness may be partially overcome, the emergence of diverse interests between organizational components, and intergroup competition and conflicts can present new organizational problems.

For example there may arise, with the introduction of increased complexity, the bifurcation of interests between the *line* and the *staff*. Line participants act as generalists concerned with executing the primary operations of the organization. In schools the primary line participants are the superintendent, principals, department heads, and the teachers. Without them, the chain of accountability would not exist. Those with staff positions act more as specialists, rendering consultation to the line participants, such as counselors, psychologists, curriculum specialists, and the evaluators. In schools, conflicts are typical between occupants of line and staff positions. The line participants may become irritated because they are urged to accept advice from staffers who do not possess a complete picture of how the school or classrooms really work. At the same time the staff participants experience frustration because they see themselves as knowledgeable and expert, even while they lack access to and leverage to influence either the school or the classrooms.

Perhaps the key issue is that members of line and staff positions gain access to different kinds of information, and each is therefore likely to entertain different strategies for accomplishing organizational goals. An example occurred in a staff with which I was consulting. During the previous several months, the staff had been complaining that the school counselor was not doing an adequate job. Disfavor with the counselor had grown to such a point that many teachers were doubting the counselor's competence. After listening to both sides, it was apparent to me that the problem was primarily structural; it had less to do with the counselor's ability and more to do with a bifurcation of interests. The counselor was spending most of his time working with parents and social agencies. The teachers only saw the students and they knew the students were not being seen much by the counselor. It was only after considerable discussion and some systematic problem solving that the counselors and teachers could recognize that while their targets for the education of youngsters were actually very similar, it was their strategies that differed. No one knows how much of a negative impact this line-staff difference had upon the school climate and student learning.

In research on business organizations, Lawrence and Lorsch (1967) found that success in achieving effective differentiation of line and staff, and collaboration between them, was determined by the organization's procedures for handling conflict. When mechanisms for resolving conflict are ineffective, as they were between the counselor and teachers described above, the tensions caused by line-staff cleavage can be destructive to the organizational climate. When conflict is openly confronted, both differentiation and collaboration can be promoted. Skillful management of line-staff conflict through collaborative problem solving can enhance school climate, as was shown in a recent empirical study by Bell (1977). Both the research by Bell as well as the industrial studies by Lawrence and Lorsch (1967) suggest that relatively flat organizations, such as elementary schools, need only a well-articulated, overlapping hierarchy for managing conflicts, whereas larger secondary schools should possess special structures for problem solving that cut across the regular, managerial hierarchy.

The multiunit structure is a useful organizational arrangement for managing role conflicts (see, Schmuck et al., 1975). The key to this structure is the link-pin role described by Likert (1961), which offers a communicative link between each level of organizational hierarchy and each team of administrators and teachers. The leadership team, for example, is the principal link with the district office, whereas team leaders act as communicative links between the leadership team and the teachers at large. Every faculty member knows someone who can communicate directly with the leadership, making flatness within hierarchy. This structure, while complex, permits direct managerial contact with those who may have different interests and therefore be in conflict. To be most effective in facilitating a psychologically supportive and informal climate, multiunit structures must have administrators and team leaders who are not only skillful at conflict management and problem solving but who also communicate accurately about everyday matters through memos and bulletins to discourage minor disagreements.

Influence

Members at the bottom of organized hierarchies often feel passive and incompetent in relationship to their authorities. In contrast, organizational members who become involved in decision-making gradually feel more powerful and are likely, eventually, to achieve a willingness to go along with organizational mandates. In many schools, the administration, either in the district office or at the school site, makes most of the major decisions, but in some schools, teachers participate actively in running the school. Research on the way schools are managed indicates that the satisfaction of teachers is associated with their perceptions of the extent to which they can influence the schools' decision-making.

Findings by Hornstein et al. (1968) and Kostman (1978) showed that teachers report greatest satisfaction with their principal and the school district when they perceive that they can influence their principal, and when their principal's reciprocal influence attempts are viewed as stemming from his or her expertise. As teachers feel more influential and begin to view their principal as an expert, they feel better about the school and manifest more emotional support in their contacts with students. As a result, when teachers become more involved in school decision-making, they take greater initiative in designing new programs for their classrooms and in getting feedback from colleagues before carrying their innovative plans to the principal or the staff.

In an ingenious laboratory study of group influence, Levine (1973) showed that the higher the total amount of control of group members over decision-making and the more equally the members shared this control, the better the groups' problem-solving performance and the higher the members' satisfaction. Levine's analysis of what occurred indicated that when control and influence were equalized and dispersed, the quality of the social–emotional interactions between members were enhanced. The implications for schools are that with more equalized and dispersed influence among staff, there will be better support for morale and cohesiveness. Indeed, other research seems to bear this out.

In schools with more equalized power relationships between administrators and staff, the quality of teacher–student relationships in the classroom also improves. In an important research project, Seeman and Seeman (1976) investigated the relationship between sixth-grade teachers' involvement with the governance of the school and their students' attitudes about school, learning, and about themselves. The teachers' degree of dialogue, decision-making, and action in school decisions were positively associated with the students' favorable attitudes. Through participation in school affairs teachers exercised power over the organizational processes of their schools and provided their own students with the feeling of power and responsibility.

Just as the influence attempts of teachers can have strong effects on classroom group processes, the principal's behavior can also affect the group processes of the school staff. Gross and Herriott (1965) showed that principals' leadership behaviors influenced staff morale, innovativeness, and professional performance and student learning. They developed a concept to describe the principal's leadership labeled as Executive Professional Leadership (EPL). A principal's EPL score was determined by how much teachers viewed the principal as being supportive, collaborative and helpful. Principals with high EPL scores (a) had constructive suggestions to offer teachers in dealing with their major problems; (b) displayed strong interest in improving quality of educational programs; (c) gave teachers the feeling that they could make significant contributions to improving performances of students; and (d) made teachers' meetings a valuable educational activity. Teachers who credited their principals with high EPL were comfortable in their school work and felt secure in being encouraged to improve by the principal. Moreover, those teachers who felt supported were not fearful of trying new educational procedures and therefore could provide a more constructive experience for their students within the classroom.

Using the same survey data but this time analyzing for sex differences among the principals, Gross and Trask (1976) found differences between male and female principals. Female principals, as a group, had higher EPL scores than male principals. These findings have also been supported by other studies comparing male and female elementary principals (Meskin, 1974). One conclusion from these analyses would be that women are more effective principals than men, but such a conclusion could be doubted. The sociology of educational administration offers other reasons to account for this discrepancy between male and female scores. Since so few women achieve line administrative positions in public schools, the women who do arrive may indeed be more competent than their male peers. Also, the characteristics of the EPL scores may be more similar to the sterotypic "feminine" qualities than they are "masculine" qualities. One argument suggests that the current valued management style emphasizing participation is a more stereotypic feminine mode of controlling and directing.

Whereas principals, whether male or female, carry the most weight in a school's decision-making, the teaching faculty as a collegial group also carries considerable influence. Chesler, Schmuck, and Lippitt (1963) found that while a teacher's willingness to try new educational practices depended greatly on the principal's support of innovative projects, the commitment of the faculty was also important. In schools where the principal was seen as supportive of innovation but the teaching staff was *not* viewed as supportive, the influence of the principal was undermined in getting teachers to try new plans. Members of a school faculty can counteract the principal's influence by dragging their heels, by letting obstacles interfere with plans, or by sabotaging change efforts that do not meet with their approval.

Informal Climate

The school's informal climate (or as some label it, the school's atmosphere) refers to the affective states that purvade the interpersonal relationships and the group dynamics of the administrators, staff, teachers, and students. It describes how organizational participants relate to one another in terms of trust, openness, closeness, social support, and cohesiveness. A school with a favorable climate is one where participants expect to support one another in doing their best, where they share high amounts of influence, where high levels of attraction exist, where norms are supportive of working diligently as well as for maximizing individual strengths, where communication is open and featured by dialogue, and where developing together as growing people are considered relevant in themselves for discussion.

It is useful to consider informal school climate as conceptually intervening between contextual factors and formal structure on the one hand and the psychological experiences of students and student learning on the other. As we have already explained, school size, the nature of the neighborhood, structural complexity, and the nature of the influence structure all serve to shape and condition the informal climate of the school. Size, for example, influences the quantity of potential social interactions and communication nets, as well as the amount of possible cognitive input—it tends to encourage the rise of impersonal bureaucratization as it increases, and to encourage closer, more personal relationships as it decreases. The culture of the neighborhood shapes interpersonal expectations, aspirations, and alienation. It presents either cultural similarities or differences between the faculty and students and gives rise to peer influences that shape what goes on in classrooms. Structural complexity puts demands on school participants for accurate communication, procedures for managing conflicts, and for carrying out collaborative problem solving. The influence structure organizes the inputs and access to decision making of the different school participants. When hierarchical, it often encourages alienation and withdrawal of those who are out of power.

All of these complex organizational dynamics and social-psychological relationships are extraordinarily difficult to systematize and to measure. In a large-scale empirical inquiry of high schools as part of Project Talent, Shaycroft (1967) put it this way: "The schools studied do vary in effectiveness, but the specific school characteristics that produce results are somewhat elusive. . . . One of the crucial differences between an ineffective school and an effective one may be something as vague as the school's atmosphere."

Let us set the stage for understanding how the informal climate performs its function in linking the school organization with student learning by reiterating some of the complex causal relationships depicted in Figure 5.1. At the start of our analysis, we are presented with students and staff members—with their many capabilities and personalities—entering a school site and coming from their respective neighborhoods, embodying the cultural perspectives of their early socialization as well as the norms of their current neighborhood. They gather together at a school site, constituting a quantity of participants that gives the schools its size. Next, the faculty and students adopt organized ways of interacting. They form into different subsystems with various degrees of complexity and they establish an influence structure for control and accountability. Both the contextual factors of size and neighborhood as well as the structural arrangements of complexity and influence are enacted through different relationships, norms, and daily procedures. Within this social context—as the interpersonal relationships play out the formal structure—the informal climate emerges to take on a life of its own. Simultaneously, events take place in the classrooms, hallways, assemblies, lunch room, and the like, during which staff climate and student climate interpenetrate each other. For the teacher's part, the complexity of this process has been nicely delineated by George and Bishop (1970). Students, for their part, develop certain perceptions, cognitions, feelings, and attitudes about the staff, academic learning, and themselves. These psychological states interact with a student's views of self as learner and feed the energy or anxiety of a student in relation to learning. Student performance on academic subjects results, as least in part, from these psychological processes.

Concepts to Understand Climate

Noteworthy contributions to the literature about climate have been made by Halpin and Croft (1963), Miles (1965), and Fox et al. (1974).

Halpin and Croft, in a classic study, coined the phrase, "the open and closed climates of schools." In differentiating between open and closed climates, they came up with four characteristics of the faculty and four characteristics of the principal. They found that schools with open climates had staffs with high esprit (morale and cohesiveness), high intimacy (trust and closeness), high engagement (collaboration and interdependence), and low hindrance (social support and facilitation of change). The principals of the open climates were characterized as showing considerateness (giving support and allowing for individual differences), manifesting thrust (initiating actions and stimulating others to act), arguing for high production (emphasizing achievement and offering formative feedback), and were low on aloofness (personal sharing, friendship, and closeness). A questionnaire of 64 items developed by Halpin and Croft to measure these eight factors has been widely used. In the last *Encyclopedia of Educational Research,* Griffiths (1969) wrote that by 1967 already over 100 studies had been done using Halpin and Croft's The Organization Climate Description Questionnaire (OCDQ).

Miles delineated several variables that he considered to be indicators of a healthy school climate. These were goal focus, communicative adequacy, power based on competence, resource utilization, cohesiveness, morale, autonomy, adaptation, and general problem-solving adequacy. While these overlap with the eight dimensions posited by Halpin and Croft, they tend to be broader and to relate better, at least theoretically, to the contextual factors and structural variables described earlier. For example, goal focus becomes more difficult as the complexity of a school increases, and having power based on competence is less likely in a highly hierarchical influence structure. Working with a score of researchers and consultants, Miles fashioned these climate concepts into a kit of instruments for local school district use (see Fox, Schmuck, Van Egmond, Ritvo & Jung, 1973).

In the most comprehensive effort yet to delineate concepts to understand climate, a 12-person team, made up of scholars and practicing administrators (Fox et al., 1974), came up with eight factors:

1. *Respect.* Shown for participants in the school seeing themselves as persons of worth with valuable ideas to share.
2. *Trust.* Reflected in confidence that others can be counted on to behave
   honestly.
3. *Morale.* Feeling relaxed about relationships and work.
4. *Opportunities for Input.* Having chances to contribute ideas and seeing
   that they are considered.
5. *Growth.* Believing in the legitimacy of personal growth for all school
   participants.
6. *Cohesiveness.* Feeling that school participants are together and thinking
   alike on important matters.
7. *Renewal.* Able to pull together to do problem solving without undue
   stress and conflict.
8. *Caring.* Feeling that participants are concerned about one anothers'
   welfare.

Using these eight factors to guide them, the team of 12 developed an
instrument for staffs to diagnose their own organizational climate. It has
been used by scores of faculties for school improvement efforts.

School Climate and Student Learning

The originators of the concepts to understand climate imply a causal
relationship between the quality of interpersonal relations among staff
members (the respect, trust, morale, etc.) and the ways teachers behave
toward their students in the classroom. The argument goes as follows: If
teachers possess feelings of comfort and rapport in relationships with colleagues, they will also be supported in their feelings of self-worth and be
better able to relate supportively with students. Contrastingly, feelings of
hostility, competition or alienation among staff members may lead to
teacher anxiety and to low levels of tolerance when interacting with students. In the parlance of our youth, if teachers are "up tight" with other
members of the faculty, they will tend to be "up tight" with their students.

One indicator of trust and openness among staff members is how often
teachers ask one another to observe in their classroom and to make suggestions for improvement. The traditional norm of professional autonomy
strongly mitigates this. Another indicator is teacher collaboration when
teachers come together informally. For example, faculty lounges are settings
that offer considerable information about staff relationships; in some schools
there are specific norms against discussing teacher-related work; in other

schools the faculty room may be where one can go to let off steam, get the support of another, or just be let alone to unwind. In some schools teachers consciously avoid the faculty room; as one teacher put it, "I've got enough problems with my students—I don't need to get involved with faculty hassles, too!"

If fear, anxiety, and competition are characteristics of a staff's relationships, innovative and creative teaching will not be encouraged, and constructive feedback among colleagues will not be for collaborative efforts at improving instruction (see Chesler, Schmuck, & Lippitt, 1963). In schools where teachers are in competition or alienated from one another, innovative ideas about classroom group processes are the property of one teacher, either because no one else knows about the ideas or because others are reticent to "steal" the ideas for their own use. The curriculum of a classroom and the constructive use of innovative instructional strategies will suffer if teachers cannot stimulate one another with new ideas and practices. As creative teaching falls off, so may student learning suffer, both as a result of students' weakened motivation and because of the lack of encouragement and reinforcement from the teachers.

While it is true that interpersonal trust and closeness among faculty members may support more creative teaching (and consequently student learning), other skills and group procedures will also be required to enhance staff members encouraging one another to teach better. Miles described these as goal focus and communicative adequacy, whereas Fox et al. wrote of the opportunities for input and the support of personal growth on the staff. For example, I have found in my consulting experiences that for staff members to stimulate and encourage one another to try instructional changes, they should be able to use the communication skills of describing behaviors without impugning others' motives, of being able to paraphrase what another person has said, of communicating about educational goals directly, and of perception checking with another colleague to see what that person is thinking and feeling. Teachers who are able to execute these communication skills when interacting with one another can both stimulate one another and more easily do the same with their students.

In one project dealing with the communication patterns of the faculty, for instance, Bigelow (1971) found that teachers used their communication skills—learned during an organization development project with their fellow staff members—in their classrooms even though none of the organization development (OD) training in communication was directly aimed at instructional change within classrooms. The teachers in Bigelow's project found ways of collaborating and solving problems together, which they also turned to good use when trying to involve their students in two-way communication in the classroom.

In addition to skillful communication, we should also emphasize the interpersonal norms and skills of *constructive openness*. Constructive openness is the sort of feedback that guides recipients supportively toward testing out alternatives for their own behavior; it does not threaten or challenge the recipient's self-concepts or feelings of competence (see, Schmuck, Runkel, Arends, & Arends, 1977). One study looked at the effect of teachers' feedback to the principal (Daw & Gage, 1967) and found favorable effects on changing the principal's role behaviors when feedback was given constructively and with the support of systematic data. Similar findings on feedback from student to teacher have also been obtained (Gage, Runkel, & Chatterjee, 1963). Indeed skill in being constructively open is a necessary part of the culture of a self-renewing school. And we do not mean mere sympathy, commiserating, or pitying by the concept of constructive openness. On many faculties there is some member who has a sympathetic shoulder, but sympathy may only ease the burden and not necessarily solve the problem that the colleague is facing. Moreover, when appropriate, constructive oppenness carries the meaning of giving critical feedback that hopefully will upgrade the recipient's role performance.

Members of staffs that use constructive openness with one another and with the students offer supportive social-emotional atmospheres for helping to solve frustrating problems. For example, in informal staff discussions, comments of colleagues about how they view the relationship between a teacher and a student may help the focal teacher to look at the student in new ways. In this manner, constructive openness serves to broaden and deepen the myopic view of the teacher involvee In some schools where I have observed or worked, the use of constructive openness has become formalized. On a regular schedule teachers observe one another with the intent of giving feedback to improve instruction or in order to present problems at faculty meetings so that group problem solving can occur. Critical evaluation that does not demean or chastise can be an important avenue for encouraging improved group processes both on the faculty and within the classroom.

The ways staff members think about human behavior can also have an impact on student–teacher interaction (see, Runkel, Schmuck, Francisco, & Arends, 1979). McGregor (1967) has distinguished between two conceptions of human motivation labeled Theory X and Theory Y. In simple terms, Theory X stipulates that people are lazy and passive, and must be pushed and prodded to action. Theory Y argues that people are curious and active and should be allowed freedom to find ways of doing things. Staffs with Theory X views tend to employ leadership characterized by authoritarianism, one-way communication, and restrictive norms. However, staffs with

Theory Y views allow for more student freedom, are more collaborative, and employ more two-way communication.

The Theory X and Y categories of McGregor are similar to the custodial and humanistic categories of Willower. Appleberry and Hoy (1969) have built on Willower's concepts to describe an educator's orientation to human behavior. Teachers who score on the custodial side of the Willower scale tend to think about students as being in need of control and training; students are viewed as lacking responsibility and self-discipline. From the custodial perspective, the school is viewed as being responsible for the students' behavior, and authority is seen as being appropriately hierarchical with administrators and teachers at the top, giving students little opportunity to make their own decisions. In contrast, teachers with a humanistic orientation view the school as a community of humans being engaged in learning through their interactions with one another. They believe that power should be shared by all participants, including the students, and that, whenever possible, decision-making decisions should be held by those who will be affected by the decision. In their research, Appleberry and Hoy found that faculties typically hold a fairly high agreement about their custodial versus humanistic assumptions for human behavior, and that these assumptions are acted out in the organizational procedures of the school. The humanistic orientation prevails in what Halpin and Croft call open schools, whereas the custodial orientation prevails in their closed schools.

PERCEPTUAL FIELDS OF STUDENTS

Students are introduced to academic learning and expected to pursue mastery of academic subjects within the school organization. In this section, I explain how the social processes delineated earlier may shape the perceptual fields of students. While the interrelation of the school's contextual factors, formal structure, and informal climate is certainly more complex than we can grasp, it does make a difference in the way students will become involved in academic learning. Furthermore, the proper starting point in understanding this social influence process is the students' perceptions of the school environment.

Perhaps the best empirical study on the relationship between the school organization and student perception is the recent one on teacher participation in educational change by Seeman and Seeman (1976). Their study traced connections among incoming teacher attributes, formal structure, informal climate, and student attitudes. It showed that when teachers with a variety of contrasting personal attributes were put into interdependent problem-solving teams with administrators, and urged to take an integral part of the influence structure by entering into what Seeman and Seeman referred to as dialogue, decision-making, and action-taking, they were influenced in their teaching to facilitate more favorable classroom climates, which in turn supported the development of more favorable student perceptions of the school. Seeman and Seeman did not collect data directly on what the informal climates of these schools were like, nor did they assess student achievement.

Lewin's simple theory for explaining the dynamics of social behavior is useful for tracing the social-psychological linkage between school and student, particularly the connections among informal climate, student perception, and student learning. He argued that behavior is caused by a concatenation of the person's perceptions of the environment and the person's personality structure. The theory was expressed in the form of a pseudo equation written as Behavior = $f(E$ and $P)$, where f stood for function of, E stood for environment, and P stood for person. We think of the school's formal structure and its informal climate as offering stimuli for the E, whereas the student's motives, attitudes, and values constitute important features of the P.

Environmental Stimuli

As I have explained, the sociological variables of size, neighborhood, formal structure, and informal climate present the organizational stage on which student academic learning takes place. These distal stimuli combine to present two proximal, environmental stimuli that impinge on students' orientations to academic learning: the stimulus of structural demands and the stimulus of staff norms and teacher expectations.

Structural Demands

The most salient proximal structure for student perception and learning is the social system of the classroom. And the most readily apparent structural feature of a class is its size. Just as we have explained previously, the size of a classroom, particularly when it exceeds 30 or 35 students, can have debilitating effects on student attitudes and learning. Whereas large group instruction can be effective for transmitting cognitive information, it typically does not offer individualized learning opportunities, nor does it raise the morale and cohesiveness of the learning group.

Hare (1962) has summarized over 60 studies which indicate that as the size of the group decreases, the strength of the affectional ties between members increases. Moreover, Hare's summary indicated that a team of about five or six members constitutes the best number for getting tasks accomplished and for performing productively. Many public school classes are too large to be either affectively supportive or cognitively productive. This was shown in the SAFE school study of the National Institute of Education (1977), which came up with the disturbing result that as class sizes rose so did the risk of being attacked and robbed. Is it any wonder that precious little academic learning goes on in large classes?

Many teachers do, of course, manage classroom instruction in ways to enhance affectional ties and cognitive growth, but I believe most of the successful cases are those in which the teacher takes initiative to create smallness out of bigness. Teachers engineer intimacy by either individualizing instruction so that each student feels more in tune with his or her own cognitive development, or by establishing learning teams of four to six so that cohesiveness becomes possible. Furthermore, through supportive reinforcement of a host of student behaviors, and through confronting either subgroup or total class disruptions, successful teachers establish a dispersed, informal support system within the peer group, thereby helping students to perform more optimally on their academic subjects.

The organizational dilemma posed by a teacher's success in constructing smallness out of bigness is the inconsistency that can arise across classes. This can be particularly troublesome in secondary schools where students move from one class to another. The inconsistencies of structures and procedures across classes, not to speak of differing leadership styles of teachers, may present a bewildering diversity for the adolescent. Frequently, the student comes to consider some teachers as nice, others as good but strict, others as permissive and perhaps weak. Psychological dissonance in relation to this diversity may be a frequent outcome for the student, leading some students to feel suspicious, mistrustful, and doubtful of the motives of adults. It could well be that the so-called generation gap increases as the variability of classroom structures and procedures increases.

Differences between classes also can be understood in terms of the different reinforcement patterns executed by both the teacher and a student's peers. In relation to the school organization, these differences can be caused by the contextual factors, formal structure, and informal climate of the school. This is particularly apparent when we consider features of the teacher's neighborhood culture along with the teacher's interactions in the school's formal and informal structures. As Dreeben (1968) and Swidler (1976) have shown, student behavior reinforced by teachers can range from "It is good to be independent" to "It is important to be collaborative." Moreover, as Seeman and Seeman (1976) have shown, teachers who are an integral part of the school's formal influence structure will tend to communicate more support for students than teachers who are removed from the influence processes of the staff.

The sad fact this analysis of the school organization presents is that even the best intentions of teachers and the most skillful teaching may lead to very little student learning when they take place in a school where most of the other teachers are performing differently. The impact of inconsistency and the resulting dissonance can, at least for students who feel insecure and doubtful about their competence, turn the students off from making an effort to learn. As we noted in the words of the student quoted first in this chapter, "Who cares?" "Why try?" "Nobody knows nothing at this school anyway!"

Staff Norms and Teacher Expectations

In part, the informal climate of a staff is constituted of a certain set of social norms. Norms are group agreements, generally implicitly established and maintained, that help guide the perceptions, thoughts, feelings, and behaviors of group members. They influence the interpersonal relationships of a staff by helping members to know what is expected of them and what they should expect from others. School goals are one sort of norm. A school's goals—whether formal or informal—are objectives that staff members believe are shared by most or at least should be shared by most.

When I discussed the informal climate previously, I mentioned research by Willower et al. (1967) on distinguishing humanistic from custodial teachers. Similar constellations of teacher attitudes can accumulate to make up the norms of a school. Indeed, the schools contrasted in the Bank Street Study approximated these two norms—the traditional school operating with custodial norms, and the modern school operating with more humanistic norms. The proximal stimuli engendered by these contrasting norms are impactful, particularly when the two norms are directly expressed through the behavioral expectations that administrators and teachers hold for how their students will act within the school or classroom.

Expectations on the part of staff members for students are communicated in various direct and indirect ways. Consider, for example, a student who has seriously broken a school rule for the first time and is called to the principal's office. If the principal says, "I'm surprised and disappointed in your behavior; explain how this happened," a different interpersonal stimulus has been presented to the student than if the principal says, "This is intolerable, but I'm not surprised; I'm going to make sure that you are not in a position to do this again." The first statement establishes that the principal did *not* expect that the student would have behaved the way he or she did, whereas the second one establishes that the principal *did* believe that the misbehavior will continue unless strong measures are taken.

Consider some of the following statements that I have heard teachers express in communicating their expectations for students in the classroom: "Don't start on your papers until I give the instructions; most of you will do it wrong anyway," or "I will have to watch the three of you very closely during the test," or "This is a very difficult story. Only a few of you will understand it. But let's try it anyway." These and many other teacher expectations for student behavior are expressed daily in the classroom. When teachers or peers come to share identical expectations for particular students, the inputs can become very powerful stimuli for the students involved.

Willower, et al. (1967) described how teachers new to a staff become socialized into the prevailing norms of the experienced staff members. The ideas that brand new teachers hold about what is good teaching often are quite different from many of the ideas of the more experienced teachers in the school. In the Willower et al. research, the neophytes differed in placing more value on a humanistic orientation, emphasizing student freedom and choice. At the same time, the new teachers were striving to feel at ease, secure, and accepted by their more experienced colleagues. Whereas a few of the new teachers maintained their personal humanistic views throughout the first year of school, most newcomers gradually succumbed to the prevailing custodial values of the staff.

That study and my own experiences indicate that staff norms can have a powerful influence on teacher attitudes and expectations and that the staff's expectations about students can shape the ways in which teachers carry out instruction and discipline in the classroom. A considerable amount of research, moreover, has established the fact that teacher expectations constitute a significant proximal stimulus for student learning (see, Schmuck & Schmuck, Chapter 3, 1979).

Personality Attributes

As the Lewinian theory stipulates, behavior is a function of both environmental stimuli and personality attributes. In relation to personality attributes, students are viewed as having a "master motive" to strive for self-esteem and self-respect. We would expect students either to seek a favorable perception of themselves as student and learner or to devalue the roles of student and learner, making them unimportant parts of the self-concept.

The classical work on personality carried out by Murray (1938) and Allport (1937), along with the theory and empirical research of McClelland and colleagues (1953) lead to the conception that striving for self-esteem takes place in at least three motivational domains: (a) the striving for achievement, also referred to as competency, efficacy, and curiosity; (b) the striving for power or influence in relation to others; and (c) the striving for affiliation and affection. According to this thinking, the most fundamental motivational questions might be: "What can I accomplish?"—"How can I exert my will?"—"Who will go along with me?"

Typical emotions resulting from frustrating these motives can be observed in most classrooms. For example, in relation to achievement, we may find feelings of inferiority and dullness that often lead to a lack of interest in academic learning and to a reduced amount of energy for work on classroom tasks. In relation to power, we often find feelings of being put down and ignored that can lead to overt aggression or covert deviousness and a heightened anxiety when called upon to perform or to cooperate. Coleman (1966) in a large-scale survey found that feelings of powerlessness inhibited student learning more than all other variables that were researched. Finally, in relation to affiliation, we often find feelings of rejection, loneliness, and even betrayal leading to insecurity, anxiety, and behavioral withdrawal or passivity. Incompetence, powerlessness, and rejection can be the most serious motivational problems within the classroom and school.

PSYCHODYNAMICS OF STUDENT LEARNING

Environmental stimuli and personality attributes combine to shape perceptual structures within students that are associated with academic learning. Those perceptions facilitate students' for either becoming involved and expending energy on learning or becoming removed and defending against academic involvement. Our understanding of the psychodynamics can be enhanced by: (a) an expectancy–valence motivational theory; (b) the circular process of interpersonal relations; and (c) a theory of personal change.

Expectancy–Valence Paradigm

A theory of motivation delineated by Atkinson and Feather (1966) is useful for describing the psychodynamics of student learning. The theory proposes that the tendency to act is determined by a motive force, an expectancy factor, and an incentive value of acting, all put together in a multiplicative relationship. The motive force is similar to our descriptions of relevant personality attributes, particularly to the motives of achievement, power, and affiliation. The expectancy factor and the incentive value, however, are presented by the environment and therefore are associated with our descriptions of environmental stimuli.

To illustrate, students who are achievement-oriented and who perceive both that their teachers expect them to do well and that they will be rewarded for showing competence will manifest a tendency to work diligently in relation to academic learning. Conversely, students with little achievement motivation and with little support or incentive from their teachers will tend to do only minimal work. In a parallel fashion, the motives of influence and affiliation support vigorous student involvement in the classroom when the environmental stimuli support their satisfaction and retard involvement when the stimuli run counter to them. Of course, those students whose motives have been frustrated regularly during early socialization will enter most learning situations with very low self-esteem and will manifest little concentration and energy in relation to academic subjects.

Circular Process of Interpersonal Relations

The combining of environmental stimuli and personality attributes within students entails both an interpersonal exchange between educator and student and an intrapsychic response on the part of both. The expectancies and incentives communicated by administrators and teachers are received by students within their own motive structures. In turn, the behavioral responses of the students affect the way faculty members subsequently communicate the expectancies and incentives, and the process goes on and on in a circular fashion.

In interpersonal exchanges between teachers and students, expectations about others interact psychologically with self-expectations and personal motives to give rise to the behavior. Those two different sorts of expectancies, about others and about the self, grow out of previous encounters with others, and through other indirect avenues such as information, cultural stereotypes, social situations, and expected role functions.

For example, staff norms that teachers have internalized undergird certain expectancies and incentives that they communicate to their students. The students read such teacher messages in terms of their own motives, self-esteem, levels of anxiety, and the like. Student responses that grow out of both their perceptions and their personal attributes are viewed by the teachers in light of the teachers' perceptual maps about themselves and their students. After teacher–student interactions of this sort have gone on over a substantial number of weeks, their relationship becomes stable, predictable, and self-fulfilling. When this occurs, a change in the relationship is difficult to engineer.

An example of a student's contrasting experiences in two classrooms can clarify circular interpersonal processes. Susan was a loving child who liked to be helpful to others. Her affiliative motive was very strong. She had been in an elementary school where there was a great deal of joint work on projects. Other students frequently wanted her to become part of their teams, and told her so. She gloried in this and blossomed because of these reinforcements, perceiving herself as a helpful and loved individual. When

Susan entered the junior high school, she went to a different set of teachers and a different student culture. There was virtually no teamwork allowed on projects. The atmosphere was competitive and individuated. She yearned for companionship, finally finding it outside the school with some former friends. Students of the junior high frequently interpreted her advances as pushiness, dependency, or even as wishing to cheat. She became disenchanted with school, gradually removing herself from extracurricular activities. In her classes she daydreamed and the teachers began scolding her for inattention and poor work.

A Theory of Personal Change

Formal interactions between faculty and students may also be understood as a social influence process, whereby the teachers offer instruction to facilitate personal changes in their students' perceptions, attitudes, and behaviors. The extent to which student changes are, at the same time, perceptual, attitudinal, and behavioral will depend in part on the nature of the influence process between teachers and students.

Kelman (1958) described three different types of social influence and their consequences for personal change: (a) *Compliance.* Students accept influence from teachers because they may gain specific rewards or because they wish to avoid specific punishments; (b) *Identification.* Students accept influence from teachers because they want to establish or maintain a satisfying relationship with the teacher; and (c) *Internalization.* Students accept influence from teachers because the ideas and actions being proposed are congruent with the students' own personal attributes.

When a teacher emphasizes reward or punishment during instruction, students learn to comply, but at a psychologically superficial level of personal change. Students conform to teacher demands primarily to avoid the threat of disapproval and rejection. The social influence process of compliance encourages public conformity without private acceptance. Thus, students' behaviors may change, particularly under the surveillance of the teacher, but their cognitions and attitudes do not change. This means that the students may behave quite differently from what the teacher intends outside the classroom or even in the same classroom when, for instance, a substitute teacher takes over.

The social influence process of identification takes place when the teacher represents an attractive model for the students. In such instances, students will tend to believe in the responses they adopt and to follow the instructional demands of the teacher; however, the specific content of instruction will be more or less irrelevant. The student adopts the teacher's instruction because it is associated with what the student defines as a desired relationship. Much of the identification process involves unconscious modeling. The student does change behavior and even some cognitions and attitudes but these changes may not persist when the teacher–student relationship comes to an end.

Internalization occurs when what the teacher offers during instruction fits the personal attributes that the student brings to the class. Thus, the student accepts influence because of the instructional content—the ideas and actions of the curriculum—and not so much because of externally administered reinforcements or the attractiveness of the teacher. Internalization tends to become a possibility as students are encouraged to choose among alternatives and as they become pursuaded of the importance of learning particular content areas or skills. Moreover, internalization is likely to occur to the extent that the instruction has avenues for satisfying the students' needs for achievement, power, and affiliation.

As has been the case in previous sections of this chapter, the complexity of the psychodynamics involved in student learning is staggering. And we have merely touched the surface. But it does seem clear that organizational life and student learning are interrelated. Environmental stimuli engendered by structural demands, staff norms, and teacher behaviors interact with the motive states of students. From the perceptual vantage points of students, the environmental stimuli become expectancies, incentives, reinforcements, demands, requests, smiles, and the like. Students' responses to those influences depend in part on the congruence between the inputs and their personality structures. Wherever students can exercise initiative or have a choice in restructuring teacher inputs to fit their own motive structures, the more likely it will be for the environmental stimuli of the school organization to be congruent with a student's personal attributes, thereby facilitating student learning.

SUMMARY AND CONCLUSIONS

The chapters in this volume address variables and processes considered by social psychologists to be most proximal to student learning. They include classroom group dynamics, teacher–student relationships, and student expectations and attitudes. In contrast, this chapter analyzes student learning from the more macro-perspective of the school organization. My argument has been that, through a complex chain of social-psychological events, the organization of the school influences the way students perceive and feel about themselves as students, and that these reactions can influence the energy available to students for pursuing academic learning.

Three classes of interrelated organizational variables serve either as facilitators or restraints to student learning. First are the contextual factors of organizational size and the culture of the neighborhoods from which the staff members and students come. Second are the formal structural variables of complexity and influence within the school. And third are the emotional aspects of the informal climate of the school including trust, openness, and morale.

These three classes of organizational variables are brought into the daily lives of the students in the form of such environmental stimuli as the structural demands of the classroom and movement from one class to another, staff norms particularly about students, and teacher expectations for student conduct and learning. Students perceive these stimuli through the cognitive maps formed by their motives for achievement, power, and affiliation along with their general self-esteem as students and learners. When the students' perceptions of the environmental stimuli and their personal attributes are combined, they create a tendency, on the students' parts, to commit various amounts of energy to academic learning.

Discrepancies between students' perceptions of environmental stimuli and their personal attributes trigger dissonance that can lead to anxiety about learning and alienation from school. Stimuli related to impersonal competition in large classes, for example, can clash with the motive for affiliation or feelings of insecurity about oneself as a student. Contrastingly, stimuli related to equalitarianism and cooperation can clash with the motive for power and the wish to control others.

While discrepancies like those, along with their attendant anxieties about academic learning, seem inevitable, they may be ameliorated by attending to more responsive and accurate two-way communication between the faculty and the students. Responsiveness can be attended to on several fronts, including classrooms, the curriculum, and the interdependence between staff governance and student governance. Teachers can facilitate responsiveness in their classes by offering choices to students about ways of carrying out learning assignments and by initiating frequent group discussions with students about how the class is going. The social studies teacher can help some students cope better with the school by offering a formal course on "learning about organizational psychology by studying our own school." Administrators can increase responsive two-way communication between the faculty and students by arranging for meetings at which teacher leaders and student leaders can carry out collaborative problem solving about organizational life in the school. But a thorough rendering of such ameliorative actions is not the province of this chapter.

REFERENCES

Allport, G. *Personality: A psychological interpretation.* New York: Henry Holt, 1937.

Appleberry, J. B. & Hoy, W. K. The pupil control ideology of professional personnel in open and closed elementary schools. *Educational Administration Quarterly,* 1969, *3,* 74–85.

Astin, A. W. *The college environment.* Washington, D. C.: American Council on Education, 1968.

Atkinson, J. & Feather, N. *A theory of achievement motivation.* New York: Wiley, 1966.

Baird, L. L. Big school, small school: A critical examination of the hypothesis. *Journal of Educational Psychology,* 1969, *60,* 253–260.

Barker, R. & Gump, P. *Big school, small school: High school size and student behavior.* Stanford, California: Stanford University Press, 1964.

Bell, W. *Impact of organization development interventions conducted by an internal cadre of specialists on the organizational processes in elementary schools.* Unpublished doctoral dissertation, University of Oregon, 1977.

Bidwell, C. The school as a formal organization. In J. G. March, (Ed.), *Handbook of organizations.* Chicago: Rand McNally & Company, 1965.

Bigelow, R. Changing classroom interaction through organization development. In R. Schmuck & M. Miles (Eds.), *Organization development in schools.* La Jolla, California: University Associates, Inc., 1971.

Boyle, R. P. The effect of high school on student's aspirations. *American Journal of Sociology,* 1966, *71,* 628–639.

Chesler, M., Schmuck, R. A., & Lippitt, R. The principal's role in facilitating innovation. *Theory Into Practice,* 1963, *2*(5), 269–277.

Coleman, J. S. *Equality of educational opportunity.* Washington, D. C.: U. S. Government Printing Office, 1966.

Daw, R. & Gage, N. Effect of feedback from teachers to principals. *Journal of Educational Psychology,* 1967, *58,* 181–188.

Dreeben, R. *On what is learned in school.* Reading, Massachusetts: Addison-Wesley, 1968.

Eisenstadt, S. N. *From generation to generation: Age group and social structure.* Glencoe, Illinois: Free Press, 1956.

Finn, J. Expectations and the educational environment. *Review of Educational Research,* 1972, *42*(3), 387–410.

Firestone, W. The balance of control between parents and teachers in co-op free schools. *School Review,* 1977, *85*(2), 264–286.

Fox, R. et al. *School climate improvement: A challenge to school administrators.* Bloomington, Indiana: Phi Delta Kappa, 1974.

Fox, R., Schmuck, R. A., Van Egmond, E., Ritvo, M., & Jung, C. *Diagnosing professional climates of schools.* La Jolla, California: University Associates, 1973.

Fox, S. D. (trans.). Emile Durkheim, *Education and sociology.* Glencoe, Illinois: The Free Press, 1956.

Gage, N., Runkel, P. J., & Chatterjee, B. B. Changing teacher behavior through feedback from pupils: An application of equilibrium theory. In W. W. Charters, Jr. & N. Gage (Eds.), *Readings in social psychology of education.* Boston: Allyn & Bacon, 1963. 173–181.

George, J. & Bishop, L. K. Relationship of organizational structure and teacher personality characteristics to organizational climate. *Administrative Science Quarterly,* 1971, *16*(4), 467–475.

Gouldner, A. W. *Patterns of industrial bureaucracy.* Glencoe, Illinois: The Free Press, 1954.

Griffiths, D. Administrative theory. In *Encyclopedia of educational research.* (4th ed.). Toronto: Macmillan, 1969.

Gross, N. *Some sociological correlates of the academic productivity of urban elementary schools with pupils of low socio-economic status.* Paper presented at the Meeting of the American Sociological Association, Miami, Florida, August 1966.

Gross, N. & Herriott, R. *Staff leadership in public schools.* New York: Wiley, 1965.

Gross, N. & Trask, A. *The sex factor in the management of schools.* New York: Wiley, 1976.

Halpin, A. W., & Croft, D. B. *Organizational climate of schools.* Chicago: Midwest Administrative Center, University of Chicago, 1963.

Handbook of Chicago School Segregation. Compiled and edited by Education Coordinating Council of Community Organization. Chicago: 1963.

Hare, A. P. *Handbook of small group research.* New York: Free Press, 1962.

Herriott, R. & St. John, N. *Social class and the urban school.* New York: Wiley, 1966.

Hornstein, H., Callahan, D., Fisch, E., & Benedict, B. Influence and satisfaction in organizations: A replication. *Sociology of Education,* 1968, *41*(4), 380–389.

Kasarda, J. The structural implications of social system size: A three-level analysis. *American Sociological Review,* 1975, *39,* 19–28.

Katz, M. B. *Class, bureaucracy, and schools: The illusion of educational changes in America.* New York: Praeger, 1971.

Kelman, H. C. Compliance, identification, and internalization: Three processes of attitude change, *Journal of Conflict Resolution,* 1958, *2,* 51–60.

Kostman, S. Shared problem solving, decision making, *Bulletin of National Association of Secondary School Principals,* 1978, *62*(414), 64–68.

Lawrence, P. R. & Lorsch, J. W. *Organization and environment: Managing differentiation and integration.* Boston: Harvard Business School, Division of Research, 1967.

Levine, E. Problems of organizational control in microcosm: Group performance and group member satisfaction as a function of differences in control structure. *Journal of Applied Psychology, 58*(2), 1973, 186–196.

Likert, R. *New patterns of management.* New York: McGraw-Hill, 1961.

McClelland, D. C., Atkinson, J. W., Clark, R. A. & Lowell, E. L. *The achievement motive.* New York: Appleton-Century-Crofts, 1953.

McDill, E., Rigsby, L., & Meyers, E., Jr. Educational climates of high schools: Their affect and source. *American Journal of Sociology,* 1969, *74*(6), 567–586.

McGregor, D. *The professional manager.* New York: McGraw-Hill, 1967.

Merton, R. *Social theory and social structure.* New York: Free Press, 1949.

Meskin, J. The performance of women school administrators—A review of the literature. *Administrator's Notebook,* 1974, *23*(1).

Meyer, J. W. & Rowan, B. Institutionalized organizations: Formal structure as myth and ceremony, Palo Alto, California: Stanford Center for Research and Development in Teaching, June, 1976.

Michael, J. A. High school climates and plans for entering college. *Public Opinion Quarterly,* 1961, *25,* 585–595.

Michaelsen, J. Revision, bureaucracy, and school reform: A critique of Katz. *School Review,* February, 1977.

Miles, M. Planned change and organizational health: Figure and ground. In R. O. Carlson, (Ed.), *Change processes in the public schools.* Eugene, Oregon: Center for Advanced Study of Educational Administration, currently Center for Educational Policy and Management, 1965, 11–36.

Minuchin, P., Biber, B., Shapiro, E., & Zimiles, H. *The psychological impact of the school experience: A comparative study of nine-year-old children in contrasting schools.* New York: Basic Books, 1969.

Moracco, J. C. The relationship between the size of elementary schools and pupils' perceptions of their environment. *Education 98*(4), 1978, 451–454.

Murray, H. A. *Explorations in personality.* New York: Oxford University Press, 1938.

National Institute of Education. A research perspective on educational improvement. Unpublished paper. Washington, D. C.: The National Institute of Education, Office of Health, Education & Welfare, October, 1977.

Pace, C. R. *Analyses of a national sample of college environments.* Final report, Cooperative Research Project, No. 50764. Washington, D.C.: Office of Education, U. S. Department of Health, Education, and Welfare, 1967.

Parsons, T. *The social system.* New York: Free Press, 1951.

Rand Corporation, *Federal programs supporting educational change.* Vol. 4: *The findings in review,* by P. Berman & M. W. McLaughlin. The Rand Corporation, R-1589/Y-HEW, April 1975.

Runkel, P., Schmuck, R., Francisco, R., & Arends, J. *Transforming the school's capacity for problem solving.* Eugene, Oregon: Center for Educational Policy and Management, 1979.

Schmuck, R., Murray, D., Smith, M., Schwartz, M., & Runkel, M. *Consultation for innovative schools: OD for multiunit schools.* Eugene, Oregon: Center for Educational Policy and Management, 1975.

Schmuck, R. A., Runkel, P., Arends, J., & Arends, R. *The second handbook of organization development in schools.* Palo Alto, California: Mayfield, 1977.

Schmuck, R. A. & Schmuck, P. A. *Group processes in the classroom.* (3rd ed.). Dubuque, Iowa: William C. Brown, 1979.

Seeman, A. & Seeman, M. Staff processes and pupil attitudes: A study of teacher participation in educational change. *Human Relations,* 1976, *21*(1), 25–40.

Selznick, P. *TVA and the grass roots.* Berkeley: University of California Press, 1949.

Sewell, W. H. & Armer, J. M. Neighborhood context and college plans. *American Sociological Review,* 1966, *31,* 159–168.

Sexton, P. C. *Education and income: Inequality of opportunity in our schools.* New York: Viking Press, 1961.

Shaycroft, M. F. *Project talent, the high school years: Growth in cognitive skills.* American Institute for Research and School of Education: University of Pittsburgh, 1967.

Stavig, G. R., & Barnett, L. D. Group size and societal conflict, *Human Relations,* 1977, *30*(8), 761–775.

Swidler, A. What free schools teach, *Social Problems,* 1976, *24*(2), 214–227.

Weick, K. Educational organizations as loosely coupled systems. *Administrative Science Quarterly,* 1976, *21*(1), 1–19.

Willower, D. J., Eidell, T., & Hoy, W. *The school and pupil control idiology.* Pennsylvania State Studies Monograph, No. 24, University Park. The Pennsylvania State University, 1967.

Wilson, A. Residential segregation of social classes and aspirations of high school boys. *American Sociological Review,* 1959, *24,* 836–845.

Winter, D., Alpert, R., & McClelland, D. The classic personal style. *Journal of Abnormal and Social Psychology,* 1963, *67,* 254–265.

chapter 6

Attitude Development and Measurement

JAMES H. McMILLAN

INTRODUCTION

The nature of pupil attitudes is important to consider. First, as a construct that influences behavior, attitudes are antecedent factors to pupil cognitive learning. Second, attitudes comprise a significant outcome of school learning, which in some cases is a far more influential consequence of schooling than cognitive knowledge attained. Although most educators agree that attitudes are important, and include "affective" objectives or goals as part of the purpose of school learning, to establish attitudes as "important" is not enough. The difficulties in working with attitudes are also well known and seem to overwhelm intent. The reality in most schools is that there is no systematic integration of attitudinal objectives with teaching. At best, it continues to be intuitive, scattered, misunderstood, and oversimplified. As an area of study of interest to social psychologists, it has direct relevance to this book, although this presentation is different from those now existing in either social psychology or education texts. The intent of this chapter is to investigate the nature of pupil attitude development. By examining the process through which attitudes are formed, the relationship between attitudes and learning in the context of the interactionist perspective can be explored more fully. Whereas some attention is also given to measuring attitudes, no attempt is made to cover traditional measurement techniques. Also, the emphasis in reviewing research is on the attitudes toward school subjects, not on attitudes toward "school" or "learning." Although

THE SOCIAL PSYCHOLOGY
OF SCHOOL LEARNING

the latter types of attitudes are not unimportant, subject matter attitudes are more clearly related to cognitive achievement (Jackson, 1968).

WHAT IS AN ATTITUDE?

Perhaps the greatest difficulty in the study of attitudes is the lack of an agreed upon definition of the construct. There are many definitions presently in the field, including the following:

> Attitudes are likes and dislikes. They are our affinities for and our aversions to situations, objects, persons, groups or other aspects of our environment [Bern, 1970, p. 14].

> A predisposition to respond in a generally favorable or unfavorable manner with respect to, or in the presence of, the object (Fishbein & Ajzen, 1972).

> An attitude is a readiness to respond in such a way that behavior is given a certain direction (Travers, 1977).

> An attitude toward an object or concept consists of the interpretations a person makes regarding its value for various purposes [Cronbach, 1977, p. 739].

> Whenever we use the word "attitude," we are making a prediction about the future behavior of a person based on our observations of his past behavior [Mager, 1968, p. 15].

> An attitude is a mental and neural state of readiness to respond that is organized through experience and which exerts a directive and/or dynamic influence on behavior (Allport, 1935).

Despite the large number of different conceptualizations of the term "attitude," there seem to be several agreed upon characteristics. Most researchers in the field agree that attitudes are learned predispositions that influence behavior, they vary in intensity, must be inferred from some type of behavior, are usually consistent over time with similar situations, and are almost always complex in their composition. Most important, it can be argued that traditional definitions of "attitude" are general and vague. This has given some persons the impression that an attitude is, similarly, a general like or dislike, for or against, or a favorable or unfavorable disposition. However, an attitude is neither general nor simple. Attitudes are multidimensional constructs that vary in different situations. Furthermore, it seems reasonable, based on the perspective of this book, that they are most meaningful only in relation to the situation with which they are considered.

The complexity of attitudes has been noted to some degree in recent educational literature. Travers (1977), Gagné (1977), and Cronbach (1977), agree that "attitudes" are best defined as having three interrelated components (a) a cognitive component; (b) an affective component; and (c) a behavioral or connotative component. This implies a more complicated structure of the concept than does the general definition that combines the components into a "disposition." The cognitive component may be defined as an intellectualized aspect of what one believes or perceives about the characteristics of some category or concept. These "cognitions" can be neutral, describing attributes of size, color, salience, etc., but are more often evaluative—valuable, worthless, useful, etc. Thus, the cognitive component is what one thinks about the object or idea; that is, mathematics is valuable to know; history is useless; Mrs. Jones is intelligent; Mr. Jones is strict. The affective component consists of the emotion or feeling associated with the cognition or belief. It is manifest in how the individual feels in the presence of the object or person and consists of automatic nervous responses. Thus, an individual feels good or bad, enjoys, dislikes, or feels comfortable or anxious, etc. Relating this component to school, a student may dislike or not enjoy doing mathematics, or feels art is fun. The behavioral component is a predisposition to act or behave in a certain way. An inclination to interact with an object or voice a favorable opinion may indicate that the individual holds a positive "attitude" toward or in regard to the object. However, other factors influence behavior, such as norms, habits, and expectancies about reinforcement. Consequently, attitudes help to direct behavior and may be inferred from behavior if these other variables are taken into consideration.

Psychological research designed to confirm the existence of the three components has not been convincing (Triandis, 1971). However, several studies report evidence that the three components are separate and independent (Bostrom, 1970; Hartman, 1972; Ostrom, 1969; Komorita & Bass, 1967, McKennell, 1974). Moreover, some psychologists argue that whereas the three components exist, they are so highly intercorrelated that separate measurement is not necessary. The components are likely to be consistent with one another, and when this occurs the attitude is strong and stable. However, it is also likely that for some students these components may be incongruous in attitudes toward school subjects. A student can like history (affective) and at the same time think it is useless (cognitive). Such a student's attitude would be favorable in one respect and unfavorable in another. A general measure of this attitude that does not differentiate between the components would not accurately reflect the student's actual feelings and beliefs toward history. Only separate measurement of each component will reveal this complexity.

The tripartite definition of attitude may be helpful in examining specific aspects of the construct and has definite implications for attitude development and measurement, which will be discussed later in this chapter. However, there is still a need to consider the pervasive influence of situation in determining attitudes and affecting the degree to which attitudes impact behavior. That is, there is a need to integrate conceptions of attitudes with the interactionist perspective in this book. Thus, with some hesitation because of the many definitions already in the field, this writer purports the following conception of attitude to specify the importance of each component and situational parameters: *An attitude refers to a set of evaluative beliefs, emotions, and behaviors which predisposes a tendency to act in a particular way toward an object in a class of social situations.* The implications of this definition are developed more fully in the remainder of the chapter.

DEVELOPMENT OF PUPIL ATTITUDES

Social psychologists have studied attitude development for many years. Although some of their research cannot be generally applied to school situations, it is useful to review their findings. The research on attitude formation and change falls into four theoretical categories: (a) classical learning; (b) operant learning; (c) cognitive restructuring; and (d) modeling. Each position will be summarized, with implications indicated for school learning. Since attitudes are learned, much like our behaviors and knowledge, the models of attitude formation correspond closely to learning theory in general.

Classical Conditioning

Classical conditioning and contiguity learning comprise the first major approach to learning attitudes. Classical, or respondent, conditioning is the primary mechanism for the development of the emotional component of attitudes. As neutral stimuli are paired with emotion-eliciting stimuli, the formerly neutral stimuli evoke a similar emotional response. Thus, when the word "no," a neutral stimulus to children when they first hear the word, is paired with a slap on the hand (which elicits an emotional response of fear and pain), the word "no" soon becomes capable of eliciting a "fear-like" response. Staats (1967) provides a summary of general laboratory studies that supports this type of learning. Leventhal (1974) has suggested that generally applying this process to nonlaboratory settings may be limited to situations where the subject has direct contact with the attitude object and its consequences, or where the effects are verbally mediated. However, it seems plausible that pupils can learn emotional responses to school and school subjects in this way. Despite the lack of systematic research in school settings, classical conditioning (or the related notion of contiguity learning) can account for much "affective" learning. To cite only a few examples: Educators provide pleasant stimuli in schools such as vending machines, pictures, interesting furniture, decorations, and carpeting to encourage student feelings of comfort and enjoyment; elementary students sing and play games; hunger and resulting responses of discomfort become associated with the class students attend just before lunch; and learning through games and other "fun" activities elicits positive feelings that are paired with the subject studied.

Bloom (1976), Mager (1968), and Glazer (1969) employ the concept of classical conditioning of attitudes in stressing the importance of providing "success" experiences for students. According to Bloom, a student's feelings toward various subjects are established over many years during which the student either succeeds or fails in mastering the subject. The notion is that as students experience pleasure, pride, and other positive emotions after achievement, this positive affect will be paired or associated with the subject. Bloom (1976) provides evidence that math students in the top and bottom fifth of their class academically develop attitudes that are congruent with their perception of ability in math. Bloom believes that "adequacy" or "success" is determined by the grade the student receives, and recommends mastery learning as an alternative to traditional grading that would maximize the positive attitudes of pupils. Although there is, clearly, a positive relationship between grades in a subject area and attitudes toward that subject, the research has been almost all correlational. Because success of "getting an A" is also a form of operant learning, the effects of rewarding and achievement will be discussed in some detail in the next section of this chapter.

Another form of classical conditioning is evident in the way we form impressions of objects and people we have little direct contact with or knowledge about. When we hear and read that a group of people display certain characteristics, for instance, we are likely to "label" that group with those characteristics. In its worst form, this process results in stereotyping. The characteristics may not directly evoke emotion, but are usually related to an affective state. Words such as "lazy," "poor," and "dumb," are likely to generate a negative affect. Sometimes called "semantic generalization," the effect of verbalizations on emotional responses has been nicely demonstrated by Staats and Staats (1958).

Another persepctive on how contiguity learning is a factor in attitude development has been suggested through research in the field of attribution (see Chapter 2). The proposition suggested is simple: Causal inference thinking affects the way we feel. Thus, as we associate success and failure with particular causes, we generate specific affective or emotional reactions. Early research in this area indicated that we maximize emotional responses, given internal causal ascriptions, and minimize responses for external ascriptions. More recent research has focused on how separate emotions are differentially experienced, depending on specific causal ascriptions. Weiner, Russell, and Lerman (1978) found that "outcome dependent" emotions, regardless of "why," were different. For success, the emotions of happy, satisfied, good, and contented were common, whereas failure elicited upset, displeasure, and uncheerful feelings. They also reported distinct emotions for different attributions. Trying hard and succeeding led to emotions of uproarious, delirious, and delighted. Luck resulted in surprise and astonishment, ability was related to confidence and competence, and failure led to feelings of incompetence and hopelessness. Also, Sohn (1977) found that attributing the cause of failure to a lack of ability results in the greatest amount of unhappiness, and that ability and effort ascriptions for success equally generate happiness. He also found that effort attributions, generally, produce more pride for success and shame for failure than those of ability.

The research of Weiner and his associates and Sohn represent important contributions to our understanding of the affective component of attitudes. However, their research, in the main, has involved contrived situations in which the subject must generate a conception of probable affect given a description of failure or success. A few studies have researched the emotional consequences of causal attributions in real life. Bailey, Helm, and Gladstone (1975) found that affect intensity (a combination of happiness, pride, satisfaction, and good–bad) was determined most by outcome, success or failure, regardless of the causal ascription. They found, for example, that positive affect was just as great for students who thought the ease of an exam was a primary determinant as for those who attributed the cause to ability or effort. This finding conflicts with Weiner's position that maximum affect is experienced with internal ascriptions. However, Frieze, Snyder, and Fontaine (1977) found internal factors generating more affect in a real-life testing situation, even though people who felt ability was the primary determinant felt better than those who attributed the success to effort, contrary to Weiner's research. Nicholls (1975) has identified other factors that may interact with causal ascriptions to determine affect. He found ability more important than effort in tasks that influenced future performance, and that the value of the task interacted with effort, such that high value, high effort courses generated most affect (pride–shame only). It seems that the research of Nicholls, especially, demonstrates the importance of the situation in determining affect, as well as the reasons people give for success or failure. That is, whereas it is reasonable to think that people experience the greatest pride in succeeding at difficult tasks and experience the greatest shame in failing at an easy task, the effort ascription that generates the feelings may be mediated by such variables as task importance, value, long-range implications, the nature of rewards, teacher characteristics, and other factors. This notion fits nicely into the perspective of this book. There is little question that how we interpret our success and failures will influence our emotions, and, as such, the affective component of our attitudes. But this idea must be considered in the context of environmental conditions and personal variables that affect the nature of the feelings.

Operant Conditioning

A large body of research exists concerning the effect of reinforcement on establishing or modifying attitudes. There are several ways in which operant conditioning is influential. Insko (1967) summarized techniques that can be used to reinforce particular behaviors that indicate a positive or negative attitude. For instance, if pupils happen to say how much they enjoyed their reading, then a teacher can affect attitude toward reading by reinforcing this positive response. Thus, we can change the behavioral component by reinforcing appropriate behaviors. This approach to developing pupil attitudes is nicely summarized, with examples for applying it in educational settings, by Mager (1968).

Operant learning is also evident when students are rewarded for achievement in a subject. Although it is unclear how the praise or incentive operates to affect the "attitude," research does seem to indicate a positive relationship between achievement in a subject area and attitudes toward the subject (McMillan, 1976). However, the evidence that grades or praise, specifically, influence attitudes is somewhat contradictory. Neidt and Hedlund (1967), in a study of 573 university students in three courses, found a small positive correlation, after partialing out aptitude, between attitudes and final course grades. Teigland (1966) also found a positive relationship between higher grades and the formation of positive attitudes with college students. However, Ryan (1968) found that there was no relationship between grade giving and attitudes in a large sample of junior high students, and Orbaker (1972) found that verbal praise did not affect the attitudes of college students toward physical education. Hake (1973) found that eighth-grade mathematics students who received written praise, personal comments, or no comments at all did not differ in the attitudes they formed. Considering the large number of studies that have indicated a positive relationship between achievement and attitude, the results of these studies seem contradictory and need to be put into perspective.

Theoretically, grades can be viewed as either extrinsic or intrinsic rewards, depending on the meaning of the grade to the student. If the grade indicates achievement and can be equated with "success," then the grade will have meaning—it will affect the self-image of the individual. This emotional feeling of competence will likely be associated with the subject and tend to foster a positive attitude toward the subject. On the other hand, if the grade is meaningless and is only an extrinsic incentive to do the work, the effect of the grade may be quite complicated, depending on the conditions under which the grade was given. Thus, the effect of the reinforcement may be a function of the perception of the contingency. This approach overlaps with another theoretical view of attitude development, cognitive learning or information processing. This perspective is illustrated in the following experimental studies of the effect of rewards on attitudes.

Deci (1971) found that the tendency of college students to engage in the intrinsically rewarding activity of solving a puzzle would lessen if money was given as a reward for performing the task. The subjects appeared to view the activity as dull if extrinsic rewards were present to "bribe" the subjects. Lepper, Greene, and Nisbett (1973) measured the effect of rewards on the intrinsic value of drawing of preschool children. Three groups of children were used in the study; one group agreed to receive a reward for drawing; the second group received an unexpected reward; and the third group was given no reward. The group that expected and received the reward showed a decreasing interest in drawing over time than the other two groups.

Kruglanski, Alon, and Lewis (1972) studied the relationship between extrinsic rewards and task enjoyment. Children 10 to 11 years old were either rewarded or not rewarded after winning various group competitions. The rewarded group rated the tasks as less enjoyable than the non-rewarded children. Kruglanski, Friedman, and Zeevi (1971) studied 15- to 16-year-olds performing several recall and creativity tasks. One group of students was rewarded by a visit to a university psychology department (this activity was previously determined to be a useful reward), the other group was not rewarded. The ratings of recall and creativity task enjoyment were higher for the no-incentive group than for the rewarded group.

Generally, the incentive-related research seems to indicate that an extrinsic reward may mitigate the instrinsic value and enjoyment of an already interesting task if administered in a certain manner. This finding is based on cognitive dissonance and attribution theory, and suggests that further research is needed with respect to the meaning of the reinforcement. It seems that it is too simplistic to apply behavioristic "laws of learning" in the development of attitudes.

Cognitive Learning

The approaches that consider a person's perceptions, beliefs, and ideas about a stimulus have been studied under the rubric of "cognitive" theories. The emphasis is on how a person's cognitive functioning under particular conditions affects attitudes. There are several areas of research related to this approach, including consistency, cognitive dissonance, persuasion, and information processing. Dissonance theory will be covered in this chapter in some detail since several studies apply this notion to student attitude formation. It is also especially relevant since it deals with the effect of rewards—a ubiquitous commodity in schools.

Cognitive Dissonance

Under a variety of conditions it is possible for a person to simultaneously hold two cognitions that are psychologically inconsistent. This creates a sense of imbalance, incongruity, or disequilibrium which is resolved by modifying the cognitions. The most common situations that manifest this inconsistency involve acting in ways that are contrary to one's beliefs and feelings, and exerting effort to reach a goal that is never attained. The latter form of generating inconsistency is especially relevant for schooling, since this is a form of behavior experienced daily. The basic notion is that when individuals exert a great amount of effort on a task they must justify that effort in some manner. Dissonance results if the effort results in unexpected or non-rewarding consequences. Under these circumstances, the individual will resolve the dissonance by cognitively placing a high value on the task activity itself and on the stimuli associated with the task. That is, the task was valuable or useful in and of itself. If rewards are present, then individuals justify their efforts by the reward they receive. Relating this notion to schools, it is possible that if a student exerts a great deal of effort and is not rewarded, then he or she may value the activity and subject. If the reward was received, the effort is justified not for its intrinsic value but for what it has gained in the form of an external reward. Thus, students will study hard for an A or for some money from their parents, and their efforts will be justified by the reward they receive. If they studied hard and do not receive the extrinsic reward then they should, theoretically, value the task and the subject matter. Dissonance theory has received support in laboratory studies but little in real-life research, and the actual conditions that affect the result described are more complicated than the simple paradigm presented earlier.

Research has demonstrated that the conditions of the situation influence whether a person experiences a dissonance effect, as found by Festinger and Carlsmith (1959), or whether greater rewards are associated with more positive attitudes, as predicted by incentive theory. Studies by Freedman (1969) and Carlsmith, Collins, and Helmreich (1966) suggest that the degree of commitment to the task is a crucial variable variable distinguishing dissonance and incentive effects (the greater the commitment the more the dissonance). However, other research has found that both high choice and high consequences are necessary conditions of the situation to result in a dissonance prediction (Frey & Irle, 1972; Sherman, 1970). Additional research has identified consequences of the behavior as yet another variable (Nel, Helmreich & Aronson, 1969; Brehm & Jones, 1970; Cooper, 1971). Thus, the literature suggests that when a task is chosen fully by the individual, is accompanied by feelings of commitment, and is important and significant (the outcome has high consequences), it is probable that extrinsic rewards will result in a dissonance prediction.

It has been pointed out that dissonance theory may apply to situations with particular conditions. Research in school settings in this area is limited, and none of the studies controls the variables of choice, consequences, and commitment. However, the basic tenant remains plausible and needs to be investigated with school learning—if a student exerts great effort with little external justification (reward), will he view the effort and activity favorably to reduce dissonance?

Two studies have examined the importance of amount of effort. Buenz and Merrill (1968) investigated the effect of effort with 66 nursing students. The subjects were divided into high and low effort groups. The low effort group was required to write one-word answers to questions that were interspersed throughout a film on nursing. The high effort group wrote a short essay justifying each answer in addition to the one-word response. The subjects were given three attitude questions, measuring the enjoyment of the experiment and perceived effort expended, and they showed that greater enjoyment was reported in the direction of the dissonance prediction. The high effort group enjoyed the learning task more than the low effort group. Kauchak (1973) studied the effects of high and low effort with 112 junior college students. In his study, one group was given the task of constructing questions and objectives concerned with Bloom's taxonomy, while the second group did the same but also wrote essays on how the taxonomy might be used to improve instruction in their particular discipline. Again, the high effort group indicated a more positive attitude toward the task than the low effort group.

Some research has studied the interaction of the degree of effort with reward. Aronson (1961) conducted a laboratory study in which subjects were required to exert either high or low effort in attaining a reward of money. The amount of money received was also high or low, producing a 2 × 2 research design. He found that in a high effort condition, high and low reward groups formed similar attitudes, whereas in the low effort condition, high reward students formed more positive attitudes than low reward students. The extrinsic reward of money was balanced by dissonance only when high effort was involved. Dissonance was not experienced in the low effort condition. In a replication of Aronson's study, McMillan (1977) found a significant interaction between an intrinsic reward and effort. College students were given high or low effort assignments and randomly given either high praise or none at all for their work. The assignments were a natural part of the class, and the students were unaware that they were subjects in an experiment. The results showed that students who exerted high effort and received high praise reported significantly more positive attitudes toward the assignment than students who exerted high effort and received no praise feedback, or exerted low effort regardless of feedback. Merrill, Yaryan, and Musser (1969) extended Aronson's design to study medical students' attitude toward programmed material. They used two levels of effort and four levels of reinforcement of correct answers. However, the dependent measure, enjoyment of the experiment, showed no dissonance or incentive effects.

In Aronson's study the reward is extrinsic. However, in theory, Aronson discusses dissonance in terms of "success," and intrinsic and extrinsic rewards are not differentiated. "Success" seems to imply an intrinsic reward of feedback that tells the individual something about his or her ability or competence. However, in the experiment the reward was extrinsic. It appears that "success" or "failure" depends on what the individual expects before the task is attempted, and how the reward or feedback relates to this expectation. Success in this sense could be either extrinsic or intrinsic, but must relate to the expectation to have an effect. For example, the previously discussed findings by Deci (1971) show than an extrinsic reward lessens interest and the intrinsic reward of praise increases interest in a task in which the expectation is that it is already valuable and/or enjoyable. In this case the praise defined "success" and thus, because effort was exerted, praise had a positive effect on the attitude. When the extrinsic reward is given, a different dynamic operates within the subject and he or she asks: "Why am I doing this?" instead of relating the praise or feedback to his or her self-image. Similarly, tasks that have high commitment, choice, and consequences probably develop expectations that allow dissonance to operate.

Most school-related tasks have many different types of rewards, and the success for any expectation is complicated. A student could receive an A in a class and thus fulfill the expection of making the Dean's List or pleasing parents, which is different from rewards such as teacher-written feedback related to competence or self-image. A real-life task has many expectations, and different rewards will relate to different aspects or stimuli associated with the task. Aronson was able to control this since the only difference in the tasks he used was the color of containers. However, in studying for an examination or writing an essay there are many aspects associated with the task, each with different expectations that different types of rewards are likely to affect. For instance, many of the experiments reviewed have measured the subject's attitude toward the task itself, not the subject matter of the task. Furthermore, the measures of the attitude have not differentiated between different components of the attitude. It is possible to value a task highly when the expectation is fulfilled and still not enjoy doing it. For example, taking a foreign language was "valuable" because it enabled a student to graduate, but it still may not have been enjoyable. The grade was an extrinsic reward related to the value of the course, yet the fact that the language was difficult to learn influenced its unpleasantness (intrinsic).

Persuasion and Modeling

A final form of cognitive restructuring has been studied as attitude change, or persuasion. There is an extensive amount of literature in this area, and only an overview of the findings will be discussed here. The empirical approach has been to investigate characteristics of the source of a message, communications, and the nature of the audience to whom the message is addressed. In an educational setting, communications—either spoken or written—are likely to have a significant effect on attitudes since they are so pervasive. Triandis (1971) summarizes research that indicates the extent to which one person can influence another, depending on the perceptions of the source of the message. If the source is viewed as competent (people who have knowledge, ability, skill, expertness), attractive (physical aspects, clothes, demographic characteristics, friendliness, pleasantness), powerful (distribution of rewards and punishments), and credibility (trustworthy intentions), he or she is most likely to be influential. The audience, depending upon their needs, will incorporate and use information related by persons with these characteristics The competence trait is related most to helping a person understand his environment, and thus would be most important for individuals who have a need for better understanding. Attractive and credible sources are especially influential to those who have personal or social needs. Relatively unenduring changes in attitude result from a need to attain rewards, and a powerful source is usually most effective when the need is focused on contingencies. Also, if the actual content of the communication is clear, able to hold attention, and induces an optimum level of anxiety or discrepancy, it will have its greatest impact.

Whereas most of the principles summarized in the previous paragraph are derived from laboratory research, the implications for developing pupil attitudes in school seem clear. Not only is it important for the teacher to be perceived as attractive, competent, and trustworthy, it is equally important that students view each other in the same way. This suggests the creation of a classroom environment that develops respect, friendships, honest and trusting communications, and a norm of supporting and caring about each other.

In this type of classroom the cognitive component can be influenced through the information shared between teacher and pupils.

The last approach to attitude development, modeling, is related to persuasion, since characteristics of the model and the needs of the learner are important determinants. If another person is admired, respected, and perceived as having good intentions, that person can influence another's behavior vicariously. This process directly influences the behavioral component of attitudes, and through the behavior affects the cognitive component.

ATTITUDE RESEARCH IN SCHOOLS

The general approaches to studying attitude change have definite implications, but the usefulness of the concepts is limited since most of the research has not been done in school settings. This section of the chapter reviews research that has been done with pupils in schools. While not usually grounded in theory as formulated through laboratory studies, this research is directly concerned with influencing pupils' attitude development toward school subjects. The research is divided into several areas. These include studies concerned with (a) identifying factors affecting attitudes; (b) instructional methods; (c) teacher attitude and enthusiasm; and (d) classroom climate.

Identifying Factors

Aiken (1970), in a comprehensive review of literature since 1960 on attitudes toward mathematics, suggested that the attitude of the teacher toward mathematics is the single most important determiner of student attitudes toward the subject. In several studies the impact of the teacher was shown to be greater than ability grouping and different curricula. Aiken also pointed out that an emphasis on relevance, meaningfulness, and games will increase positive attitudes, as will simply getting a student to associate mathematics with something pleasant. The final factor Aiken stressed is enabling the student to feel successful. Students who consistently fail in a subject lose self-confidence and develop a dislike for the subject. Aiken identified success as the reward students receive, and suggested that learning should be structured so that the student feels competent with the subject. Aiken did not discuss how grade giving and other forms of feedback from the teacher affect students' feelings of success.

In a later review of attitudes toward mathematics, Aiken (1976) concluded that "changes in attitudes toward mathematics involve a complex interaction among student and teacher characteristics, course content, method of instruction, instructional materials, parental and peer support, and methods of measuring these changes [p. 302]." In particular, Aiken stated that certain personality characteristics, such as self-concept, achievement motivation, intuitiveness, and attitudes of parents are related to attitudes toward mathematics. Specific methods or courses have not had a significant impact on college, elementary, or secondary school students' attitudes toward mathematics. Aiken cited several studies that do not support the contention that the teachers' attitudes are related to pupils' attitudes, but stated that the research, overall, supports the impact of teachers' attitudes. Studies of the use of calculators and other instructional devices gave conflicting results, and behavior modification techniques were generally successful in reducing anxiety toward mathematics. The reviews by Aiken show that the number of studies on mathematics attitudes has increased sharply over the past 10 years. However, general conclusions are less evident. While the teacher seems to be the most important classroom variable, there are many conflicting results. This is due, in part, to different instrumentation and definitions of "attitude," varying degrees of sophistication in research design, comparing results across grade levels, and the interaction of personality factors with attitudes.

Several studies suggest that school-related attitudes are influenced before the student begins school, and that these prior attitudes have an important impact on subsequent attitude development. Poffenberger and Norton (1959) questioned 390 freshmen at the University of California concerning their attitudes toward mathematics and the attitudes and expectations of their parents. They found that the students' attitudes were positively related to the fathers' attitudes toward mathematics and the expectations for achievement in mathematics held by both parents. Aiken (1972) also found a high correlation between the attitudes of students and parents. Osborn (1971) took a sample of 398 high school students and concluded that student attitudes toward educational achievement was positively related to the educational level of their parents. Hansen (1969) found that the attitudes of fourth graders toward reading was positively correlated with the extent of parent involvement with the child's reading activities; showing concern, encouragement, interest, and giving help. Ramsett, Johnson, and Adams (1974) studied three college economics classes. They used regression analysis to conclude that prior attitudes were most highly related to measures of the attitudes toward economics taken at the completion of the course. Cangemi (1972) found the same results in college chemistry classes. Ryan (1968) researched the effects of modern and conventional mathematic curricula on student attitudes of 126 pairs of ninth grade classes. Each teacher taught one conventional and one modern class. Ryan found that teacher grade-giving and curriculum materials did not account for different student attitudes, but that prior attitudes toward mathematics accounted for the attitude differences.

Callahan (1971), in an informal survey of 366 eighth grade students, asked them to give reasons for liking or disliking mathematics. The most frequent reasons stated for liking math included "needed for life, interesting, fun, and good teachers [p. 753]" while reasons for disliking math were "not good in math, boring, no value [p. 753]." A study by Namazi (1969) found similar results. Namazi asked 1170 fifth- and sixth-grade students to recall "critical" moments in their school experience that affected their attitude toward physical education. The pupils reported that teachers who used demonstration and explanation, provided a variety of games and activities, and in general did something to provide fun and enjoyment had the most positive impact on their attitudes. These studies seem to indicate that classroom activities that depend upon teacher behavior may influence attitude formation.

Moore (1973) randomly selected a national sample of 373 tenth-, eleventh-, and twelfth-grade students to determine predictors of student attitudes toward science and scientists. He found that the sex of the student, the impression of the teacher as "liked" or "smart," and self-concept of present and future academic ability were significant predictors. These results support the findings of other research. Self-concept is a factor similar to parental influence since it is determined prior to a school experience, while the teacher is confirmed as the most important variable in the classroom. Haney (1964), in a study of high school students' attitudes toward science, found that the teacher is more important than the sex of the student, socioeconomic status, IQ, or grade point average in changing science attitudes.

McMillan (1976) reviewed 124 dissertations written between 1969 and 1975 which studied factors related to pupil attitude formation toward school subjects. I found that 84% compared different instructional approaches, but very few of those reported significant differences. The most significant relationships resulted from studies of teacher behavior and student-related variables such as self-concept, background, parents, and previous attitudes. My conclusion was that research comparing two or three types of curriculum, textbook, class structure, set of objectives, etc., was generally not related to attitude formation. Rather, positive self-concept, teacher enthusiasm toward and knowledge of the subject, positive attitudes of parents, and favorable attitudes in the past consistently resulted in significant relationships with attitude formation. This represents a nonexperimental artifact, however, and it is not clear whether the various factors caused the attitudes or the attitudes resulted in positive self-concept, perception of teacher enthusiasm, etc.

In a review of attitudes toward reading, Alexander and Filler (1976) reached several conclusions with regard to variables associated with attitude development. They cited several studies that show some relationship between achievement and attitudes, and suggested that certain instructional methods and programs may improve attitudes. Student self-concept and teacher and parent interests, attitudes, and interaction with students may affect attitudes toward reading. In a less extensive review of studies, Squire (1969) indicated that liking or disliking reading may depend on the interaction between background factors, revealed in interest "preferences" and reading materials. Squire generalized from several studies to suggest that the environment in which reading is taught may affect student attitudes, but that most findings with regard to classroom approaches are sporadic and disappointing. Squire concluded his review by stating that personal qualities of the teacher are critical in developing pupils' attitudes toward reading.

McMillan and May (1979), interviewed a random sample of 53 junior high school students to assess perceptions of school influences on their attitudes toward science. Questions focused on influences of the teacher, amount of effort in studying science, parents' feelings about science, rewards, and the relationship between enjoyment and perception of usefulness. Results showed that the best-liked aspect of the curriculum involved active participation, that teacher characteristics (personality and behavior) are crucial influences both positively and negatively, that effort exerted toward science was important (the more effort the better the attitude), and that students differentiated between liking science and thinking it was useful.

In summary, the literature identifying factors that affect attitude development seems to suggest that a few variables are especially influential. These include factors related to the teacher in the class (the teacher's enthusiasm and attitude toward the subject, how well-liked the teacher is by students, the teacher's system of reward giving, the way in which the teacher keeps the subject relevant or interesting) and factors that affect attitudes before the students enter a particular classroom (parental attitudes, the student's self-concept and prior attitudes toward a subject). The problem with much of this research, however, is that many of the "important" factors are difficult to specify in hypothesizing a general theory of attitude formation. What is "relevant" in one class is boring in another. What does a "positive attitude" of a teacher toward a subject consist of, and is this attitude manifest in a similar way across subjects and grade levels? That is, it is difficult to suggest, from this research, what specific activities or behaviors teachers could engage in to improve student attitudes.

A number of correlational studies have examined the relationship of one or two factors to attitudes. An important word of caution is needed in interpreting this research, since results do not imply that a certain factor caused the change in attitude. First, the direction of inferred influence cannot be determined. It is just as likely, for instance, that a favorable attitude helped to create a positive classroom climate as the climate influencing the attitude. Second, other unmeasured factors associated with the factory may be more important. Thus, a positive climate may be highly related to self-concept, and it could be the latter variable that is the most influential. Given these limitations, the correlational research is important in suggesting studies to determine causal relationships.

Instructional Methods

Some studies report a relationship between specific instructional methods and attitude development. It seems likely that many of these instances were successful in altering the classroom climate, teacher-pupil interaction, self-concept, or other conditions that result in more positive attitudes. For example, Kokovich and Matthews (1971) found that sixth graders with poor self-concepts who tutored first graders in reading developed more positive self-concept and attitudes toward reading. Healy (1965) found that fifth-grade students developed positive attitudes toward reading if they were allowed to choose reading groups, select reading material, plan creative activities, and use reading partners. Teaching methods that result in closer student-teacher contact show more positive attitude development (MacDonald, Harris, & Mann, 1965–1966; Marita, 1966–1967). Gurney (1966) used a special program of individualized instruction in reading with fourth graders that resulted in better attitudes toward reading. Self-concept of ability in reading could have been affected using this method. As already indicated, Bloom (1976) has reported a positive relationship between attitudes and the use of a mastery approach in teaching. Doyle (1978) suggests that attitudes toward subject matter are influenced by classroom task ambiguity and risk. These affect-generating factors are the result of how academic tasks are structured. Thus, it appears that curriculum, class activities, and classroom organization can affect attitudes, but that the causal variable is determined by how these factors influence the social-emotional climate of the classroom.

Other studies of specific methods do not clearly relate to generic factors such as self-concept, classroom climate, and teacher–student relationships. For example, Smith (1967) demonstrated that the assignment of creative writing tasks prior to reading a short story favorably affected the attitudes formed toward the story. Although other studies indicate that a specific instructional approach or activity can promote more positive attitudes, several researchers have reported that most of this type of research has produced insignificant results (Aiken, 1970, 1976; Alexander & Filler, 1976; McMillan, 1976; Squire, 1969). Gardner (1975), for instance, reviewed about 30 studies that compared innovative and traditional science curricula, and concluded that there was little difference in pupil attitudes toward science as a result of enrollment in a specific curriculum. Even significant results only mean that a particular method, used with certain students under certain conditions had at one time affected attitudes. This type of conclusion is severely limited in external validity, and mitigates its uselessness with respect to theory development and confirmation.

Teacher Attitude and Enthusiasm

Several correlational studies have supported the general finding that teacher attitude and enthusiasm is an important factor in student attitude development. In a survey of 1672 earth science students and 43 teachers in 28 schools, Yoveff (1972) found a statistically significant positive correlation between student interest in the course and student ratings of teachers. Phillips (1973) traced pupil attitudes back through fourth, fifth, and sixth grades and found similar positive correlations. Garner (1963) administered an inventory to measure 45 first-year algebra teachers' and their 1063 students' attitudes toward algebra. He found a significant relationship between teachers' attitudes toward algebra and student attitudes toward algebra, and teachers' and students' judgments concerning the practical value of algebra. However, Lawrenz (1975) measured teacher and pupil attitudes toward science in 236 secondary science classes in 14 states and failed to find a significant relationship.

In a well-designed and carefully conducted study, McConnell (1977) found several significant relationships between teacher behaviors and ninth-grade student attitudes toward algebra. His sample included 50 classes from 13 Chicago suburban high schools. He used class means as the unit of analysis and regressed post-test attitudes against pre-test aptitudes, achievements and attitudes, then correlated residuals with teacher behavior measures. He found that both pupil and observer assessments of teachers who demonstrated more clarity, enthusiasm, and task orientation were significantly related to positive attitude development. He also found that teachers whose pupils rated them as emphasizing analysis questions and activities over other forms of cognition viewed mathematics as harder, duller, and less attractive.

Classroom Climate

Another variable related to teacher behavior is the classroom climate the teacher fosters and the impact of this climate on student attitudes. Walberg (1969) used bipolar adjective scales to measure three aspects of students' attitudes toward physics; interesting–dull, exciting–boring, and stimulating–monotonous. He also measured the classroom climate of the physics classes of these students, using the Learning Environment Inventory (LEI) (Walberg & Anderson, 1972). This instrument measures class organization, goals, student cliques and friendships, difficulty of class work, and other aspects of the atmosphere of the class. He found a statistically significant and positive correlation between the LEI and physics interest and between the LEI and the enjoyment of doing class work.

Several other studies have found a significantly positive relationship between the classroom climate as determined by the LEI and attitudes toward the subject matter of the class (Anderson, 1970; Anderson & Walberg, 1968; Walberg, 1971; Walberg & Anderson, 1972). However, Lawrenz (1975), in his study of characteristics of secondary science teachers and their classes did not report a significant relationship between the LEI and pupil attitudes. Rees and Peterson (1965) found a positive correlation between cooperative attitudes, and important aspects of climate, and favorable evaluations of poetry. Johnson and Johnson (1974) cite several other studies, which show that students' attitudes toward school subjects were more favorable in cooperative rather than competitive environments.

Summary

The literature reviewed, while neither plentiful nor conclusive, has suggested that certain factors and conditions influence students' attitude development. Prior attitudes certainly will influence attitude development in the future. A second factor that seems to be important is the attitude and enthusiasm of the teacher toward the subject taught. The evidence indicates a positive relationship between a teacher's favorable attitude and enthusiasm toward a subject and attitudes of his students. Some evidence suggests that a positive class environment is related to positive attitudes toward the subject of the class. Classroom activities, themselves, that are relevant, fun, challenging, or enjoyable constitute a fourth class of variables which may have a positive impact on attitude development.

There is no clear indication of how rewards influence the attitudes students develop toward school subjects. The impact of rewards seems to depend on (a) whether the rewards are intrinsic or extrinsic; (b) whether the rewards follow an already interesting task or a boring task; (c) to what the individual attributes the outcome; (d) how choice, commitment, and consequences are perceived; and (e) the degree of effort put forth in the task. There is evidence that rewards which are intrinsically meaningful will affect student attitudes toward school subjects, whereas extrinsic rewards probably do not have much effect on attitudes toward a specific subject (with the exception that an extrinsic reward for an enjoyable task may lessen subsequent interest in the task and the subject related to the task).

It is encouraging to note that many of the factors that seem to influence attitudes can be manipulated by the teacher. That is, the teacher is primarily responsible for establishing a positive climate—providing meaningful success experiences, dispersing rewards, making assignments that require high or low effort—and for the attitudes, enthusiasm, and knowledge that he or she presents to the students. It is also encouraging that these behaviors and factors are not bound by either grade level or subject matter. Few studies have found that a particular curriculum or instructional method has a consistent effect on attitudes. This suggests that the everyday teacher–student interactions and relationships that determine classroom climate, rewards, and other factors which influence attitudes toward school subjects are the most critical variables, regardless of instructional materials. Further experimental research of these variables may lead to generic theories to explain how attitudes are formed, and those specific teacher behaviors that can promote more favorable attitudes.

METHODS OF RESEARCH

While it is helpful to understand attitude development to improve students' attitudes, an objective study of attitudes depends on sensitive and accurate measurement. The purpose of this section of the chapter is to consider methodological issues related to attitude measurement. The focus is on analyzing how instruments can be developed and used to provide school personnel with information to improve pupil attitudes.

A great number of existing instruments measure pupils' attitudes. Table 6.1 indicates by grade level and area the attitude instruments reviewed for use by existing sources. However, many of these instruments have not been very useful for establishing general theories of attitude improvement. They suffer from a lack of systematic, agreed upon criteria for interpretation of results, are often unreliable across time and situations, and rarely demonstrate construct validity. Several factors are important in considering the rather dismal state of the art, including (a) the definition of "attitude" adopted; (b) our knowledge of attitude development; (c) content area being

Table 6.1
A SUMMARY OF ATTITUDE INSTRUMENTS REVIEWED BY EXISTING SOURCES[a]

Source	Elementary (K–8) General attitudes toward school and learning	Reading	Math	Science	Other	Secondary (7–12) General attitudes toward school and learning	Reading	Math	Science	Other
Alexander, Filler, 1976		15					10			
Beatty, 1969	3	1			5	2	1			3
Buros, 1972	1				2	1				3
Buros, 1974	2				4	4				3
Chun et al., 1975	5				2	8				3
Frith, Narikawa, 1972	4	3	3	3	8	3	2	2	2	8
Gephart, Ingle, Marshall, 1976	2				1	2				5
Henerson, Morris, Fitz-Gibbon, 1978	5				5	3				3
Hoepfner, CSE test evaluations series, 1971–1974	12				4	25	1	2		29
Johnson, 1976	17	2	3	1	7	11	2	2	2	19
Payne, 1974	1					3				2
Shaw, Wright, 1967					1	3		2	1	7
Summers, 1977		13	1	1			8			
Test Collection Bulletin 1970–1978	9	3	1		14	6		1		8
Zirkel, Greene, 1976		10					2			

[a] This table indicates the number of instruments reviewed by each source in each category. Backer (1977) has summarized information about a large number of sources that review tests, including those cited in this table. Kevin F. Spratt helped locate and review sources for inclusion in this table.

measured; and (d) strengths and weaknesses of different types of instruments. The discussion will not review the traditional methods of measuring attitudes, since several sources are available that adequately explain these approaches (Anderson, Ball, & Murphy, 1975; Backer, 1977; Green, 1977; Henerson, Morris & Fitz-Gibbon, 1978; Payne, 1974; Severy, 1974; Summers, 1970, and Triandis, 1971).

Perhaps the most serious problem with most existing instruments is the definition of attitude explicit in the items and scoring. Well-known techniques such as Likert, Guttmann, and Thurstone scales are unidimensional. They give a single evaluative continuum that measures the attitude as a generalized pro–con/favorable–unfavorable/positive–negative/like–dislike continuum (McKennell, 1974). It has already been stressed that an attitude is multidimensional and situation specific, and such a general measure as "attitude toward school" or "attitude toward math" is at best a gross approximation of the actual feelings of the students. It is not surprising, since most studies have used unidimensional instruments, that research in this area is often contradictory and difficult to replicate. One should choose or develop instruments for measuring attitudes with the understanding that an "attitude" is comprised of three components—affective, cognitive, and behavioral—and that the situation or context of the question is important. The instrument, then, should be multidimensional to reflect these factors. For instance, math can be valuable (cognitive) and enjoyable (affective) in the context of Mr. Jones's class, but useless and boring in Mrs. Brown's class. Or, a student could report that history is mundane while in class or in the context of schooling, but that it is necessary and valuable information outside of class.

Content area is a third variable that influences the multidimensional nature of the construct and should also be reflected in the instrument. There is little meaning, for instance, in determining an attitude toward "school." Rather, it is necessary to determine attitudes toward school rules concerning behavior, length of classes, principal, grades, competition, testing, teachers, and other aspects of the "school." Similarly, "science" consists of biology, physics, human anatomy, astronomy, laboratory exercises, difficult terminology, and other components.

These three considerations, definition of attitude, content area, and situation are represented in Figure 6.1. Each of the boxes can be thought of as a different dimension to be measured. It is likely that not all of the interactions are meaningful and need to be tapped, but as a way of conceptualizing what should be covered in the instrument the approach is far more accurate than developing a unidimensional, general measure. Not only will the responses to a multidimensional instrument be more accurate but they will also allow the teacher to identify specific areas of strength and weakness

Content area analysis (i.e., "science")

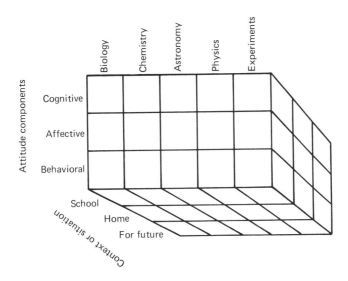

Figure 6.1. Factors contributing to item construction.

in developing positive attitudes. A general measure which reports that "students don't like English" conveys nothing about particular aspects of English that are viewed unfavorably.

The second factor noted, knowledge of attitude development, is especially useful for understanding how we can foster more positive attitudes. By extending the basic processes of attitude development to school settings and incorporating research of school variables that influence attitudes, a list of factors can be identified and measured along with the assessment of the status of the attitude. Such factors as classroom climate, meaning of rewards, enthusiasm of the teacher, and enjoyment of instructional activities can be measured to determine their impact on attitudes. This would emphasize, once again, constructing instruments to assist teachers in developing more positive attitudes. By making the information specific and individual it will be more useful. Bills (1975, 1976) provides further elaboration on this point and describes effective procedures for assessing attitudes by school district for use in improvement efforts. He describes how the unique research setting of the school, including attitudes of the staff and needs of the school, should be considered in constructing instruments that provide immediate and useful feedback.

The fourth area concerns the nature of the attitude instruments. The characteristics of each type of instrument—strengths and weaknesses, time, money, and personnel needed—need to be integrated with the purpose of the assessment. A multimethod approach is preferred to increase construct validity and reduce error. It is also important to consider nontraditional and creative approaches to measurement. It is not necessary to always use a Likert, semantic differential, or sentence completion type of instrument. Nonreactive measures, observational techniques, phenomenological approaches, and other devices have unique advantages that could be effectively developed. Sinaiko and Broedling (1976) have summarized how alternatives to traditional survey approaches can be useful.

There are three examples of recently developed instruments that illustrate some of the previous suggestions. Johnson (1974) has described the development of the Minnesota School Affect Assessment (MSAA), an instrument designed to "assess affective reactions of students," and "feed results back to the school district . . . for action planning to improve the instructional program [p. 108]." Areas for assessment were generated from school personnel and represented a number of categories. Through pilot testing, using a semantic differential format, two dimensions were identified and incorporated for each category, "important–unimportant," and "pleasant–unpleasant." Though not consciously planned to come out this way, the dimensions clearly reflect the cognitive and affective components, respectively, of the tripartite definition of attitudes. Thus, the MSAA is capable of measuring specific aspects of schooling (i.e., "learning about animals and plants," "being a good student," "choosing what I want to learn") and separating cognitive and affective dimensions for each aspect.

Another example of instrument development, which is based on the premise that attitudes are not unidimensional or global, is reported by Engin, Wallbrown, and Brown (1976). They performed a factor analysis of 853 fourth-, fifth-, and sixth-graders' attitudes toward reading, and identified four definite factors (difficulty, reading as reinforcement, reading as enjoyment, alternate reading modes) and three tentative factors (reading group, silent versus oral reading, and comic books). These dimensions appear to reflect causal factors as well as the measure of attitude, and if replicated, can provide important information to educators for improving attitudes. The finding that reading group and type of reading (silent or oral) may be independent factors of students' feelings about reading suggests a need for more investigation of these practices and their effect on attitudes.

Kahn (1978) used pictorial stimuli and self-ratings of 8-year-olds with teacher-rating of pupils to measure attitudes toward school, teacher, self, and independence. The multimethod approach used is laudible but rarely done, and showed that teachers tended to rate students on a single dimension, a general disposition, while pupils' attitudes were more differentiated.

Kahn's study is a good example of utilizing the strengths of different types of assessment, balancing the weaknesses of the self-report (acquiescence, social desirability, faking) and ratings by others (selective perception, forgetting, halo effect) to more accurately assess the attitude in question.

In summary, this brief discussion of methodological issues has suggested that increased attention be given to developing instruments and methodologies to measure causal factors and components of attitudes with respect to situational characteristics. This multidimensional perspective is complex but much more accurate than relying on global, sometimes meaningless, measures that do little to help improve attitudes. The approach advocated is specific and pragmatic, to promote positive growth of pupil attitudes.

INTEGRATION WITH COGNITIVE SOCIAL-PSYCHOLOGICAL MODEL OF LEARNING

The nature of pupil attitudes can be integraged with the cognitive social-psychological model of learning in two ways. The first is to conceive of attitudes as determinants of behavior, directly as measured by the behavioral component, and indirectly as a factor that influences the feedback an individual attends to and in turn has an impact on behavior. For example, if the cognitive component of a student's attitude is positive, it seems reasonable to assume that the student will focus on information related to the area of interest. That is, a student who believes it is very important to learn about the environment is more likely to incorporate feedback from a science teacher critiquing an opinion than a student who does not believe it is important to study the environment. Or, consider the young adolescent who considers it both fun (affective component) and useful (cognitive component) to learn about sex, relating to others, vocations, and other topics closely related to their development. Other persons, both adults and peers, who can provide experience with and information about these areas will be able to hold attention and influence subsequent behaviors.

Not only will attitudes help determine behavior, but because it is not possible to measure the construct "attitude" directly, the attitude components assessed can be thought of as behaviors. Thus, the first part of the cognitive social-psychological model could be interpreted as "the behavior or attitude of a person in a situation," influenced by the factors summarized. The research summarized earlier suggesting that teacher enthusiasm and classroom climate affect pupil attitudes is a good example of how the social environment can influence attitudes, and in this case the affective component. Modeling, the influence of significant others and reference groups, and expectancy are well documented factors that show the impact of social interaction on attitudes. Although not empirically researched, it also seems likely that general attitudes toward school and learning are a result of institution characteristics. The established norms, rules, and bureaucratic patterns must have an impact on how students feel about school.

SUMMARY, IMPLICATIONS, AND SUGGESTIONS FOR FURTHER RESEARCH

The purpose of this chapter has been to present a particular perspective concerning pupil attitude development and measurement. The approach has considered an "attitude" to be a multidimensional construct, consisting of cognitive, affective, and behavioral components in the context of a given situation. Variables that affect pupil development were discussed, in both a general sense from traditional social-psychological research and from data gathered in studies specific to students in school. A strong point was made to construct instruments to measure attitudes that reflect the tripartite definition and situational parameters, and identify causal factors that will provide educators with specific information to implement affective improvement programs.

The importance of positive attitudes has always been recognized but underestimated. Lasting and influential effects of schooling are often affective in nature, and there is little question about the positive impact of good attitudes on cognitive learning in specific subjects. Student attitude development can be considered a "basic skill," because it is a prerequisite to effective cognitive learning and positive mental health. However, there has been relatively little research of causal factors of attitudes. There is a need for basic research in this area, to better specify the conditions that promote positive attitudes. This research should be careful to represent real-life situations as accurately as possible and to consider idiosyncrasies of students and environments as important, interrelated factors. New approaches to measure attitudes, which could provide accurate, specific, and useful information, need to be developed. This includes observational, unobtrusive, and ethnographic approaches. Finally, there is an unexplored domain of individuals' interactions with school organizational and group characteristics, and the way these interactions affect attitudes. This chapter has limited much of the discussion to students' attitudes toward school subjects, an area closely related to achievement. There are, of course, other types of attitudes that could also be explored using the perspective of this chapter, including attitudes toward learning, school, teachers, peers, parents, vocational areas, ethnic groups, sex-role identity, and other areas children develop during their school years.

REFERENCES

Aiken, L. R. Attitudes toward mathematics. *Review of Educational Research,* 1970, *40,* 551–596.

Aiken, L. R. Biodata correlates of attitudes toward mathematics in three age groups and two sex groups. *School Science and Mathematics,* 1972, *72,* 386–395.

Aiken, L. R. Update on attitudes and other affective variables in learning mathematics. *Review of Educational Research,* 1976, *46,* 293–311.

Alexander, J. E., & Filler, R. C. *Attitudes and reading.* Newark, Delaware: International Reading Association, 1976.

Allport, G. W. Attitudes. In C. Murchison (Ed.) *Handbook of social psychology,* Worcester, Massachusetts: Clark University Press, 1935, 798–844.

Anderson, G. J. Effects of classroom social climate on individual learning. *American Educational Research Journal,* 1970, *7,* 135–152.

Anderson, G. J., & Walberg, H. J. Classroom climate and group learning. *International Journal of the Educational Sciences,* 1968, *2,* 175–180.

Anderson, S. B., Ball, S., & Murphy, R. T. *Encyclopedia of educational evaluation.* San Francisco: Jossey-Bass, 1975.

Aronson, E. The effect of effort on the attractiveness of rewarded and unrewarded stimuli. *Journal of Abnormal and Social Psychology,* 1961, *63,* 375–380.

Backer, T. *A directory of information on tests.* TM Report 62. ERIC Clearinghouse on Tests, Measurements, and Evaluation, Princeton, New Jersey, 1977. (ED 152802).

Bailey, R. C., Helm, B., & Gladstone, R. The effects of success and failure in a real-life setting: performance, attribution, affect, and expectancy. *Journal of Psychology,* 1975, *89,* 137–147.

Beatty, W. H. (Ed.). Improving educational assessment and an inventory of measures of affective behavior. Washington: Association for Supervision and Curriculum Development, NEA, 1969.

Bem, D. J. *Beliefs, attitudes, and human affairs.* Belmont, California: Brooks/Cole, 1970.

Bills, R. E. *A system for assessing affectivity.* University: The University of Alabama Press, 1975.

Bills, R. E. Affect and its measurement. In W. J. Gephart, R. B. Ingle, and F. J. Marshall (Eds.), *Evaluation in the affective domain,* CEDR Monograph, Phi Delta Kappa, 1976.

Bloom, B. S. *Human characteristics and school learning.* New York: McGraw-Hill, 1976.

Bostrom, R. N. Affective, cognitive, and behavioral dimensions of communicative attitudes. *Journal of Communication,* 1970, *20,* 359–360.

Brehm, J. W., & Jones, R. A. The effect on dissonance of surprise consequences. *Journal of Experimental Social Psychology,* 1970, *6,* 420–421.

Buenz, R. Y., & Merrill, I. R. Effects of effort on retention and enjoyment. *Journal of Educational Psychology,* 1968, *58,* 154–158.

Buros, O. K. (Ed.). *The seventh mental measurements yearbook.* Vol. 1. Highland Park: The Gryphon Press, 1972.

Buros, O. K. (Ed.). *Tests in print II,* Highland Park: The Gryphon Press, 1974.

Callahan, W. J. Adolescent attitudes toward mathematics. *The Mathematics Teacher,* 1971, *64,* 751–755.

Cangemi, M. A. *A study of relationships among verbal interaction, student achievement, and attitude in selected two and four year college general chemistry classes.* Unpublished doctoral dissertation, New York University, 1972.

Carlsmith, J. M., Collins, B. E., & Helmreich, R. L. Studies in forced compliance: I. The effect of pressure for compliance on attitude change produced by face-to-face role playing and anonymous essay writing. *Journal of Personality and Social Psychology,* 1966, *4,* 1–13.

Chung, K., Lobb, S., & Frunch, J. R. P., Jr. *Measures for psychological assessment.* Survey Research Center, Institute for Social Research, University of Michigan, Ann Arbor, 1975.

Cooper, J. Personal responsible and dissonance: The role of foreseen consequences. *Journal of Personality and Social Psychology,* 1971, *18,* 354–363.

Cronbach, L. J. *Educational psychology* (3d ed.). New York: Harcourt Brace Jovanovich, 1977.

Deci, E. L. Effects of externally mediated rewards on intrinisci motivation. *Journal of Personality and Social Psychology,* 1971, *18,* 105–115.

Doyle, W. *Task structures and student roles in classrooms.* Paper presented at the Annual Meeting of the American Educational Research Association, Toronto, March 1978.

Engin, A. W., Wallbrown, F. H., & Brown, D. H. The dimensions of reading attitude for children in the intermediate grades. *Psychology in the Schools,* 1976, *13*(3), 309–316.

Festinger, L., & Carlsmith, J. Cognitive consequences of forced compliance. *Journal of Abnormal and Social Psychology,* 1959, *58,* 203–210.

Fishbein, M., & Ajzen, I. Attitudes and opinions. *Annual Review of Psychology,* 1972, *23,* 487–544.

Freedman, J. L. Role playing: Psychology by consensus. *Journal of Personality and Social Psychology,* 1969, *13,* 107–114.

Frey, D., & Irle, M. Some conditions to produce a dissonance and an incentive effect in a forced compliance situation. *European Journal of Social Psychology,* 1972, *2,* 45–54.

Frieze, I. H., Snyder, H. N., & Fontaine, C. M. *Student attributions and the attributional model during an actual examination.* Paper presented at the annual meeting of the American Psychological Association, San Francisco, 1977.

Frith, S., & Narikawa, D. (Eds.). *Attitudes toward school K–12* (Rev. ed.). Los Angeles, California: Instructional Objections Exchange, 1972.

Gagné, R. M. *The conditions of learning* (3d ed.). New York: Holt, Rinehart & Winston, 1977.

Gardner, P. L. *Science curricula and attitudes to science:* A review, The *Australian Science Teachers Journal,* 1975, *21*(2), 23–40.

Garner, M. V. *A study of the educational background and attitudes of teachers toward algebra as related to the attitudes and achievements to their Anglo-American and Latin American pupils in first year algebra classes of Texas.* Unpublished doctoral dissertation, North Texas State University, 1963.

Gephart, W. J., Ingle, R. B., & Marshall, F. J. (Eds.). *Evaluation in the affective domain.* Bloomington, Indiana: Phi Delta Kappa, 1976.

Glazer, W. *Schools without failure.* New York: Harper Row, 1969.

Green, D. H. Attitudes. In S. Ball (Ed.), *Motivation in education,* New York: Academic Press, 1977.

Gurney, D. The effect of an individualized reading program on reading. *Reading Teacher,* 1966, *19,* 277–280.

Hake, C. T. *The effects of specified written comments on achievement in and attitude toward algebra and geometry.* Unpublished doctoral dissertation, Pennsylvania State University, 1973.

Haney, R. E. The development of scientific attitudes. *The Science Teacher,* 1964, *31,* 33–35.

Hansen, H. S. The impact of the home literary environment in reading attitude. *Elementary English,* 1969, *46,* 17–25.

Hartman, D. D. *The determination of the applicability of the Fishbein model of attitudes in ascertaining the attitudes toward science held by high school students.* Unpublished doctoral dissertation, University of Wisconsin, 1972.

Healy, A. K. Effects of changing children's attitudes toward reading. *Elementary English,* 1965, *42,* 269–272.

Henerson, M. E., Morris, L. L., & Fitz-Gibbon, C. T. *How to measure attitudes.* Beverly Hills: Sage, 1978.

Hoepfner, R., et al. (Eds.). *CSE test evaluation series, 1971–1974.* Center for the Study of Evaluation, UCLA Graduate School of Education, Los Angeles, 1971–1974.

Insko, C. A. *Theories of attitude change.* New York: Appleton-Century-Crofts, 1967.

Jackson, P. W. *Life in classrooms.* Holt, Rinehart & Winston, 1968.

Johnson, D. W. Affective outcomes. In H. J. Walberg (Ed.), *Evaluating educational performance: A sourcebook of methods, instruments, and examples.* Berkeley, California: McCutchan, 1974.

Johnson, D. W., & Johnson, R. T. Instructional goal structure: Cooperative, competitive, or individualistic. *Review of Educational Research,* 1974, *44,* 213–240.

Johnson, O. G. *Tests and measurements in child development: Handbook II.* Vol. 2. San Francisco: Jossey-Bass, 1976.

Kahn, S. B. A comparative study of accessing children's school-related attitudes. *Journal of Educational Measurement,* 1978, *15*(1), 59–66.

Kauchak, D. P. *Attitude change as a function of essay writing.* Unpublished doctoral dissertation, Washington State University, 1973.

Kokovich, A., & Matthews, G. E. Reading and the self-concept. *National Elementary Principal,* 1971, *50,* 53–54.

Komorita, S. S., & Bass, A. R. Attitude differentiation and evaluative scales on the semantic differential. *Journal of Personality and Social Psychology,* 1967, *6,* 241–244.

Kruglanski, A. W., Alon, S., & Lewis, T. Retrospective, misattribution and task enjoyment. *Journal of Experimental Social Psychology,* 1972, *8,* 493–501.

Kruglanski, A. W., Friedman, I., & Zeevi, G. The effects of extrinsic incentive on some qualitative aspects of task performance. *Journal of Personality,* 1971, *39,* 606–617.

Lawrenz, F. The relationship between science teacher characteristics and student achievement and attitude. *Journal of Research in Science Teaching,* 1975, *12,* 433–437.

Lepper, M. R., Greene, D., & Nisbett, R. E. Undermining children's intrinsic interest with extrinsic rewards: a test of the "over-justification" hypothesis. *Journal of Personality and Social Psychology,* 1973, *28,* 129–137.

Leventhal, H. Attitudes: Their nature, growth, and change. In C. Nemeth (Ed.), *Social psychology: Class and contemporary integrations.* Chicago: Rand McNally, 1974, 52–126.

MacDonald, J. B., Harris, T. L., & Mann, J. S. Individual versus group instruction in first grade reading. *The Reading Teacher,* 1965–1966, *19,* 643–646, 653.

Mager, R. F. *Developing attitudes toward learning.* Belmont, California: Fearon, 1968.

Marita, M. Beginning reading achievement in three classroom organizational patterns. *The Reading Teacher,* 1966–1967, *20,* 12–17.

McConnell, J. W. *Relationships between selected teacher behaviors and attitudes/achievements of algebra classes.* Paper presented at the Annual Meeting of the American Educational Research Association, New York City, April 4–8, 1977.

McKennell, A. C. *Surveying attitude structures.* Amsterdam: Elsevier, 1974.

McMillan, J. H. Factors affecting the development of pupil attitudes toward school subjects. *Psychology in the Schools,* 1976, *13*(3), 322–325.

McMillan, J. H. The effect of effort and feedback on the formation of student attitudes. *American Educational Research Journal,* 1977, *14*(3), 317–330.

McMillan, J. H., & May, M. J. A study of factors influencing science attitudes of junior high students. *Journal of Research on Science Teaching,* 1979, *16,* 217–222.

Merrill, J. R., Yaryan, R. B., & Musser, T. S. The effects of effort and reinforcement on retention and enjoyment of programmed instruction. *Journal of Medical Education,* 1969, *44,* 184–192.

Moore, B. E. *Predictors of high school students' attitudes toward involvement with science and perceptions of the scientists.* Unpublished doctoral dissertation, Kansas State University, 1973.

Namazi, A. *Critical teaching behaviors influencing attitude development of elementary school children toward physical education.* Unpublished doctoral dissertation, University of Maryland, 1969.

Neidt, C. O., & Hedlund, D. E. The relationship between changes in attitude toward a course and final achievement. *The Journal of Educational Research,* 1967, *61,* 56–58.

Nel, E., Helmreich, R., & Aronson, E. Opinion change in the advocate as a function of the persuasability of his audience: A clarification of the meaning of dissonance. *Journal of Personality and Social Psychology,* 1969, *12,* 117–124.

Nicholls, J. B. Causal attributions and other achievement-related cognitions: Effects of task outcome, attainmemt value, and sex. *Journal of Personality and Social Psychology,* 1975, *31,* 379–389.

Orbaker, E. F. *The effects of verbal reinforcements on attitude toward physical education.* Unpublished doctoral dissertation, West Virginia University, 1972.

Osborn, M. The impact of differing parental educational levels on the educational achievement, attitude, aspiration and expectation of the child. *Journal of Educational Research,* 1971, *65,* 163–167.

Ostrom, T. M. The relationship between the affective, behavioral, and cognitive components of attitude. *Journal of Experimental Social Psychology,* 1969, *5,* 12–30.

Payne, D. A. *The assessment of learning: Cognitive and affective.* Lexington, Massachusetts: D. C. Health & Co., 1974.

Phillips, R. B., Jr. Teacher attitudes as related to student attitude and achievement in elementary school mathematics. *School Science and Mathematics,* 1973, *73,* 501–507.

Poffenberger, T., & Norton, D. A. Factors in the formation of attitudes toward mathematics. *Journal of Educational Research,* 1959, *52,* 171–176.

Ramsett, D. E., Johnson, J. D., & Adams, C. An interinstitutional study of student attitudes toward principles of economics. *The Journal of Experimental Education,* 1974, *42,* 78–85.

Rees, R. D., & Peterson, D. M. A factorial determination of points of view in poetic evaluation and their relation to various determinants. *Psychological Reports,* 1965, *16,* 31–39.

Ryan, J. *Effects of modern and conventional mathematics curricula on pupil attitudes, interests, and perceptions of proficiency.* Contract OEC-5-10-051, Washington, D. C.: Office of Health, Education, & Welfare, 1968.

Severy, L. J. *Procedures and issues in the measurement of attitudes.* TM Report #30, ERIC, Princeton, New Jersey: Educational Testing Service, 1974.

Shaw, M. E., & Wright, J. M. *Scales for the measurement of attitudes.* New York: McGraw-Hill, 1967.

Sherman, S. Effects of choice and incentive on attitude change in a discrepant behavior situation. *Journal of Personality and Social Psychology,* 1970, *15,* 245–252.

Sinaiko, H. W., & Broedling, L. A. (Eds.). *Perspectives on attitude assessment: Surveys and their alternatives.* Champaign, Illinois: Pendleton, 1976.

Smith, R. J. The efforts of reading a short story for creative purpose on student attitude and writing. Research and Development Center for Cognitive Learning, Technical Report No. 28, University of Wisconsin, Madison, 1967.

Sohn, D. Affect-generating powers of effort and ability, self attributions of academic success and failure. *Journal of Educational Psychology,* 1977, *69*(5), 500–505.

Squire, J. R. What does research in reading reveal about attitudes toward reading? *English Journal,* 1969, *58,* 523–533.

Staats, A. W. An outline of an integrated theory of attitudes. In M. Fishbein (Ed.), *Readings in attitude theory and measurement,* New York: Wiley, 1967.

Summers, E. G. Instruments for assessing reading attitudes: A review of research and bibliography. *Journal of Reading Behavior,* 1977, *9*(2), 137–165.

Summers, G. F. (Ed.). *Attitude measurement.* Chicago: Rand McNally, 1970.

Teigland, J. J. The relationship between measured teacher attitude change and certain personality characteristics. *Journal of Educational Research,* 1966, *60,* 84–85.

Test Collection Bulletin. Vols. 4–12. Princeton, New Jersey: Educational Testing Service, 1970–1978.

Travers, R. M. W. *Essentials of learning* (4th ed.). New York: MacMillan, 1977.

Triandis, H. C. *Attitude and attitude change.* Wiley, 1971.

Walberg, H. J. The social environment as a mediator of classroom learning. *Journal of Educational Psychology,* 1969, *60,* 443–448.

Walberg, H. J. Models for optimizing and individualizing school learning. *Interchange,* 1971, *3,* 15–27.

Walberg, H. J., & Anderson, G. J. Properties of the urban behavioring class. *Journal of Educational Psychology,* 1972, *63,* 381–385.

Weiner, B., Russell, D., & Lerman, D. Affective consequences of causal ascriptions. In J. H. Harvey, W. J. Ickes, and R. F. Kidd (Eds.), *New Directions in Attribution Research.* Vol. 2. New Jersey: Lawrence Erlbaum, 1978.

Yoveff, S. L. *Student achievement in and attitude toward earth science courses in secondary schools.* Unpublished doctoral dissertation, Western Michigan University, 1972.

Zirkel, P. A., & Greene, I. F. Measurement of attitudes toward reading in the elementary grades: A review. *Reading World,* 1976, *16*(2), 104–113.

Author Index

Numbers in italics refer to the pages on which the complete references are listed.

Subject Index

A

Achievement motivation, 56, 57, 206, 207
Aptitude treatment interaction, 7, 8, 11
Attitude change, 218
  persuasion, 226
Attitude development, 218–234
  classical conditioning of, 218–221
  classroom activities, effects of, 229
  classroom environment, effects of, 226, 231, 233
  cognitive learning, 222–227
  effort, 223–225
  instructional methods, effects of, 229–232
  modeling, effects of, 227
  operant conditioning, 221, 222
  parents' influence, 228
  prior attitudes, influence of, 228–230
  related to grades, 221, 222
  rewards, effects of, 223–225, 230
  school factors affecting, 230, 233, 234
  self concept, effects of, 229
  teacher, effects of, 221, 227, 228, 232, 234
  teacher enthusiasm, effects of, 229, 230, 232
Attitude measurement, 217, 225, 226, 234–239
  alternatives to traditional assessment, 238
  construction questionnaires, 237
  content area, 236, 237
  definition of attitudes, 236–238
  examples, 238, 239
  existing instruments, 235, 238, 239
  factors in item construction, 236–238
  limitations, 234, 236
  multidimensional scales, 236–239
  multimethod approach, 238, 239
  related to attitude development, 236, 237
  unidimensional scales, 236–239
Attitude research in schools, 227–234
Attitudes
  affective component, 216–221, 236–238
  affective reactions to performance, 47–49, 64, 68, 219–221
  as general disposition, 216, 217
  behavioral component, 217
  cognitive component, 216, 217, 236–239
  definition, 216–218
  goal structures, effects of, 136
  integrated with model of learning, 239, 240
  related to peer groups, 187
  situational influences, 218, 220
  suggestions for research, 240
Attitudes and behavior, 217, 239, 240
Attitudes related to achievment, 219, 220
Attitudes toward mathematics, 227–229, 232, 235

EDUCATIONAL PSYCHOLOGY

continued from page ii

Harvey Lesser. Television and the Preschool Child: A Psychological Theory of Instruction and Curriculum Development

Donald J. Treffinger, J. Kent Davis, and Richard E. Ripple (eds.). Handbook on Teaching Educational Psychology

Harry L. Hom, Jr. and Paul A. Robinson (eds.). Psychological Processes in Early Education

J. Nina Lieberman. Playfulness: Its Relationship to Imagination and Creativity

Samuel Ball (ed.). Motivation in Education

Erness Bright Brody and Nathan Brody. Intelligence: Nature, Determinants, and Consequences

António Simões (ed.). The Bilingual Child: Research and Analysis of Existing Educational Themes

Gilbert R. Austin. Early Childhood Education: An International Perspective

Vernon L. Allen (ed.). Children as Teachers: Theory and Research on Tutoring

Joel R. Levin and Vernon L. Allen (eds.). Cognitive Learning in Children: Theories and Strategies

Donald E. P. Smith and others. A Technology of Reading and Writing (in four volumes).

> *Vol. 1. Learning to Read and Write: A Task Analysis (by Donald E. P. Smith)*
>
> *Vol. 2. Criterion-Referenced Tests for Reading and Writing (by Judith M. Smith, Donald E. P. Smith, and James R. Brink)*
>
> *Vol. 3. The Adaptive Classroom (by Donald E. P. Smith)*
>
> *Vol. 4. Designing Instructional Tasks (by Judith M. Smith)*

Phillip S. Strain, Thomas P. Cooke, and Tony Apolloni. Teaching Exceptional Children: Assessing and Modifying Social Behavior

EDUCATIONAL PSYCHOLOGY

continued from page ii

Harvey Lesser. Television and the Preschool Child: A Psychological Theory of Instruction and Curriculum Development

Donald J. Treffinger, J. Kent Davis, and Richard E. Ripple (eds.). Handbook on Teaching Educational Psychology

Harry L. Hom, Jr. and Paul A. Robinson (eds.). Psychological Processes in Early Education

J. Nina Lieberman. Playfulness: Its Relationship to Imagination and Creativity

Samuel Ball (ed.). Motivation in Education

Erness Bright Brody and Nathan Brody. Intelligence: Nature, Determinants, and Consequences

António Simões (ed.). The Bilingual Child: Research and Analysis of Existing Educational Themes

Gilbert R. Austin. Early Childhood Education: An International Perspective

Vernon L. Allen (ed.). Children as Teachers: Theory and Research on Tutoring

Joel R. Levin and Vernon L. Allen (eds.). Cognitive Learning in Children: Theories and Strategies

Donald E. P. Smith and others. A Technology of Reading and Writing (in four volumes).

> *Vol. 1. Learning to Read and Write: A Task Analysis (by Donald E. P. Smith)*
>
> *Vol. 2. Criterion-Referenced Tests for Reading and Writing (by Judith M. Smith, Donald E. P. Smith, and James R. Brink)*
>
> *Vol. 3. The Adaptive Classroom (by Donald E. P. Smith)*
>
> *Vol. 4. Designing Instructional Tasks (by Judith M. Smith)*

Phillip S. Strain, Thomas P. Cooke, and Tony Apolloni. Teaching Exceptional Children: Assessing and Modifying Social Behavior